CORRECTING YOUR ENGLISH

CORRECTING
YOUR ENGLISH

Harry Blamires

BLOOMSBURY

This edition published in 1996

First published in 1994 as *The Queen's English* by
Bloomsbury Publishing Plc
2 Soho Square
London, W1V 6HB

A copy of the CIP entry for this book is available from the British Library

ISBN 0 7475 2515 3

10 9 8 7 6 5 4 3 2 1

Typeset by Hewer Text Composition Services, Edinburgh
Printed in Britain by Cox & Wyman Ltd, Reading, Berkshire

CONTENTS

INTRODUCTION

Codes which consist of prohibitions sometimes have more clarity than positive recommendations. Perhaps the Ten Commandments are a case in point. Useful guidance may rely a good deal on telling people what not to do. You have to imbibe much negative instruction when you first learn to drive. 'Don't drive too close to the vehicle in front of you. Don't try to overtake on a blind bend. Don't try to join a fast stream of traffic without allowing plenty of space for the vehicles coming behind you.' We know what good driving is precisely because we recognise what bad driving is. We drive well because we avoid the errors committed by bad drivers.

We shall begin to write well by learning to recognise bad English and to avoid the practices which make it bad. Most books written to encourage the correct use of our language are quite properly planned in such a way as to present the reader with a tidy progress through the rules of good usage. That approach can be invaluable, but it is not the only possible approach. This book starts instead with the questions: What errors are regularly being committed today in the use of English? What currently are the bad habits which the would-be writer needs to be forewarned against? What are the pitfalls to be avoided?

It so happens that this is a good time to explore error in English usage. There is a lot of it about. We hear complaints about falling standards of literacy in our country. We hear claims that our educational system is not doing its job in this respect. We may well wonder how justifiable the complaints are. No doubt there are always individuals for whom criticising the current state of our language is a favourite pastime, like criticising the state of our railways. There are always those who relish writing letters to the press in protest against some contemporary fad in English usage. Recently, however, doubts about the level of literacy in our country have assumed a new urgency. The concern has ceased to be a minority interest.

Where can we turn for hard evidence of how bad the use of our own language is? After all, if we are going to do something about national standards of literacy, we need to know exactly how low those standards currently are. We need data and we need yardsticks. If bad practices are becoming habitual, they should be exposed. A finger should be pointed at the actual faults in current usage. Errors which are habitually made should be identified and listed before us in black and white.

Correcting Your English has been written to meet this need. It is a survey of the climate of literacy, or illiteracy, in which we operate today. It is designed to give body and point to a controversy which so far has produced more noise than substance. Daily papers and other current journals have been ransacked for evidence. I collected over 3,000 specimens of bad English – sentences which exemplify current misusage in respect of grammar, syntax, logic, vocabulary, and so on. The sentences were derived from about 120 publications. *The Times* and *The Independent* were each scrutinised for weeks at a time to ensure that what is called the 'quality press' should be fully represented in the survey. For the rest, journals were selected from what was generally available on bookstalls, in an attempt to do justice to various interests from hunting and the countryside to railways and the stockmarket. The sentences were labelled and card-indexed, and I arranged them in groups according to the kind of error they exemplified. Time and time again, I found, a recognisable body of faulty practices marred the work of writers from widely different sources. It has thus been possible to produce from the gathered material a systematic account of where we go wrong.

About half the total number of sentences collected have been used in the book. The survey analyses each kind of error exemplified and supplies corrections. In the interests of tidy and economic presentation, corrections are always given in italic type. One aim has been to try to illustrate a given error at contrasting levels of crudity and sophistication. Another aim has been to try to illustrate a given error at varying degrees of gravity. Though these two aims overlap, they are basically different. An error does not become less grave because it is half-hidden in a mass of pretentious verbiage. One of the side-effects of presenting the material thus is that sophisticated writers sometimes emerge as temporary bedfellows in error with some very simple souls.

Precisely because certain errors are exemplified at very different levels of gravity, there will be sentences at one end of the scale which are grossly illiterate, and sentences at the other end of the scale which seem barely to fail the test of acceptability. Something is to be learned, not only from those sentences whose howlers grate on the literate ear, but also from those sentences which carelessly abuse the kind of liberties we take in conversation, liberties which we would deny ourselves in speech-making and which are quite out of place on the printed page. Thus not every sentence quoted in this book deserves the same kind of blue-pencil treatment.

No scheme was made beforehand for arranging the material that follows. The sentences were collected, the errors labelled, and the cards sorted until groupings emerged. But of course there is many a sentence here which might have been differently placed, either because it contains errors of two or more different kinds, or because what is centrally wrong with it is something which overlaps two categories of error. For instance, there are sentences in the section headed 'Illogicality' which have syntactical faults that could have given them a place under a different heading, and many more sentences under other headings that have an element of illogicality.

A word must be said about the method of correction adopted. On many occasions, in studying a bad sentence, I have thought, 'If I were trying to say what this writer is trying to say, I wouldn't start like that.' But to correct a faulty sentence by writing a completely different one would not be very helpful to readers. So it has been my practice throughout, wherever possible, to correct a sentence without tampering with the basic pattern adopted – to free the faulty construction of error rather than to change the construction. There are occasions when the result is a sentence which, though correct, is clumsy or too wordy, and sometimes an alternative and more thorough re-drafting is suggested.

In some respects the borderline between what is acceptable and what is unacceptable is not fixed but changes from decade to decade. The language develops. Where our parents would have said 'The meeting was resumed at 2 o'clock', we now say 'The meeting resumed at 2 o'clock'. We have turned what was exclusively a transitive verb into one with an intransitive use. There is nothing wrong with this process of change. It has been happening for centuries. That kind of development in linguistic convention is not what this book is primarily concerned with. The important rules of grammar are not inhibitions devised by pedants, but are largely formulated commonsense. For this reason, the aim in this book has been to reduce to a minimum the use of grammatical terminology. It cannot be totally eradicated of course, but wherever possible I have tried to make error stand out by citing parallel cases which exaggerate or parody the mistake. My overriding aim has been to display the *absurdity* of error, by appealing to the reader's commonsense, rather than to some assumed familiarity with grammatical formulations. Indeed, one of the results of making this survey is the discovery that failure to think straight is at least as prevalent a cause of error as ignorance of grammar.

Perhaps this should not cause surprise. For I have known people who would have been incapable of writing a grammatically faulty sentence and yet would wave their hands dismissively in the air in total incomprehension if one used any grammatical terminology more advanced than 'noun' and 'verb' in speaking to them. Perhaps the seeming paradox is explicable, as the people in question were in the habit of reading and they had plenty of commonsense. Perhaps those two ingredients make up a recipe for a high level of literacy. However, reading can only do its job of infecting the receptive with literacy if what is read is itself literate. And here we have cause for concern, as my survey will prove.

Readers may be shocked, as indeed I was myself, to discover the sheer quantity of error in current journalism. They may be astonished to find how large is the proportion of error culled from the quality press and smart magazines. Assembling the bad sentences together *en masse* brings home to us that we have come to tolerate a shocking degree of slovenliness and illogicality at the level of what is supposed to be educated communication.

In this connection the question may be asked: Why is there so little material here from the much despised tabloid press? In the first place, it would have been foolish to bother with any of those journalists who, knowingly and often semi-comically, exploit ungrammatical colloqui-alisms as a device of supposedly amusing populist appeal. But this was not the sole reason for largely neglecting the tabloids. When I turned to the tabloid press in its soberer sections, I discovered that it was not a fruitful source of material for my purposes. It is easy to explain why. Suppose you wanted to discover what was the standard of literacy in a city's schools. You would not spend a lot of time examining the work of nursery school children who were learning to pen sentences such as 'The cat sat on the mat', if that is how they begin these days. Such children are not treating the written word as a vehicle for thought. They are not attempting to use the English language to reason or reflect. In the same way, a glance at the tabloids reveals that their journalists are all too often preoccupied with a level of utterance so basic and unreflective that they can scarcely go wrong. Writers need to get beyond the 'Janet and John' level of articulacy if they are to aspire to the dignity of interesting error. There is a moral here of course. To cultivate simplicity and directness in expression is a safeguard against error. Neglect of this safeguard accounts for many of the specimens of bad writing from *The Times* and *The Independent* that follow in this book. And leader-writers are among the offenders.

This book is not, however, an examination of the English press designed to show which periodicals deserve bad marks and which deserve good marks. Too few periodicals have been surveyed for that purpose to be justly served. I happened to scrutinise *The Times* and *The Independent* for some months. Had I subjected *The Daily Telegraph* and *The Guardian* to the same treatment, I should still be collecting material. As it was, the reader will see that I studied a few issues of *The Guardian* and *The Daily Telegraph*, but I soon concluded that these two papers did not differ notably from the other two in respect of the amount of error, or, more relevantly from my point of view, in respect of the character of the error. There came a point at which it seemed fruitless to accumulate more and more instances of the same kinds of error.

I have done what I can to satisfy curiosity about the source of my materials. After each quotation the name of the publication from which it is derived is cited. A reference number directs the reader to the Appendix where the date of publication is given. The writer (where known) is also named. This applies to journalists and celebrities, not to people who have written letters to the press.

I must leave others to assess the relevance of my survey to the current debate about English in education. Certainly the material gathered here raises the question whether an educational system can be expected to do much to lift standards of literacy when the young are pitchforked into an adult world in which professional writers and editorial staff are so careless of good usage.

ACKNOWLEDGEMENTS

At several points in this book there is mention of judgments made by 'Fowler'. The reference, of course, is to H. W. Fowler's *A Dictionary of Modern English Usage* (1926) and to the earlier work, *The King's English* (1906), in which H. W. Fowler collaborated with his brother, F. G. Fowler. Subsequent defenders of good English have learned a lot from them.

An expression of my gratitude to the writers who have supplied material for this survey might strike them as churlishly ironic. Yet they must surely sympathise with the general purpose of this book, and I hope therefore that I can justifiably thank them in advance for taking my borrowings in good part. In return I must apologise in advance if, in spite of my best efforts, any writer has been misquoted or misrepresented.

Harry Blamires

– I –

Comparing and Contrasting

1 'Like/unlike'

'Like' and 'unlike' are adjectives which we use to indicate similarities or contrasts between one thing and another or between one person and another. Care has to be taken to ensure that there is no mismatch in these comparisons or contrasts. For all too often, as 'like' and 'unlike' are used today, writers fail to make clear exactly what is being matched with what or who is being matched with whom. Various forms of mismatch can be identified.

1 Total detachment

We say 'Thomas is like/unlike his mother'. Here the words 'like/unlike his mother' derive their validity from their attachment to the noun 'Thomas'; this represents the correct usage.

> Unlike a building society, there are no penalties for withdrawing cash before a term is up. *Moneywise*[1]

This statement (recommending a unit trust) leaves the phrase 'unlike a building society' hanging in the air, unattached to any word in the sentence. The institution which is unlike a building society is not mentioned, yet it is the basis of the contrast. *Unlike a building society, the trust imposes no penalties for withdrawing cash before a term is up.*

> Unlike many jails in Britain, there is no overcrowding. *Independent*[2]

Similarly the sentence here (about the Maze Prison in Northern Ireland) leaves 'unlike many jails in Britain' hanging in the air. The prison that is the starting-point of the contrast is not mentioned. *Unlike many jails in Britain, the Maze does not suffer from overcrowding.*

> Unlike previous speeches, he emphasised the advantages rather than the drawbacks of the treaty . . . *Times*[3]

Peter Riddell seems to be telling us that 'he' (Mr Major) is unlike his previous speeches. *Unlike previous speeches, this one emphasised the advantages rather than the drawbacks of the treaty.*

> There are no Victoria Crosses, unlike the Falklands campaign when two were awarded. *Daily Mail*[4]

1

Again the phrase 'unlike the Falklands campaign' hangs in total detachment. The campaign (the Gulf War) which is 'unlike' the Falklands campaign is not cited. *There are no Victoria Crosses for the Gulf War, unlike the Falklands campaign for which two were awarded.*

> I don't have a car and, unlike New York, everyone tells me not to walk. *Times*[5]

What is unlike New York? Grammatically it appears that 'everyone' is. We know from the previous sentence that the writer is talking about New Haven, but that does not make the grammar here any less slipshod. Either 'unlike' must go – *In contrast to what happens in New York, everyone here tells me not to walk* – or 'New Haven' must come in: *Here in New Haven, unlike New York, everyone tells me not to walk.*

> Those that have not turned back on finding that, unlike the Thames, there are no lock keepers and very few 'facilities' will soon have reached Garston Lock . . . *Waterways World*[6]

There has to be something cited which is 'unlike the Thames'. The passage is about the Kennet and Avon Canal, and it must be mentioned: *Those that have not turned back on finding that, unlike the Thames, the canal has no lock keepers.*

2 Personal mismatch

Especial care is needed when the subject of the sentence is personal, whether a noun or a pronoun. There is always the danger of making a likeness or unlikeness attach to someone to whom it cannot possibly belong, thus producing an absurdity.

> Unlike most holidays, you feel better at the end than when you start. *Moneywise*[7]

The writer seems to be telling you that you are unlike most holidays, but it is a certain kind of holiday that is being recommended as 'unlike' others, and it must be cited. *Unlike most holidays, this one leaves you feeling better at the end than when you start.*

> Unlike some offers, YOU don't have to buy anything. *Daily Mirror*[8]

Again it is not 'You' who are unlike some offers, as the statement suggests. Mention must be made of what really is unlike them. *Unlike some offers, this one does not compel you to buy anything.*

> Room rates range from £165 for a single to £375 for a suite, but, unlike the Randolph, you will find neither kettle nor teabags for a warming midnight brew. *Times*[9]

2

'You' are here seemingly told that you are 'unlike' the Randolph. There is no mention of the hotel which is the true subject of the likeness. *Unlike the Randolph, the hotel in question supplies neither kettle nor teabags for a warming midnight brew.*

> But unlike some accounts, you won't have to wait to collect your windfall. *Daily Mail*[10]

Lloyds Bank's way of flattering is to suggest that you lack any resemblance to certain inferior accounts. The account in question must be mentioned to make sense of 'unlike'. *But unlike some accounts, this one doesn't make you wait to collect your windfall.*

> So, unlike Yoga, you don't have to be a contortionist to find the correct position. *Company*[11]

Others have told you that you are unlike most holidays, unlike a hotel, and unlike certain bank accounts. You are assured by this Tampax advertisement that you are 'unlike' Yoga. The intention was different. *You don't have to contort yourself as you might in Yoga in order to find the correct position.*

> Unlike many banks and building societies, every Firstdirect customer without exception receives a cheque card that not only guarantees cheques to the value of £100, but has a SWITCH facility too. *Independent*[12]

It is the turn now of *every* customer to appear to be unlike many banks and building societies. The intended message was different. *Unlike many banks and building societies, Firstdirect gives every customer without exception a cheque card.*

3 Possessive mismatch

Errors frequently occur when a writer confuses people or things with their attributes. You would not make the mistake of saying or writing 'My hair is like my mother' instead of 'My hair is like my mother's'. Yet this kind of mistake is very common.

> His hair doesn't flop over his forehead like a spaniel . . . *Tatler*[13]

The image of a dog hanging over a man's forehead is what is actually pictured here by the terms used. The mismatch is absurd. *His hair doesn't flop over his forehead like a spaniel's.*

> Like many people, Carol's love of antiques began with an interest in the decorative and embellished look that's typical of Victoriana and Art Nouveau . . . *Ideal Home*[14]

Here we see the same mistake. It is implied that Carol's love of antiques is like many people. That will not do. The love and the people do not

3

match. Once more an apostrophe is needed to make the parallel clear. *Like many people's, Carol's love of antiques began . . .*

The more complicated the sentence, the more easily this error can be overlooked.

> Whether this hyperactive excitability, like children at a birthday party, is suited to making instant long-term decisions is another story. *Times*[15]

This 'excitability' must not be compared with children but with children's excitability. Either an apostrophe must be added – like children's – or an impersonal pronoun ('that of') introduced: *Whether this hyperactive excitability, like that of children at a birthday party.* This treatment is often called for, as in the next example.

> Conventional stalks take care of windscreen wipers and lights, though unlike most European cars, indicators are operated by the right hand stalk. *Cumbria Life*[16]

English indicators must be matched with continental indicators, not with continental cars: *unlike those of most European cars.*

> They rob drugstores, they hustle; and unlike the fully paid-up members of society, their lives are short. *Gentlemen's Quarterly*[17]

Their short lives are not 'unlike' other people, they are unlike other people's. If 'unlike those of the fully paid-up members of society, their lives are short' is too clumsy, then re-write: *Unlike the fully paid-up members of society, they die young.*

> NEDC, a creature of corporation whose nickname Neddy sounds appropriately like a pantomime horse, somehow survived the quango-cuttings of the 1980s. *Times*[18]

The nickname doesn't sound like a pantomime horse. It sounds like the name of a pantomime horse. Either use an apostrophe 's' – *whose nickname Neddy sounds like a pantomime horse's* – or add 'that of': *whose nickname Neddy sounds like that of a pantomime horse.*

> Like so many prominent Trinity men in the seventeenth and eighteenth centuries Sumner's *curriculum vitae* shows a multi-faceted career embracing the army, the church and academe, being at various times, major, chief engineer, fellow and professor. *History Today*[19]

Here the error of matching Sumner's *curriculum vitae* with Trinity men instead of with those men's CVs has to be tackled first: *Like so many prominent Trinity men's in the seventeenth and eighteenth centuries, Sumner's* curriculum vitae . . . But observe too that 'being' can only

4

qualify '*curriculum vitae*'. So the CV is here said to have been a major, a chief engineer, and so on. This second error requires a bigger change: *. . . a multi-faceted career embracing the army, the church and academe. He was at various times major, chief engineer . . .*

4 Other forms of mismatch

Extraordinary ingenuity is displayed in the misuse of 'like' and 'unlike' (see Chapter V, 3). Here we illustrate further mismatches.

> Like most businesses, success requires careful planning. *Money-Maker*[20]

Success cannot be 'like' any businesses. If 'success' is kept, then 'like' must go: *As in most businesses, success requires careful planning.*

> Trevor Cooper, a retired squadron leader, has been owner of The Star for three years and, like many pubs in Hampshire, has gone up-market with his food. *Times*[21]

The squadron leader has surely not behaved like many other pubs in going up-market. He has behaved like other innkeepers: *. . . and, like many other pub-owners in Hampshire . . .*

> Unlike other European markets there has been little room for foreign investment or domestic launches – with only a few niche titles . . . *Marketing Week*[22]

There is no mention in this sentence of the market which is 'unlike' the others. In fact it is the German market, and it must be cited: *Unlike other European markets, the German market allows little room.*

> Like all emotional movements, many strands of society are swept along on a tide of truths, half-truths and non-truths. *The Field*[23]

The strands are said to be 'like' emotional movements. This is not what the writer means. 'Like' is the wrong word and should be replaced by 'as in': *As in all emotional movements, many strands of society are swept along.*

> But unlike America, where fear of Japan's economic might is currently in one of its periodic 'yellow peril' phases, the British have no present-day fears or quarrels to stand in the way of a closer relationship with these other great islanders. *Times*[24]

Here the country (America) is matched with the people (the British). To correct the mismatch either 'America' must be changed – *But unlike the Americans, whose fear of Japan's economic might is currently in one of its 'yellow peril' phases, the British have* – or else 'the British' must be changed: *But unlike America . . . Britain has no present-day fears or quarrels.*

Unlike the Thatcher years, Mr Major's good relations with other leaders give Britain the opportunity to exercise greater influence. *Times*[25]

This erroneously offsets Mr Major's relations with other leaders against the Thatcher years instead of against Mrs Thatcher's relations with other leaders. It appears that political delicacy is at work: *Unlike Mrs Thatcher's, Mr Major's relations with other leaders.* It is surprising to see once more how often an apostrophe can solve the problem of a mismatch after 'like' or 'unlike'.

What makes the task especially difficult is that, unlike Victim Support where there is always a victim, and Bereavement Support where someone has always died, each phone call is very different. *Options*[26]

The phone calls to Missing Persons are clearly *not* 'unlike' the other organisations, but unlike their phone calls: *unlike the calls received by Victim Support, which always involve a victim, and Bereavement Support, which always report a death, the phone calls reaching us are very various.* For our correction of 'where' see Chapter II, 3.

2 'MORE/LESS THAN'

The errors that can trap us when we are paralleling like with like or contrasting opposite with opposite are equally prevalent in sentences in which distinctions are made between what is greater and what is less. Once more the habit of mismatching the subjects of comparison is widespread. For instance, there is the same tendency to confuse a person or a thing with the attributes attaching to them.

1 Possessive mismatch

The weather was already noticeably cooler than southern Florida . . . *Complete Traveller*[1]

Weather in one place may be matched with weather in another place, but not, as in this case, eastern Florida's weather with southern Florida. An apostrophe would correct this: *The weather was already noticeably cooler than southern Florida's.* The same error occurs in comparing the attributes of people.

If he is, as I postulate, a *lowly* bureaucrat, his salary is unlikely to be greater than the supplicant before him. *Times*[2]

The writer, Bernard Levin, should have inserted an apostrophe here: *his salary is unlikely to be greater than the supplicant's.*

6

. . . the food is much better than the average Greek island. *Go Greek*[3]

At first hearing it sounds as though someone has been trying to eat a Greek island. Clearly the island must be distinguished from its food: *the food is much better than that of the average Greek island*

> More importantly, the 14.3 per cent rise to 17.5p is likely to prove the lowest of the ten privatised groups. *Independent*[4]

This passage on Anglian Water compares the company's business results with other companies instead of with their business results. You would not write 'The pocket-money rise of 50p per week was the smallest of the three boys'. Yet that mistake is perpetrated in the financial pages of the press day after day. The match between cash rise and cash rise must be preserved: *the 14.3 per cent rise to 17.5p is likely to prove the lowest increase of the ten privatised groups*.

2 Mismatch of place or time

Two of the examples given above have to do with comparing the situation in one place with that in another in respect of the weather and the food. Mistakes abound in making such comparisons.

> . . . cycling in the US is no more dangerous than England. *Complete Traveller*[5]

Cycling abroad cannot be either more or less dangerous than England – *cycling in the US is no more dangerous than it is in England*

> There must be more swimming pools than Beverly Hills. *Lancashire Life*[6]

(The passage is about the Algarve.) Gramatically, the sentence seems to be telling us that there are more swimming pools than Beverly Hills in the Algarve. 'There are more swimming pools than golf courses' is a sentence that would make sense, for golf courses, like swimming pools, are scattered about the world, while Beverly Hills are not. There is no escape here from using more words: *There must be more swimming pools than there are in Beverly Hills*.

> But the charm is that sooner than any city in the world you become an 'insider'. *Complete Traveller*[7]

You are here told that you can beat any city in the world in the race to become an insider (the piece is about Bangkok). The sentence can be corrected by the insertion of a single preposition – *sooner than in any city in the world* – though it might be better to adjust word order too: *But the charm is that you become an 'insider' here sooner than you do in any city in the world*.

Not all errors in this category are as easily detected as these few we have cited so far.

> The Chanas painted the ceilings upstairs in darker shades to give the rooms a more subdued effect than downstairs, where they wanted a light, airy atmosphere. *Ideal Home*[8]

The 'effect' is not more subdued than 'downstairs': it is more subdued than the effect downstairs. We may regret that English usage is not more concise in this respect, but logic demands more words: *to give the rooms a more subdued effect than that (achieved) downstairs.*

What goes wrong in comparing the situation in one place with the situation in another also tends to go wrong in comparing what happens at one time with what happens at another.

> Although the £3.7bn new consumer credit advanced in June was lower than the previous three months, retail sales volume in June was revised upwards . . . *Daily Mail*[9]

The figure for June was *not* lower than the previous three months; it was lower than the figure for the previous three months: *was less than the sum advanced in the previous three months.*

> Nick Georgano agreed with me that the Citroën truck shown on page 62 of the December issue (*Finds & Discoveries*) looked older than 1948. *Automobile*[10]

You would not say 'My son looks older than 1972' if 1972 was his birthday. We cannot keep 'older' or younger' if the date of origin is to be the basis of comparison: . . . *that the Citroën truck . . . appeared to date from earlier than 1948.*

> Vintage differences are a fascination of drinking claret, but, because 1990 and 1989 were both exceptionally hot summers, their wines resemble each other more closely than any other year of the last thirty, except 1982. *Wine Society leaflet*[11]

A nice point arises here. Established usage would allow one to write '1990 and 1989 were vintages that resembled each other', and to add 'more closely than any other vintage except 1982'. But the writer has denied himself that freedom by defining 1990 and 1989 as 'summers', not as vintages. Quite properly therefore he speaks of '*their* wines'. He must be consistent in what follows: *their wines resemble each other more closely than those of any other year of the last thirty, except 1982.*

3 More complex errors

Hitherto we have for the most part considered instances of error which could be corrected by the insertion of a phrase such as 'that of'. Now we turn to errors whose correction requires something different in the way of grammatical change.

> When such emphatic style appears on the catwalk at Hartnell, it is clear that the revival of a couture house celebrated more for dressing dowagers than its chic is finally complete. *Times*[12]

In 'celebrated more for keeping cats than dogs' it is clear that the dogs as well as the cats are are the objects of the verb 'keeping'. Just so, in 'celebrated more for dressing dowagers than its chic' it might appear that 'its chic', like dowagers, has to wear clothes. (See Chapter V, 5.) Repeat the preposition 'for': *a couture house celebrated more for dressing dowagers than for its chic.*

> Switzerland, Austria, Canada and the countries of Scandinavia have all done better by most economic indicators than the continental economies on whose borders they thrived. *Times*[13]

Here is a straight mismatch. Some 'countries', it is said, have done better than some 'economies'. Either economy should be matched with economy – *The economies of Switzerland, Austria, Canada . . . have all done better . . . than the continental economies* – or country should be matched with country: *Switzerland, Austria, Canada . . . have all done better . . . than the continental countries.* Since the contrast is established *by most economic indicators*, there is no need to introduce the word 'economy', and the second alternative is therefore the better.

> Britain's greater scope for allowing its currency to fluctuate against the other exchange-rate mechanism units also ties its hands less than the hard core members of the currency grid. *Times*[14]

Now we are in deeper water. Consider the basic sentence pattern used here ('Tea costs me less than dinner'). If read accordingly, the above would appear to mean that the hard core members of the currency grid tie Britain's hands more than does Britain's greater scope . . . But the intended comparison is between the degree of freedom enjoyed by Britain and the inhibitions accepted by other countries. *Britain's greater scope for allowing its currency to fluctuate against the other exchange-rate mechanism units permits greater freedom than is permitted to the hard core members of the currency grid.*

We turn to some more tangled mismatches.

> Hunting on the other hand has two possible outcomes; either the fox is killed, usually more quickly and cleanly than most of the alternative methods or it gets away to live another day. *Cumbria Life*[15]

This seems to imply that most alternative methods are killed slowly and dirtily. The colloquial short-cut makes nonsense. Although the insertion of a single preposition would mend matters – *usually more quickly and cleanly than by most of the alternative methods* – it would be preferable to be more precise: *usually more quickly and cleanly than it would be by most of the alternative methods*.

> However, an Auntie Clara, who stayed with us to escape the London blitz, used to take me to the LM&SR station in Avenue Road where platform entry was less formal than the stuffy restrictions of platform tickets at the nearby Great Western station. *Steam Railway*[16]

This enthusiast for steam trains who lived at Leamington Spa manages to contrast platform entry at one station with stuffy restrictions at another: *the LM&SR station in Avenue Road, where the regulations for entry on to the platform were far less strict than they were at the nearby Great Western station.* For a more subtle failure to keep one's head consider the following on the Robert Maxwell case:

> The loss adjusters conclude in a lengthy report that the evidence suggesting that the publisher took his own life is 'more compelling than any other cause' . . . *Times*[17]

The evidence cannot be more compelling than 'any other cause' because the evidence is not a cause. Evidence must be matched with evidence, cause with cause. *The loss adjusters conclude . . . that the evidence pointing to suicide is more compelling than the evidence pointing to any other cause of death.*

In most of the cases dealt with so far there has been mismatch of substance. That is to say, the writer has been talking about an economy when he should have been talking about a country, about children when he should have been talking about their excitability, or about a locality when he should have been talking about its weather. These errors represent material failures of parallelism. Sometimes, however, writers keep their heads in this respect but nevertheless lose control of the grammatical construction used.

> Indeed he was usually keener to talk to a visitor about the latest play or painting he had seen or book he had read than reiterating his well-known views on his own playing. *Times*[18]

In this obituary notice on Claudio Arrau there is a cross-over from one construction to another. You cannot say that a man was keener to talk than reiterating. You must opt for the one construction – *Indeed he was usually keener to talk to a visitor . . . than to reiterate his well-known views* – or the other: *Indeed he was usually happier talking to a visitor . . . than reiterating his well-known views.* Condensing one's meaning colloquially can produce similar error.

I achieve a richer, more subtle surface than mixing the colours on a palette. *The Artist*[19]

The surface is surely not more subtle than mixing. The writer needs to use more words. *I achieve a richer, more subtle surface than I do by mixing the colours on a palette.*

4 Comparative overkill
We must resist the temptation which besets some writers to indulge in what might be called 'comparative overkill'.

Among those who rated confidence high on their lists, there was a higher proportion of those who drank over the limit – more so than among those who wished to project other qualities. *New Woman*[20]

What are we to make of 'more so'? It seems to pile comparative upon comparative. It does not compensate for the omission of 'than there was' which it appears to replace. *Among those who rated confidence high on their lists there was a higher proportion of those who drank over the limit than there was among those who wished to project other qualities.*

The administration does not want a sudden, uncontrolled mass exodus to the United States, still less if unsavoury elements are included and the purpose is to help the Castro government. *Times*[21]

'Still less' than what? The words suggest an emphasis which they cannot grammatically supply. They should be replaced by 'especially'.

The *Daily Telegraph* and *The Independent* devote as much space, if not slightly more, to unit trusts as opposed to share prices. *Meridian*[22]

'As opposed to' is another instance of overkill. Again it appears to represent an attempt to suggest an emphasis which it cannot grammatically supply. If these newspapers devote more space to unit trusts than they do to share prices, it should be said in exactly those words.

Unlike any previous effort to enlist Western financial support, the Soviet Union's present claims for aid are more structured and sophisticated. *Independent*[23]

This is a rarer form of overkill. You might say 'Unlike his brother, John is greedy', or you might say 'John is greedier than his brother'. What you must not do is to telescope the two constructions into 'Unlike his brother, John is greedier', which makes nonsense. So does the above, from which 'more' must be deleted: *Unlike any previous effort . . . the Soviet Union's present claims for aid are structured and sophisticated.*

5 Adverbial comparatives

Generally speaking, the method of making adverbial comparisons is by the use of 'more' and 'most' ('Smith treated me generously', 'Jones treated me more generously', 'Harris treated me most generously'). However, there are some few adverbs which have comparatives matching those of adjectives ('often', 'oftener', 'oftenest'). There are also some adjectives whose comparative and superlative forms are used adverbially ('Smith ran faster, but Jones ran fastest'). Good writers tend to be hesitant about extending these usages to other adverbs.

> You can earn a free return ticket from London to the US easier than on other airlines. *Daily Mail*[24]

You cannot earn anything 'easier'. You can earn it 'more easily'.

> Paraquat is one of the most well known herbicides . . . *Lancashire Life*[25]

The adverb 'well' has the comparative and superlative forms 'better' and 'best'. *Paraquat is one of the best-known herbicides.*

> The bone can actually heal stronger than it was originally. *Sun*[26]

'Heal stronger' is grammatically undesirable; 'heal more strongly' would be clumsy. Better change the construction. *The bone can actually be stronger after healing.*

3 'RATHER THAN'

'Rather than' is used in expressing a preference between two alternatives. The two alternatives should match each other grammatically. 'I smoke a pipe rather than cigarettes.' There the noun 'cigarettes' matches the noun 'pipe'. 'I like to walk rather than to drive.' There the verb 'to drive' matches the verb 'to walk'. Failure to follow this simple pattern is widespread.

1 The intrusive gerund, simple

What we might call the 'intrusive gerund' is popular at every level of sophistication, and is the most common cause of mismatch after 'rather than'. Journalists of the 'quality' press and experts on the specialist magazines provide us plentifully with examples.

> It was cheating to aim deliberately rather than firing immediately, and if proved would certainly lead to a conviction. *The Field*[1]

(The article is about duelling.) Here the gerund 'firing' does not match the infinitive 'to aim'. *It was cheating to aim deliberately rather than to fire immediately.*

> But they have tended to take the first offer they have received rather than juggling with a number of options, which is the usual pattern here. *Independent*[2]

In this sentence about university students who are applying for jobs the error appears again. You would not write 'I tend to stand rather than sitting'. 'They have tended to take the first offer . . . rather than juggling' is just as awkward. *But they have tended to take the first offer they have received rather than to juggle with a number of options.*

> And the young contingent chooses to sleep soundly in Bournemouth boarding houses rather than camping out to great fanfares on the beach below the town's conference centre. *Times*[3]

Again there must be an infinitive to match 'to sleep': *And the young contingent chooses to sleep soundly in Bournemouth boarding houses rather than to camp out to great fanfares on the beach.* It will be observed that the more words there are separating the words that fail to match, the less obvious the mismatch becomes.

> The procedure is a source of wonder, derision and disgust to the rest of the world, but these are emotions which draw in the public to watch the show, rather than ignoring it. *Independent*[4]

Here we have a learned theologian reviewing a book and writing scathingly about the Roman Catholic practice of canonisation. He ought to sense that 'ignoring' cannot match 'to watch': *these are emotions which draw in the public to watch the show rather than to ignore it.*

2 The intrusive gerund, complex

In the instances given above the use of the intrusive gerund was generally able to be corrected by directly substituting another form of the verb, usually the infinitive. Sometimes, however, the correction cannot be so so easily made.

> Rather than taking short positions in markets where that facility may be in doubt, they will probably opt for London. *Economist*[5]

'They will probably opt for London rather than (for) Paris' illustrates a natural usage. Equally natural would be 'They will probably opt for London rather than *for* taking short positions in markets'. But that construction cannot be very happily reversed ('Rather than for taking short positions . . . they will probably opt for London'). It is often awkward to use 'rather than' as the first words of a sentence. Replace 'rather than' here by 'instead of', which is properly followed by a gerund: *Instead of taking short positions . . . they will probably opt for London.*

'Instead of' can be used with greater flexibility than 'rather than'. 'Rather than' expresses a degree of prior choice or eligibility, and is involved in comparing items in terms of preferability. The concept of relative priority is not necessarily involved in use of 'instead of', which is concerned with substitution.

> If you haven't actually managed to pin down what sort of work you're looking for, it can make job-hunting more difficult rather than widening your horizons. *Catch*[6]

Correcting this by bringing 'widening' into line with 'can make' ('it can make job-hunting more difficult rather than widen your horizons') would be less natural than using 'instead of': *it can make job-hunting more difficult instead of widening your horizons.*

> If moving to a larger house with a growing family, check out existing endowments and top up existing policies, rather than cashing them in. *Bella*[7]

The writer presents us with a similar problem here. You cannot say 'Stand up rather than sitting'. Nor can you say 'Check out . . . and top up . . . rather than cashing'. 'Rather than' strictly requires the imperative verbs 'check out' and 'top up' to be matched by another imperative ('check out existing endowments and top up existing policies rather than cash them in'), which would be intolerably unnatural. Here again use 'instead of': *instead of cashing them in.*

> Hazel nuts eaten by mice or voles usually have just a small hole in the shell rather than being broken open. *Waterways World*[8]

What possible forms of words can follow 'rather than' in this sentence? 'Hazel nuts . . . have just a small hole . . . rather than a big one' makes grammatical sense. But there is no grammatical parallel between 'have just a small hole' and 'being broken open'. A complete re-write is required here. *When hazel nuts have been eaten by mice, they will usually have just a small hole in the shell instead of being broken open.*

> Car drivers are less prone to travel sickness than passengers, probably because they are forced to look straight ahead rather than allowing their gaze to wander. *Living*[9]

Here 'rather than' is quite unnecessary: *probably because they are forced to look straight ahead and not allow their gaze to wander.*

14

Unfortunately the letter from the 6000LA crossed with one from York telling the Association that, rather than being allowed to take the 'King' back to Hereford for its overhaul to begin, it was to become the prime attraction at the Great Western Museum. *Steam Classic*[10]

You might get away with 'Rather than being allowed to eat the trifle, he was sent to bed' ('instead of' would be better). But you cannot say 'Rather than being allowed to eat the trifle, it is to be thrown away', where the subject of 'rather than being' is forgotten. Better scrap 'being allowed' here: *instead of going back to Hereford for its overhaul to begin, the 'King' was to become the prime attraction.*

3 Comparative overkill

Comparative overkill occurs when the comparative function of 'rather than' is improperly combined with another comparative expression such as 'more than' or 'better than'. For instance, you might properly say 'It's cheaper to go than to stay', but not 'It's cheaper to go rather than to stay'. The combination of 'cheaper' and 'rather' constitutes comparative overkill.

It's more cost effective to have this all done at once rather than having to keep calling the various tradesmen back to do a room at a time. *Annabel*[11]

To correct the gerund 'having' ('It's more cost effective to have this all done at once rather than to have to keep calling') still leaves us with a faulty sentence, for 'rather' is redundant. *It's more cost effective to have this all done at once than to keep calling the various tradesmen back to do a room at a time.*

This frees the estates to invest more in their vineyards and cellars rather than in bottling equipment and storage space . . . *Decanter*[12]

This time either 'more' or 'rather' is redundant. The writer must sacrifice either 'more' – *This frees the estates to invest in their vineyards and cellars rather than in bottling equipment and storage space* – or 'rather': *This frees the states to invest more in their vineyards and cellars than in bottling equipment.*

The length of your maternity leave will depend on your employer, but according to psychologists Jo Douglas and Naomi Richardson it will be easier for you if you leave when she is six months old rather than waiting until she is at the clinging stage. *New Woman*[13]

The obvious way to improve this might seem to be to correct the mismatch before and after 'rather than' ('if you leave when she is six months old rather than wait until she is at the clinging stage'). However, here again 'rather than' duplicates the comparative impact of 'easier', and must be omitted. And correct the impression that it is a question of not waiting until the employer reaches the clinging age: *it will be easier for you to leave when baby is six months old than to wait until she is at the clinging stage.*

I am addicted to sharper flavours in summer rather than in winter, to things that are sour, sharp or even spicy and hot. *Independent*[14]

The duplication of comparatives ('sharper' and 'rather') will not do. The writer must choose between 'sharper – *I am addicted to sharper flavours in summer than in winter* – and 'rather': *I am addicted to sharp flavours in summer rather than in winter.* He cannot have both.

Once you know that you are better suited to a particular activity on some days rather than others, you will become far more confident in your abilities . . . *New Woman*[15]

You would say 'I am better pleased with this than (with) that', not 'I am better pleased with this rather than with that'. 'Better suited' requires the same treatment. 'Rather' must go. The preposition 'on' might well be repeated: *Once you know that you are better suited to a particular activity on some days than (on) others.*

4 Repetition of preposition
The last example shows how a comparison using 'rather than' can be clarified by repetition of a preposition. This is an improvement which can frequently be made.

For example, the nylon is cut with a hot soldering iron rather than scissors to ensure that the cut ends don't fray. *Cumbria Life*[16]

Greater clarity is achieved by repetition of 'with'. *For example, the nylon is cut with a hot soldering iron rather than with scissors.* In wordier sentences the need for this clarification is often greater.

You will experience the clarity of Modern architecture properly executed and connect Foster with his Classical forebears rather than the grim modern buildings that, for the most part, have desecrated London over the past 50 years. *Independent*[17]

Clarify the meaning, in this article on the architect Sir Norman Foster, by repeating the preposition 'with': *You will . . . connect Foster with his Classical forebears rather than with the grim modern buildings.*

When Reni died he moved his studio into Bologna, taking over something of his old rival's style as well as his clientele, which was perhaps a pity, though probably the result of modesty rather than adapting to the market. *Spectator*[18]

Again repetition of the preposition 'of' is to be recommended: *which was perhaps a pity, though probably the result of modesty rather than of adapting to the market.* There are cases where failure to be strict about this might result in ambiguity. The sentence 'The bad news was the cause of frustration rather than sickness' might leave one wondering whether 'sickness' is the alternative to 'bad news' or to 'frustration' (in conversation inflection would remove doubt). The reader has no doubts about 'The bad news was the cause of frustration rather than of sickness'.

In the same way, comparisons involving 'rather than' will have greater clarity and precision if 'to' is repeated in the infinitive forms that follow verbs of wishing and preferring.

> National Garden Gift Tokens are ideal Valentine gifts for people who prefer to grow their own roses rather than be given a bouquet. *Ideal Home*[19]

Amend this by repeating 'to': *people who prefer to grow their own roses rather than to be given a bouquet.*

For more on the need to repeat prepositions see Chapter V, 5.

4 OTHER CONSTRUCTIONS

1 'similar/same' etc.

When we use 'similar' or 'same' in making comparisons we need to take the usual precautions lest we mismatch the items that are being compared.

> I am sure many readers have had a similar problem to my brother Laurie who . . . damaged a tile . . . *Ideal Home*[1]

Readers might here assume that the writer's brother Laurie was a 'problem'. But it is clear from the context that the problem was Laurie's not Laurie: *a similar problem to my brother Laurie's.*

> To me, the presentation of a dish is as important as its quality – an idea similar to nouvelle cuisine, although I am more generous with my portions. *Family Circle*[2]

The 'idea' is surely not similar to nouvelle cuisine but to the principles of nouvelle cuisine. If 'an idea similar to those of nouvelle cuisine' sounds too stiff, get rid of 'similar': *an idea adapted in nouvelle cuisine.*

Although purists might argue that newer Amish quilts are not pure 'Amish', all the work is done in the same way as older quilts . . . *Period Living*[3]

'I do it in the same way as he does' makes sense because of the match between 'I do' and 'he does'. The words 'all the work is done in the same way as' must be followed by some such expression as 'it always was'. The work and the way it is done is the subject of the comparison. The words 'older quilts' run the comparison into a grammatical cul-de-sac. *Although purists might argue that newer Amish quilts are not pure 'Amish', they are made in exactly the same way as older quilts.*

To become a teacher as part of a life which includes child-rearing and home-making and mixes periods of part-time and full-time participation, is to make a rounded contribution to society. But it does not require the same material reward as the dedicated professional who gives a career completely to teaching. *Times*[4]

The comparison between 'it' (mixing part-time teaching and home-making) and the 'dedicated professional' will not do. The comparison must be between two persons or two things. *But it does not require the same material reward as the dedicated professionalism of the person who gives a career completely to teaching.*

What applies to the use of 'similar' and 'same' applies to certain constructions which serve the same purpose of matching like with like.

Whatever the outcome, the case will have conferred upon the band a degree of notoriety approaching the Sex Pistols and Frankie Goes to Hollywood. *Independent*[5]

The band's notoriety must be likened, not to the Sex Pistols, but to the Sex Pistols' notoriety: *the case will have conferred upon the band a degree of notoriety approaching that of the Sex Pistols.*

Veronica Hanlon, a teacher at Newsome High School, in Kirklees, West Yorkshire, claimed that she was doing work of equal value to three men who were on higher grades. *Independent*[6]

The work was not equal to three men but to three men's work, or rather, we may assume, to the work done by any one of the three. *Veronica Hanlon . . . claimed that she was doing work of equal value to that of any one of three men who were on higher grades.* This may sound over-precise, but legal claims demand precision.

. . . but the Butentown Historic Railway Society's No80150 remains very much in the condition that it left Barry for the short journey to Cardiff. *Steam Classic*[7]

A comparable sentence, 'I remain in the condition that I left home', will perhaps bring out what has gone wrong here: . . . *No80150 remains very much in the condition in which it (was when it) left Cardiff.*

2 'compared with/to'

The most common error in sentences containing 'compared with' or 'compared to' is again the failure to preserve parallelism between things compared.

> But while the goods are sometimes cheap compared with high street prices, they are grotesquely overpriced against their cost. *Times*[8]

Goods must be compared with goods, prices with prices. Either 'goods' must go – *But while the prices are sometimes low compared with high street prices* – or 'prices' must go: *but while the goods are sometimes cheap compared with high street goods.* The purist may amend further: *goods are sometimes cheap compared with those sold in the high street.*

> Each officer took 11.6 days sick leave in 1990 compared to seven or eight days in manufacturing. *Daily Express*[9]

(The subject is Britain's police force.) So many days in 1990 ought not to be compared to so many days in manufacturing. A few more words are needed to correct this. *In 1990 each officer took 11.6 days sick leave compared to seven or eight days taken by employees in manufacturing.*

> Although a fall in the mortgage rate brought about a 5.2 per cent fall in housing costs compared with last month, that was offset . . . *Guardian*[10]

This month's fall must not be compared with last month but with last month's fall. The apostrophe 's' will correct the error: *Although a fall in the mortgage rate brought about a fall in housing costs compared with last month's.*

> At its worst the Firth of Forth can be a fearsome place . . . but even its most tempestuous mood pales to insignificance compared with times past. *Country-Side*[11]

As the fall in the mortgage rate could not be compared with last month, so the tempestuous mood of the Firth of Forth cannot be compared with times past: *but even its most tempestuous mood pales to insignificance compared with the upheavals of time past.*

> Compared to the early career of Disraeli, the contrast is stark. *History Today*[12]

(The subject is Robert Peel.) The mind boggles here. The writer ought surely not to compare a contrast with a career. *His early career contrasts starkly with Disraeli's.*

> In the case of forced intercourse by a steady date (and, to some degree, a forced date) compared with a stranger, men were less likely to regard it as rape than women. *New Woman* [13]

'Compared with' is wrong. Replace it by 'as opposed to': *In the case of forced intercourse by a steady date . . . as opposed to a stranger.*

3 'as opposed to'

We have just cited a case where 'as opposed to' was the appropriate expression to use. The contrast directly matches the 'steady date' and the 'stranger' in grammatical equivalence. Where such a direct match cannot be made, the expression ought not to be used.

> Thus there is no proof of the efficacy of drug treatment in the management of mild high blood pressure, as opposed to the small number of cases with very high blood pressure. *Times* [14]

What is being opposed to what here? Grammatically, mild high blood pressure is contrasted with a small number of cases instead of with very high blood pressure. *Thus there is no proof of the efficacy of drug treatment in the management of mild high blood pressure as opposed to very high blood pressure, which affects only a small number of cases.*

> But both owner-occupiers and tenants now need to have lived in the property as their main residence for only a year in order to qualify for a payment, as opposed to the old five-year qualifying limit. *Moneywise* [15]

You can say 'I favoured a patio as opposed to a flower-bed' because the 'flower-bed' stands in direct contrast to 'patio'. It would be grammatically correct to say 'I lived there a year as opposed to five years', but it would not be very good English because of the weakness of the contrast between one year and five. Here the writer speaks of people living in a residence for only a year as opposed to a qualifying limit. A 'year' cannot be 'opposed to' a 'qualifying limit', and re-phrasing is needed. *But, in order to qualify for a payment, both owner-occupiers and tenants now need to have lived in the property as their main residence for only a year, as opposed to the five years required under the former regulation.*

4 'different from/other than'

Sticklers would rather have 'different from' than 'different to' but some good writers (including Charlotte Brontë) have given 'different to' respectability. We shall not distinguish here.

. . . yet its handling and performance were no different from a conventional narrowboat. *Waterways World*[16]

The mismatch here is what we have got used to in investigating the use of 'like', 'unlike', and 'similar'. The handling and performance of one boat cannot be compared with another boat, only with another boat's handling and performance: *yet its handling and performance were not different from those of a conventional narrowboat.* If that sentence seems too stiff, there is an alternative correction: *yet in handling and performance it was no different from a conventional narrowboat.*

The magazine market in the East is as different to the West as it ever was . . . *Marketing Week*[17]

It is wrong to contrast the market in the East with the West instead of with the market in the West. *The magazine market in the East is as different to that of the West as it ever was.*

The chakras or inner energy centres of women are totally different from men . . . *Independent*[18]

Women's constitutions cannot be in any respect different from men but only from men's: *totally different from men's.*

Because the structure of UK agriculture is somewhat different from that of the continent . . . *Times*[19]

Here is an interesting error. 'That' must refer back to either 'structure' or 'structure of UK agriculture'. If the former is assumed to be the case, then the structure of our agriculture is being compared to the structure of the continent. If the latter is assumed to be the case, then the structure of UK agriculture here is being compared to the structure of UK agriculture on the continent. To make sense, 'UK' must cease to qualify 'agriculture': *Because the structure of agriculture in the UK is somewhat different from that of the continent.*

However, international acceptability of products such as microwave ovens and vacuum cleaners has not been matched by conventional gas and electric cookers. *Times*[20]

Degrees of acceptability can be compared and products can be compared, but acceptability cannot be balanced against products. Keeping 'acceptability' as the subject would be awkward ('international acceptability of products such as microwave ovens and vacuum cleaners has not been matched by the acceptability of conventional gas and electric cookers'). Better change the subject: *Conventional gas and electric cookers have not matched products such a microwave ovens and vacuum cleaners in international acceptability.*

There is ample parking in and around the spacious market place other than on a Friday when the world and its wife visit the weekly market. *Dalesman*[21]

It is obvious what the writer means here and he should have said it: *There is ample parking space in and around the market place except on a Friday.* The tendency to imagine that 'other than' is a rather smart alternative to 'except' has no basis.

The danger is that words such as 'other than' will take on a function collectively that encourages the writer to grow careless of the grammatical limitations imposed by each word separately. It also happens with 'far from' and 'in line with'.

Far from the feared lack of demand, the original moorings were soon taken up and, stage by stage, the moorings extended along the sides of the canal. *Waterways World*[22]

Grammatically speaking, the first phrase here would appear to be defining the location of the moorings ('Far from home, he wandered over the hills'). One way to correct this would be to replace 'far from' by 'in spite of': *In spite of the feared lack of demand, the original moorings were soon taken up.* If 'far from' is preserved, more words will be needed: *Far from there being any lack of demand, as was first feared, the moorings were soon taken up.*

5 *'as/as with/in line with'*

As with the new car or the foreign holiday, people have had to postpone their divorces. *Tatler*[23]

(The article is concerned with the effects of economic recession.) Much is said elsewhere about overuse of the word 'with' (see Chapter V, 4). Another over-used and much abused word 'like' has to be recommended here in place of 'as with': *Like the new car or the foreign holiday, people have had to postpone their divorces.*

Village Farm Cottage dates from the 16th century and, as with many modest buildings, has been extended and altered over the years. *Old-House Journal*[24]

Again 'as with' is out of place and 'like' would be right. *Village Farm Cottage dates from the 16th century and, like many modest buildings, has been extended and altered over the years.*

As with so many other south Lebanese Shia clerics, Abdul Karim Obeid's fate was decided by Ayatollah Khomeini and the Iranian revolution. *Independent*[25]

The only satisfactory way to eliminate 'as with' here is to re-shape the sentence. *Abdul Karim Obeid's fate, like that of so many other south Lebanese Shia clerics, was decided by Ayatollah Khomeini and the Iranian revolution.*

> Now it is generally accepted as valid art although, as everything, it has its detractors. *Viva*[26]

'As' here appears to have the same force as 'as with' in the two previous sentences. It should be replaced by 'like'. *Now it is generally accepted as valid art although, like everything, it has its detractors.*

> This will contain . . . moving robotic dinosaurs as might be seen in a horror movie. *Viva*[27]

'As' was used for 'like' above. Here it is made to do the work of 'such as': *moving robotic dinosaurs such as might be seen in a horror movie.*

> But a proposed law requiring British Standard riding hats to be worn has been held up, thanks to the EC and their policy of only allowing laws which are in line with member countries. *Woman*[28]

Laws cannot be said to be either in line or out of line with member countries, only with their laws: *thanks to the EC and their policy of only allowing laws which are in line with those of other member countries.*

> Anglian will be less immediately well placed than others because of its increasing workforce, in line with expanding sales volume. *Independent*[29]

It is difficult to see what purpose is served by introducing the expression 'in line with' here. If it is used merely to stress that the two developments belong together, then it would be better replaced by 'and': *because of its increasing workforce and its expanding sales volume.* If it is used in order to imply a causal connection between the one development and the other, then it would be better to make the point explicitly: *because of the increasing workforce necessitated by its expanding trade volume.*

– II –
ADDING AND ELABORATING

1 ELABORATION

We have looked at the pitfalls that can upset us when we relate things or people together to make comparisons or contrasts. We now turn to the matter of running concepts together, side by side, to give additional information or to elaborate what has already been said. In the sentence 'Charlotte Brontë, daughter of a Yorkshire parson, became a famous novelist', the words 'daughter of a Yorkshire parson' are put side by side with 'Charlotte Brontë' to shed further light on her by explaining her parentage. In this present section we are concerned with that process of elaboration. And once more we find that the main threat to good writing arises from failing to preserve due parallelism, the parallelism that exists above between 'Charlotte Brontë' and 'daughter of a Yorkshire parson'. Here again mismatches are all too easy to find.

1 Apposition (after)
By the device of apposition in its simplest form a writer adds one noun in parallel to another. In 'Charles Dickens, the novelist, lived here', the words 'the novelist' stand in apposition to the words 'Charles Dickens'.

> It is usual also to obtain a Street Traders' Licence from the Local
> Authority, usually a very nominal sum. *Money-Maker*[1]

Here the phrase 'usually a very nominal sum' stands in apposition to a missing word. It adds to our information about something which has not been mentioned, the cost of the licence. In grammatical construction the sentence implies that the Local Authority is usually a very nominal sum. If the appositional phrase is to be kept, what precedes it must be drastically altered: *It is usual also to put down money for a Street Traders' Licence from the Local Authority, usually a very nominal sum.* There 'a very nominal sum' stands in apposition to 'money'. It would, however be simpler to re-write: *It is usual also to obtain a Street Traders' Licence from the Local Authority, which can be done at little cost.*
Money matters seem to encourage carelessness of this kind.

> . . . Kodak's technically excellent Cinema Digital Sound (CDS) is
> limited by the fact *that* it requires an expensive sound-processing
> device attached to projectors – a cost many exhibitors can do
> without. *Gentlemen's Quarterly*[2]

The words 'a cost' stand in seeming apposition to a missing noun, for the word 'expensive' is an adjective and 'a cost' cannot stand in apposition to it. Some word to match 'cost' must be inserted if the appositional construction is to be kept. *Kodak's technically excellent Cinema Digital Sound (CDS) . . . requires outlay on an expensive sound-processing device attached to projectors – a cost many exhibitors can do without.* There 'a cost' stands in apposition to 'outlay'. Alternatively drop the appositional construction and insert 'at' before 'a cost': *an expensive sound-processing system attached to projectors – at a cost many exhibitors can do without.*

> The daughter of a Polish officer who fought with the British during the war, Miss Cierach was born and brought up in Rhodesia, a life that she loved. *Times*[3]

This sentence contains two appositional constructions – one at the beginning ('The daughter of a Polish officer') quite properly describing Miss Cierach, and one at the end ('a life that she loved') which hangs in the air. You cannot say 'I was born and brought up in Wigan, a life that I loved'. There is no word for 'a life' to relate to in these sentences. Either 'life' must go – *Miss Cierach was born and brought up in Rhodesia, a place that she loved* – or the appositional construction must go: *Miss Cierach was born and brought up in Rhodesia, and she loved the life there.*

> Erith wrote frequent papers for archaeological journals, most of which were beautifully illustrated by drawings and diagrams of his finds, a gift which he shared with his elder brother Raymond . . . *Times*[4]

Here again the word 'gift' stands in apposition to a missing noun. You can say 'Tom had a flair for house-decoration, a gift he shared with his brother', where 'gift' stands in apposition to 'flair'. But you cannot say 'Tom's sitting-room was tastefully decorated, a gift he shared with his brother' because there is no word for 'a gift' to attach itself to. If the appositional construction is kept, an anchorage must be found for it: *. . . most of which were beautifully illustrated by drawings and diagrams of his finds, evidence of a gift which he shared with his elder brother Raymond.*

It seems that elaborating on personal attributes often seduces writers into errors of this kind.

> He made no pretension to scholarship but he had abundant common sense and was physically and mentally 'tough' in the best sense of the word, qualities that naturally reached their peak under the pressures of war. *Independent*[5]

'Qualities' cannot stand in apposition to the adjectival phrase 'physically and mentally "tough"'. Substitute a noun and the sentence can be rescued: *but he had abundant common sense as well as physical and mental 'toughness', qualities that naturally reached their peak under the pressures of war.*

2 Apposition (before)

In one of the sentences above we saw an instance of an appositional construction placed before the noun it related to, and correctly handled ('The daughter of a Polish officer . . . Miss Cierach was born'). It is not hard to find the construction incorrectly handled.

> A Victorian love story, it's a sensitive role but one which David still manages to cram with plenty of sex appeal. *19*[6]

In this review of a film the mismatch is obvious. The Victorian love story is not a 'sensitive role'. The film and the acting role in it are two different things, so that the appositional construction is out of place. *The sensitive role in this Victorian love story is one which David manages to cram with plenty of sex appeal.*

> More than a mere biography of Louis IX, who ruled from 1226–1270, the author examines the emergence of the territorial unity of the French state . . . *History Today*[7]

The review here, this time of a book, may be at a more exalted intellectual level, but the mismatch is no less gross. The author is implied to be something more than a mere biography. Change 'author' to 'book' to get the right parallel. *More than a mere biography of Louis IX, who ruled from 1226–1270, the book examines the emergence of the territorial unity of the French state.*

> Now an isolated ruin lying one mile from the village, it is only too easy to visualise the two desperate brothers who, mounted and in full armour, plunged their blindfold steeds over the ramparts. *In Britain*[8]

The 'isolated ruin lying one mile from the village' constitutes an isolated phrase lying detached from any grammatical mooring. There must be a subsequent noun for it to relate to, or it must go. As so often in the case of stray appositional constructions, it would be better to make a new sentence or clause: *It is now an isolated ruin lying one mile from the village, and it is only too easy to visualise.*

> A favourite haunt of Ruskin, many tales are told of its origin . . . *Cumbria Life*[9]

26

(The subject is the old Bridge House at Ambleside.) This represents our first instance in which an appositional construction is made to relate to a possessive pronoun (or noun) as though it were not a possessive. You can say 'A handsome dog, I loved it', where 'it' is parallel to 'a handsome dog'. But you cannot say 'A handsome dog, I cooked its dinner' because 'its dinner' does not parallel 'dog'. Similarly, 'A favourite haunt of Ruskin' is not parallel to 'its origin'. The origin of the house was no more Ruskin's favourite haunt than the dog's dinner was the dog. Cite the favourite haunt. *A favourite haunt of Ruskin, many tales are told of the origin of the house.*

This appositional mismatch involving the possessive pronoun occurs frequently in portrayals of people.

> Still a student at the Royal College of Art, his strangely amorphous designs take their forms from architecture, ethnology and . . . underwater life. *The World of Interiors*[10]

Here 'his strangely amorphous designs' are implied to be still a student at the Royal College. 'Still a student at the Royal College' must be anchored in what follows. *Still a student at the Royal College of Art, he derives his strangely amorphous designs from architecture.*

> The first person to fly the Atlantic solo from east to west, Beryl Markham's reputation rests on her best-selling memoir, *West with the Night. Times*[11]

The possessive mismatch appears again; Beryl Markham's reputation was not a person and did not fly the Atlantic. *The first person to fly the Atlantic solo from east to west, Beryl Markham is now remembered for her best-selling memoir.*

> The winner of every children's award going (and inaugural winner of the Guardian's in 1967), his adventures in country houses, seaports and back alleys echo and meet the challenges of Fielding and Dickens . . . *Guardian*[12]

To say 'his adventures' when you mean the adventures of 'his' characters is inelegant at best. More importantly, his adventures were not in fact 'the winner' of any awards. Better abandon the appositional construction: *He is the winner of every children's award . . . His characters' adventures in country houses.*

3 Unattached adjectival phrase
Just as we must ensure that appositional constructions are properly attached where they belong, so too we must ensure that adjective phrases do not get detached from the nouns they qualify.

27

> Eager to avoid the cluttered look associated with the Victorian era, simply wrought iron furniture was used to create a more modern look. *Laura Ashley brochure*[13]

Who is 'eager to avoid' something? Their identity remains a mystery. Grammatically, it appears that 'simply wrought iron furniture' is eager to avoid something. The word 'eager' is misplaced, and demands anchorage to a person. *Eager to avoid the cluttered look associated with the Victorian era, we used simply wrought iron furniture.* Alternatively change the construction. *In order to avoid the cluttered look associated with the Victorian era, simply wrought iron furniture was used.*

> Positive that we could match their skills, it was back on court for two more hours to put all the theories into practice. *Elle*[14]

Here 'Positive that we could match their skills' is left hanging in the air. As so often, the error results from evasion of what is most simple and natural. *Positive that we could match their skills, we went back on court for two more hours.* The writer was ensnared by the jaunty flourish of 'it was back on court' and forgot that 'it' could not be 'positive'.

> Personally impressive, trilby hat tipped over bald head, gregarious, ever ready with smiles but producing a calculated temper when needed, his own dance record commanded respect from every dancer he directed . . . *Independent*[15]

Here the writer is even more forgetful. He gives a series of descriptive introductions to the citing of a person and then forgets to mention him. Instead he tells us that someone's dance record is gregarious and wears a trilby hat. *Personally impressive . . . ever ready with smiles but producing a calculated temper when needed, he had a dance record which commanded respect.*

4 'as' (in the capacity of)

Wherever phrases perform the kind of descriptive function we have been investigating, there is the danger that they may float away from their proper anchorage. In the sentence 'As a violinist, he was outstanding', the words 'as a violinist' are anchored to the subject 'he'. Yet writers frequently allow comparable phrases to become inattached.

> As a listed building, electrical wiring and lights have been well camouflaged. *Period Living*[16]

The electrical wiring and lights are not a listed building, as the above suggests. The force of 'as' appears here to be vaguely causal, and it would be better to make this causal element explicit: *Because it is a*

28

listed building, electrical wiring and lights have been well camouflaged.

As a member of the National Breakdown your car is covered 24 hours a day, 365 days a year, anywhere in the UK. *Independent*[17]

It appears here that membership of the National Breakdown is granted to cars and not to their owners. *As a member of the National Breakdown, you have your car covered 24 hours a day.*

As a single mother with two school-age children, moving is not practicable. *Times*[18]

But moving is not a 'single mother'. *As a single mother with two school-age children, she finds moving impracticable.*

John Rich's command of the spoken word was erratic, his memory unreliable. But as the dumb Harlequin, this did not matter. *Vivid*[19]

The phrase 'as the dumb Harlequin' is meant to relate to John Rich, but in the sentence in which it occurs it relates to 'this'. *John Rich's command of the spoken word was erratic, his memory unreliable. But when he played the part of the dumb Harlequin, this did not matter.*
In longer sentences the error tends to get lost to sight.

As Prime Minister for 12 months and Chancellor before that, the sharp stabbing pains caused by unemployment rising above 2.5 million undoubtedly falls into the category of self-inflicted injury. *Times*[20]

There are three grave grammatical errors here. A plural subject governs a singular verb ('the sharp stabbing pains . . . undoubtedly falls'). The 'gerciple' ('by unemployment rising') (see Chapter III, 5) should be scrapped ('by the rise of unemployment'). More immediately, we cannot have stabbing pains functioning 'as prime minister'. *As Prime Minister for 12 months and Chancellor before that, John Major ought to regard the sharp stabbing pains caused by the rise of unemployment above 2.5 million as a self-inflicted injury.*
It is interesting to speculate about how much idiomatic freedom can be allowed in the use of this construction.

Her own interest in the subject took root as a child in a household where turning off unwanted lights was a duty. *Country Living*[21]

This so clearly identifies her interest 'as a child' that it cannot be allowed. *Her own interest in the subject took root when she was a child.*

As a pianist, his own technique was formidable, encompassing the strength and breadth of colour of an orchestra . . . His public career began early, at the Wigmore Hall aged four, and he had become a well-known prodigy in Europe by 11. *Independent*[22]

Strictly considered, 'As a pianist, his own technique was formidable' implies that his technique was a pianist. Yet idiomatic usage would allow 'His technique as a pianist was formidable' just as it would allow 'His career as a conductor was a fruitful one'. Nevertheless we cannot allow 'his public career' to be said to be 'aged four'. *His own technique at the piano was formidable, encompassing the strength and breadth of colour of an orchestra . . . His public career began early, at the Wigmore Hall when he was only four, and he had become a well-known prodigy in Europe by the age of 11.*

2 ADDITION

In the sentence 'Charlotte Brontë, daughter of a Yorkshire parson, became a famous novelist', the phrase 'daughter of a Yorkshire parson' sheds further light on the subject 'Charlotte Brontë'. In the sentence 'Charlotte Brontë, along with her sisters Emily and Anne, wrote novels that have survived', the phrase 'along with her sisters Emily and Anne' adds to the subject 'Charlotte Brontë' by accumulating parallel concepts in concurrence with it. In using expressions which operate in this accumulative way, we have to guard against mismatches once more.

1 'together with, along with' etc.
You can say 'Together with my friends I sampled the baked beans', which aligns your friends with yourself in the same act, or you can say 'Together with the bacon I sampled the baked beans', which aligns the bacon and the beans in the same process. But you ought not to say 'Together with two other cans of beans, the source of the bacon was the local supermarket'. Yet that is something like what happens in the sentence below.

Together with the two other early Norman castles in the City of London, Monfichet Tower and Baynard's Castle, the origins of the Tower can be traced back to the winter of 1066/67 . . . *History Today*[1]

This aligns 'two early Norman castles' with the 'origins' of the Tower, instead of with the Tower itself. *Together with the two other early Norman castles in the City of London, Monfichet Tower and Baynard's Castle, the Tower has origins dating back to the winter of 1066/67.*

Work was speeded up together with alterations to the water supply, to be finished by June 1940. *British Railways Illustrated*[2]

What is the force of 'together with' here? Grammatically it would appear to suggest that not only was the work speeded up but alterations to the water supply were speeded up too. Yet those alterations were part of the work. *Work, which included alterations to the water supply, was speeded up, to be finished by June 1940.*

> Together with the evidence of recession from the output figures and the monthly industrial trends surveys, there is justification enough on domestic grounds for another cut in rates. *Independent*[3]

(The subject is a CBI report on factory gate prices.) This is like saying 'Together with the sausage and mash, the meal was a good one'. The sausage and mash were part of the meal, just as the 'evidence of recession' is part of the 'justification'. 'Together with' must be disentangled from its present connection with 'justification'. *Together with the evidence of recession from the output figures and the monthly industrial trends surveys, figures from the domestic market provide justification for another cut in rates.*

> Along with our new look, we have streamlined our advance booking, making it easier for you to book tickets for the coming season. *ENO circular*[4]

The English National Opera authorities do not really mean that they have streamlined their new look as well as their advance booking, but that is what they say. Presumably the reform of the booking system is additional to the acquisition of a new look. *In addition to acquiring a new look, we have streamlined our advance booking.* But perhaps 'new look' is current code for a general shake-up which includes box office matters: *As part of our reformation we have streamlined our advance booking.*

> 'The Triumph of Bacchus' is one of a pair of unique 16th century Brussels tapestries. Along with 'The Labours of Hercules', once cleaned both will hang in the King's Apartments at the Palace when it re-opens to the public in July. *Old-House Journal*[5]

'Joan is one of two twins. Along with Jill, both are going to school.' How many children are there? How many tapestries are there if 'both' will hang along with 'The Labours of Hercules'? *'The Triumph of Bacchus' and 'The Labours of Hercules' are a pair of unique 16th century Brussels tapestries. Once cleaned, they will hang in the King's Apartments at the Palace.*

> This compact size, in common with all the other Sunmed south coast resorts, makes for a very friendly holiday. *Go Greek*[6]

You can say 'Tom Jones, in common with all his class-mates, had strong biceps', but you cannot say 'Tom's strong biceps, in common with all his class-mates, made for athletic prowess'. There has to be clear understanding of what is 'in common with' what. *The island of Matala, in common with all the other Sunmed south coast resorts, has a compact size which makes for a very friendly holiday.*

> The determination of some of the boutiques not to release their wines until they think they are ready, coupled with other wineries being more pragmatic and putting wines out when they are drinkable, in the short term, means that there is going to be a diversity of styles within each varietal group. *Decanter*[7]

You cannot say 'My determination to travel, coupled with my wife being happier at home, has caused a domestic rift'. But you could say 'My determination to travel, coupled with my wife's preference for staying at home, has caused a domestic rift'. 'Determination' must be 'coupled with' a matching noun: *The determination of some of the boutiques not to release their wines until they think they are ready, coupled with the greater pragmatism of other wineries in putting wines out when they are drinkable.*

2 'as well as/besides'

'As well as' links two items. 'As well as sandwiches we took cans of beer.' 'Sandwiches' and 'cans of beer' match in partnership.

> . . . 'The History of British Trade Unionism, c. 1770–1990' by Keith Laybourn (24), which charts the rise and decline of the trade union movement in Britain, as well as a historiographical review of the debates on the movement that have divided historians over the years. *History Today*[8]

You can take cans of beer as well as sandwiches, but you cannot chart 'the rise and decline of the trade union movement as well as a historiographical review'. The review is not something to be charted. Eliminate 'as well as': . . . *which charts the rise and decline of the trade union movement in Britain, and makes a historiographical review of the debates on the movement.*

There is a temptation to use 'as well as' to convey a vague enthusiasm for aggregation without reference to grammatical fitness.

> As well as the river's commanding presence, the countryside here is plain and solid . . . *The World of Interiors*[9]

The temptation is here at its most damaging. *The river here has a commanding presence, and the countryside is plain and solid.*

As well as how it will operate, the plan is likely to include a cashflow projection (predicting the flow of money in and out of the business during the first year of trading) . . . *Money-Maker*[10]

Re-arrange the wording and the error is brutally exposed ('the plan is likely to include a cashflow projection as well as how it will operate'). If 'as well as' is used, then 'projection' must acquire a partner: *As well as an explanation of how it will operate, the plan is likely to include a cashflow projection.*

Errors abound when 'as well as' is used to partner processes rather than items. 'The treatment was intended to give him pleasure as well as to restore his health.' Parallelism must be thus maintained between the partnered processes (to give pleasure, to restore health).

Tony Lacey succeeded Kaye Webb as chief editor of Puffin books and proved remarkably astute in the way he increased Puffin's popularity as well as upgrading much of its fiction list. *Annabel*[11]

Once more 'as well as' proves a snare. 'The way he increased . . . as well as upgrading' will not do. It is rarely correct to follow 'as well as' by a gerund. (It is correct only when one gerund is partnered by another: 'He enjoyed hunting as well as fishing'.) Take out 'as well as': . . . *proved remarkably astute in the way he increased Puffin's popularity and upgraded much of its fiction list.*

As well as giving me confidence I gained a thorough knowledge of the modelling world, from learning make-up and grooming to how to keep my books for the tax man. *Catch*[12]

(This piece is about a course at the London College of Fashion.) The thing that is 'giving' confidence must be cited. 'As well as giving me stomach-ache, the pudding made me sick' would make sense, but not 'As well as giving me stomach-ache, I lost an ear-ring'. Eliminate 'giving' – *As well as confidence I gained a thorough knowledge of the modelling world* – so that 'confidence' and 'knowledge' are appropriately partnered as objects of 'gained'.

It's vital to know when a baby's due so that you can organise antenatal care and parentcraft classes, as well as beginning all the preparations you and your partner need to make. *Parents*[13]

Here is more evidence that 'as well as' is almost always better avoided. Simply replace it by 'and'. *It's vital to know when a baby's due so that you can organise antenatal care and parentcraft classes, and begin all the preparations you and your partner need to make.*

The Prime Minister, using the Royal Prerogatives, enjoys immense power to make war; sign treaties; agree to European Community legislation; appoint ministers, peers, archbishops and judges; as well as determining who will head our public institutions – all without a legal requirement to consult anyone. *Independent*[14]

We see here how, at a more sophisticated level, misuse of 'as well as' may be almost lost to sight in a welter of words. Tony Benn (for it is he) would probably not write 'He has power to stay as well as going', for he would keep his head through the construction and write 'He has power to stay as well as to go'. Yet here he slips into just such a mistake. Correct as before: *The Prime Minister . . . enjoys immense power to make war, sign treaties, agree to European Community legislation; appoint ministers, peers, archbishops and judges; as well as to determine who will head our public institutions.*

Before writing the phrase 'as well as', we should recall Fowler's observation that the strict meaning of the expression is not 'besides' but 'and not only'. 'Besides' means 'in addition to'.

> Besides a sporty past and present – tennis is still a great love – the Bishop enjoys gardening at home at Hartlebury Castle, Kidderminster . . . *Gateway*[15]

The word is misused here, for the Bishop does not enjoy a sporty past in addition to gardening at home, though that is the message conveyed. *A man with a sporty past and present – tennis is still a great love – the Bishop enjoys gardening at home.*

3 'not only (just) but also'
Strict parallelism must be preserved in the use of this construction. Mistakes arise through carelessness over word order.

> Manchester's MBA deals with what is termed 'corporate responsibility', which covers not only environmental concerns, but also raises questions on social and political policy related to business management. *Green Magazine*[16]

You can say 'He enjoys not only cricket but also football', but you cannot say 'He enjoys not only cricket but also plays football'. That is the error committed above. Change the positioning of 'not only' and all is well: *'corporate responsibility', which not only covers environmental concerns but also raises questions on social and political policy related to business management.*

> A particularly pleasant way of doing so is to put yourself into the hands of the Maison Tolbooth, which is not only an exceptional restaurant but it also has featured, albeit as a humble cottage, in Constable's painting *The Vale of Dedham*. *In Britain*[17]

Where two verbs are partnered by 'not only . . . but also' ('not only sings well but also plays the piano') 'not only' and 'but also' must precede the respective verbs, here 'is' and 'has featured': *the Maison Tolbooth, which not only is an exceptional restaurant but also has featured . . . in Constable's painting.* (The intrusive 'it' of 'but it has also featured' compounds the error.) In fact, even corrected, the construction is awkwardly out of place here and would be better dropped: *. . . which is an exceptional restaurant and has featured . . . in Constable's painting.*

> Agricultural buildings raise not only the question of money for repairs but of use. *Times*[18]

It would be correct to detach 'not only' from 'the question' and relate it to 'of money' – *Agricultural buildings raise the question not only of money for repairs but also of use* – but it would be better to repeat 'the question': *raise not only the question of money for repairs but also the question of use.*

> His appointment further strengthens the company's management team as it not only continues to meet popular demand for its wide range of quality new homes but also as it plans for the expected general upturn in the housing market later in the year. *Investors Chronicle*[19]

There were two possible alternatives here: *strengthens the company's management team as it not only continues to meet popular demand . . . but also plans*, and *strengthens the company's management team not only as it continues to meet popular demand . . . but also as it plans.* What we have got is an improper mixture of the two.

> With this arrangement, not only is the traveller spared the trouble of having to arrange insurance for each overseas visit, but, it also eliminates this cost element of overseas travel. *Meridian*[20]

If you begin 'not only is the traveller fleeced', you must complete the sequence, 'but he is also flogged'. Here 'not only is the traveller spared' opens a sequence that is never completed. The sentence must be re-written and the dangerous words, 'with' and 'not only' eliminated. *This arrangement spares the traveller the trouble and expense of arranging insurance every time he travels.*

> The variety of the work and level of responsibility of the positions requires that the successful applicants are not only possessed with a good academic ability but also be practical and have aspirations to move into the management of the operations. *Daily Telegraph*[21]

There is something sinister about wanting people 'possessed with' something or other. And the advertisement requires that the candidates *are* not only this but also *be* that. Bring the verbs into line: *requires that the candidates are not only academically able but also practical and ambitious to move into the management.*

> English-language competence is the passport not only to success at work, but also a more fulfilling life. *Independent*[22]

This exemplifies another trap for the careless in use of 'not only'. It is not that word-order needs to be changed but that the preposition ('to') needs to be repeated: . . . *the passport not only to success at work, but also to a more fulfilling life.* (See too Chapter V, 5.)

4 'apart from'

When properly used, 'apart from' isolates something. It defines an exception. The modern practice of using it to mean 'besides' or 'in addition to' is difficult to justify.

> Apart from the more familiar destructive patterns of anorexia, compulsive over-eating or self-mutilation by which women try to 'punish' their bodies, sex is another way in which they may express self-loathing. *New Woman*[23]

Clearly 'apart from' here is not introducing exceptions but a list of habits to which 'another way' is added, and becomes merely a device for emphatically piling instance upon instance. Use 'in addition to': *In addition to the more familiar destructive patterns of anorexia, compulsive over-eating or self-mutilation by which women try to punish their bodies, sex is another way . . .*

> Apart from displaying Rembrandt at his best, the occasion has a didactic purpose, which becomes apparent at the end of the exhibition of pictures and drawings. *Vivid*[24]

'Apart from' is again not the most suitable expression. Use 'as well as', 'in addition to' or 'besides'. *In addition to displaying Rembrandt at his best, the occasion has a didactic purpose.*

> Like sponsors of similar issues, Lloyds points out that, over the medium to long term, the shares of UK smaller companies have outperformed their bigger brethren apart from the last two years. *Investors Chronicle*[25]

This implies that the 'last two years' are 'bigger brethren' that have not been outperformed, whereas it is *during* 'the last two years' that performance is excepted from the general rule: *the shares of UK smaller companies have outperformed their bigger brethren except during the last two years.*

Kathy had missed England acutely: she had no gift for languages and apart from the obvious pleasures of warmth and beautiful landscape, Kathy always felt lonely in France. *Independent*[26]

You could say 'Apart from the mathematics, she enjoyed her studies', where 'apart from' clearly links 'mathematics' and 'studies', but you could not say 'Apart from hatred of the mathematics she always felt happy at school' because a grammatical sequence is there left incomplete. Get rid of 'apart from': *she had no gift for languages and, although she shared the obvious pleasures of warmth and beautiful landscape, Kathy always felt lonely in France.*

3 RELATIVE CLAUSES

We started our study of apposition with the sentence 'Charlotte Brontë, the daughter of a Yorkshire parson, became a famous novelist'. The same meaning might have been conveyed by the sentence 'Charlotte Brontë, who was the daughter of a Yorkshire parson, became a famous novelist'. The relative clause ('who was the daughter of a Yorkshire parson') is another device for adding explanatory material. In using relative clauses, many of which begin with 'who', 'which' or 'that', we have to exercise the same care as we did with appositional constructions and adjective phrases to ensure that they are properly connected to the words they qualify.

1 'who/whom'

Writers sometimes slip up over the use of the relative pronoun 'who'. I may refer to the man 'who kicked me' (where 'who' is the subject of the verb 'kicked') or to the man 'whom I kicked' (where 'whom' is the object of the verb 'kicked'). Clearly commonsense demands that there should be no confusion over who kicks and who is kicked. Nevertheless misuse of 'who' in place of 'whom' is widespread. Here are instances in which 'who' must be corrected to 'whom'.

I was expecting to be faced by a formidable *grande dame*, maybe a touch severe and remote like Queen Mary who she had recently played on television . . . (Peggy Ashcroft obituary) *Independent*[1]

Catherine Walker, who Marion profiles this month, gives brides no such problems . . . *Tatler*[2]

The children . . . live in Norway with their mother, Anne Britt Kristiansen, who Cash never married. *Esquire*[3]

. . . one of those marvellously forthcoming women who shy people dread and journalists love. *Options*[4]

It'll be her husband Rob – who she sees about eight times a year . . . *Woman*[5]

. . . she had a particular problem with one team member who she had not confronted herself. *Nursing Standard*[6]

The research examined couples for who mortgage rescue was the best chance of staying in their homes. *Times*[7]

It is less easy to find 'whom' where 'who' is wanted, though not impossible.

Some of the clearest, sprightliest prose comes from the pen of Alessandra Ponte, whom one imagines was not born in Bedford. *Spectator*[8]

Here we must substitute 'who' and also change the punctuation: *Alessandra Ponte, who, one imagines, was not born in Bedford.*

Today Vanessa is in a relationship with a man whom she says is equally as jealous as she is . . . *Bite*[9]

Apply the same treatment: . . . *in a relationship with a man who, she says, is as jealous as she is.* 'Who' is needed in these two sentences because the pronoun is the subject of following verbs ('who . . . was not born' and 'who . . . is as jealous').

Although 'whom' does not often masquerade as 'who', there is a curious tendency to use 'whomsoever' where 'whosoever' would be correct. Even a Home Secretary (Kenneth Baker) can so offend.

The police will continue to do their duty . . . and to take effective action against offenders, whomsoever they may be. *The Field*[10]

In 'I shall distrust him, whoever he is', 'him' is the object of the verb 'distrust', but 'whoever' agrees with 'he' as subject of 'is'. *The police will continue . . . to take effective action against offenders, whosoever they may be.*

'Tomorrow, as the noonday bell tolls,' she says, 'whomsoever passes through the city gate will be your ruler.' *Opera Now*[11]

This is exactly the same grammatical mistake as saying 'Him went through the gate' instead of 'He went through the gate': *whosoever passes through the city gate will be your ruler.*

2 'whose/who's'

Confusion over this distinction ought surely to be expected only in the lower forms of our schools. 'Who's' is an abbreviation of 'who is' or 'who has'. Unless one of these can be substituted for 'who's' then 'who's' is wrong.

> She is a storyteller who's timing and planning is as rich as a full bodied mature wine. *Spare Rib*[12]

She is a storyteller whose timing and planning . . .

> And stars characters who's bodies turn with their head. *Private Eye*[13]

This caption accompanies a cartoon in the comic strip about the BBC. One would like to believe that there is some subtle, ironical joke here, perhaps even at the expense of the reader. Nevertheless, even at the risk of seeming humourless, I must correct it. *And stars characters whose bodies turn with their heads.*

3 'which/that'

In 'He was late home for dinner, which had gone cold', 'which' relates directly back to the single word 'dinner'. In 'He was late home for dinner, which annoyed his wife', 'which' relates back to the whole clause preceding it. Both uses of 'which' are legitimate, but it is important to avoid phrasing which seems to hover between the two usages, leaving the reader slightly uncomfortable even though the usage cannot always be declared incorrect.

> Females of all ages are more commonly affected than males. It has been suggested this is due to hormonal factors, which is backed up by the fact that women are most prone to travel sickness during menstruation and pregnancy. *Living*[14]

It would be better here to clarify the relationship of 'which' to what precedes it: *It has been suggested that this is due to hormonal factors, a theory which is backed up by the fact that women are most prone to travel sickness during menstruation and pregnancy.*

> They do, however, treat them for flystrike in June which is approved by the Soil Association . . . *Cumbria Life*[15]

Again it would be more elegant to clarify the function of 'which'. *They do, however, treat them for flystrike in June, a practice which is approved by the Soil Association.*

> Only in this way could the possibility be avoided of purchasing a boat which subsequently might prove not to be up to standard and which the cost of bringing up to standard proved to be prohibitive. *Waterways World*[16]

You cannot say 'Here is a house which the cost of buying I cannot afford'. You need to use the words 'whose cost'. Amend this accordingly: . . . *purchasing a boat which subsequently might prove not to be up to standard and whose repair to the required standard might prove to be prohibitively costly.*

'That' is often used as an alternative to 'which' or 'who'. The same rules govern its usage.

> . . . he is on the look-out for a suitable property that would be his last move. *Cumbria Life*[17]

Here the misuse of the relative 'that' is at its worst. There must be a noun or a clause for 'that' to relate to, and here it relates back neither to 'suitable property' nor to the fact that 'he is on the look-out'. The construction must be changed: *he is on the look-out for a suitable property so that he can make his last move.*

> The place that one usually expects to find tiles is on the roof . . . *Traditional Homes*[18]

You cannot say 'the place that I live' when you mean 'where I live'. *The place where one usually expects to find tiles is on the roof.*

> In response to the controversies the Securities and Investments Board (SIB) recently announced that it would review all the ways that financial products are sold to the public . . . *Money-wise*[19]

Colloquially we may refer to 'the way that he does it', but the proper usage remains 'in which': *SIB recently announced that it would review all the ways in which financial products are sold to the public.*

> The Booker Prize is one way that we recognise outstanding ability and reward excellence. *Times*[20]

You might say 'one way in which we recognise' (which corrects the misuse of 'that') but 'way' is not the best word here: *The Booker prize is one device for recognising ability and rewarding excellence.*

4 'when/where'

Used to introduce a relative clause, used adjectivally that is, 'when' must relate to a noun with a temporal meaning. You can speak of 'the day when I arrived' or 'the period when I was a bookmaker', but you cannot speak of 'the concert when I fainted'. It must be 'at which'.

> The decisive engagement between the Roman general Sulla . . . and the army of Mithridates . . . took place near monuments to an earlier battle, when Philip II of Macedon, father of Alexander the Great, broke the power of the Greek city states in 338 BC. *Times*[21]

40

You cannot refer to a 'battle when Philip' did this or that. The construction is 'in which': . . . *took place near monuments to an earlier battle, in which Philip II of Macedon . . . broke the power.*

> The vertical shape of the painting adds to the strained atmosphere and the girl is very much *against* the background, unlike John's treatment of other subjects, when the area around the figure is broken by spots of subtle colour. *The Artist*[22]

(For the misuse of 'unlike' see Chapter I, 1.) The word 'when' cannot depend on 'treatment of other subjects': *John's treatment of other subjects, in which the area around the figure is broken by spots of colour.*

> AXA 527 is a late 1933 registration by when most Austins had a more modern appearance. *Automobile*[23]

'1933 registration' are not words on which a 'when' clause can hang. *AXA 527 is a registration dating from 1933, by which time most Austins had a more modern appearance.*

What applies to 'when' also applies to 'where' in introducing a relative clause.

> Swimming lessons, where your child goes into the water with a teacher, start at 3 or 4 years old . . . *Parents*[24]

'Where' here introduces a clause qualifying 'swimming lessons': *Swimming lessons, in which your child goes into the water with a teacher . . .*

> Whichever mask you buy, it must enclose the nose, to counter the effects of mask squeeze (where your eyes pop out). *Outdoors illustrated*[25]

You can say 'He squeezed me where it hurts' because the 'where' clause there qualifies the verb 'squeezed', but not 'I like the kind of squeeze where you feel like jelly', because the 'where' clause there is made to qualify 'the kind of squeeze': . . . *to counter the effects of mask squeeze (which makes your eyes pop out).*

> First impressions of Pinero are of rustic charm and cleanliness but what will remain with you is a different South American experience, where conservation is being allowed to work. *Green Magazine*[26]

'Where' cannot refer back to the adjective 'South American' or to the noun 'experience'. If 'where' stays, 'South America' must somehow come in: *what will remain with you is experience of a different South America, where conservation is being allowed to work.*

> The guidelines, drawn up with the Joint Consultants Committee, come after concern that the GP fund-holding scheme, where

doctors can buy hospital care, was leading to a two-tier service. *Times*.[27]

Replace 'where' by 'in which', 'by which' or 'under which': *the GP fund-holding scheme, under which doctors can buy hospital care.*

(For further treatment of 'when' and 'where' clauses see Chapter V, 2.)

– III –
HANDLING PARTICIPLES & GERUNDS

We turn now to constructions which probably produce more errors in current usage than any other, and it would have been easy to multiply the number of faulty sentences cited in this section from the material collected.

1 DETACHED PRESENT PARTICIPLE

We have already investigated the kind of descriptive addition represented by apposition ('Charlotte Brontë, daughter of a Yorkshire parson, became a famous novelist') and the kind represented by a relative clause ('Charlotte Brontë, who was the daughter of a Yorkshire parson, became a famous novelist'). There is another kind of descriptive addition, 'Charlotte Brontë, writing in a remote Yorkshire village, became a famous novelist'. In the first of these descriptive additions, 'daughter of a Yorkshire parson', there is no verb. In the second, 'who was the daughter of a Yorkshire parson', there is a straightforward verb, 'was'. In the third, however, 'writing in a remote Yorkshire village', there is a verb 'writing' which acts adjectivally by its descriptive connection with the subject 'Charlotte Brontë'. The verb used thus adjectivally is a 'participle', and the participle, being adjectival, cannot function except in agreement with a noun or noun-substitute. In 'Walking down the street, I met an old friend', the present participle 'walking' agrees with 'I', and all is well. But you cannot say 'Walking down the street, the rain began to fall' for the simple reason that the rain was not walking down the street. There is nothing for the adjectival 'walking' to attach itself to. We call it a 'detached participle', examples of which now plague the press.

1 Crude mismatch

> Listening to Mr Gorbachev's post-summit presentation, his ignorance was certainly striking. *Times*[1]

Who was 'listening'? According to the rules of grammar, his 'ignorance' was listening. If the participle is to be kept, then a noun or pronoun must be supplied for 'listening' to attach itself to: *Listening to*

Mr Gorbachev's post-summit presentation, I found his ignorance striking.

> Knowing it was certain to rain sometime during the day, gaberdines were always essential baggage. *Dalesman*[2]

It was not the gaberdines that knew it was going to rain. *Knowing it was certain to rain sometime during the day, we always took gaberdines.*

> Screeching to a halt just round the corner for the best croissants in the town at The Brasserie, my spectacular diagonal parking is somehow more acceptable in a car of this character. *Esquire*[3]

As wordiness increases the error is less exposed. This writer says that his spectacular diagonal parking screeched to a halt. He must not be so shy of mentioning himself. *Screeching to a halt just round the corner for the best croissants in town at The Brasserie, I found my spectacular diagonal parking somehow more acceptable.*

> Reading the total grant figures this answer provides, and then putting them alongside the more limited figures the department revealed to us, its coyness is immediately explained. *Guardian*[4]

Here the department's coyness is said to have read the figures and put them alongside others. *Reading the total grant figures . . . and then putting them alongside the more limited figures . . . I immediately understood why the department was so coy.*

> That evening, leaning on the exquisitely inlaid bar (from Sotheby's) conversation meandered over the priceless contents of the Uffizi Gallery . . . *Homes & Gardens*[5]

It was not the conversation that leaned over the bar. *That evening, leaning on the exquisitely inlaid bar . . ., we allowed our conversation to meander over the priceless contents of the Uffizi Gallery.*

> . . . and it is a mark of his intelligence and skill that, never letting the tonal dangers inherent in such brilliant colours exceed his control and destroy his sculptural modelling, his figures take on an enhanced monumentality and seem to be by Donatello, come to life. *Harpers & Queen*[6]

Here 'never letting' has nothing to agree with except 'his figures' which are said to be in control of the work: *. . . and it is a mark of his intelligence and skill that he never lets the tonal dangers inherent in such brilliant colours exceed his control . . . so that his figures take on an enhanced monumentality.*

2 Local descriptions

In descriptions of places and routes there seems to be a special danger of lapsing into use of detached participles.

> Going around the county, these buildings stand out as beacons amid the mediocrity of the last two decades. *Spectator*[7]

But these buildings are not going round the county. *Going round the country, I find that these buildings stand out as beacons.*

> Climbing higher still, the Pepper Pot is reached. *Country Walking*[8]

But the Pepper Pot is not climbing higher. *Climbing higher still, the walker reaches the Pepper Pot.*

> Leaving Dornoch and driving on north, the views become even more spectacular. *In Britain*[9]

But the views are neither leaving Dornoch nor driving north. *Leaving Dornoch and driving on north, we encounter even more spectacular views.*

> Stepping out of the pergola to the other side, the colour schemes become more riotous. *Homes & Gardens*[10]

But the colour schemes do not step out of the pergola. *As one steps out of the pergola to the other side, the colour schemes become more riotous.*

> Descending the moor, the magnificent hills of Glen Coe and Glen Etive come into view . . . *Complete Traveller*[11]

But the hills do not descend the moor: *As you descend the moor . . .*

3 'being'

Failure to attach the participle 'being' to an appropriate noun or pronoun can produce absurdities.

> Being Tommy Steele . . . West End musical star and sculptor, it was all just a matter of time. *Daily Mirror*[12]

Tommy Steele being what he is . . . it was all just a matter of time.

> . . . being a typical night club in Ibiza, it's debatable whether anyone would have minded . . . *New Woman*[13]

. . . since it was a typical night club in Ibiza, it's debatable . . .

> They filmed inside his office, as well as outside, and he says he was assured the film would not be as raunchy as the book, being the BBC. *Time*[14]

Here Hunter Davies is describing the making of a TV version of Melvyn Bragg's novel *A Time to Dance*. There is no word for the phrase 'being

45

the BBC' to attach itself to, nothing mentioned that can 'be' the BBC':
. . . he says he was assured the film would not be as raunchy as the book, the BBC being in charge.

Let us now look at the peak of illiteracy in this respect.

A Rover 200 for under £10,000 . . . Life's full of surprises . . . Of course, being a Rover, you won't be suprised to find a high level of refinement across the entire range. Being a Rover, you'll be suitably impressed with the superb ride the suspension system delivers. Being a Rover, you can also expect a wide range of engine alternatives. *Times*[15]

You are left in no doubt at all that you are a Rover.

4 Appointments advertisements

Advertisements of vacant posts abound in detached participles.

Working closely with the Managing Director, this will incorporate the attainment of agreed sales and profits targets for each brand . . . *Times*[16]

It is not 'this' but the unmentioned appointee who will work with the Managing Director. If the participle construction is to be preserved, the appointee must be mentioned: *Working closely with the Managing Director, the appointee will . . .*

Working as a member of a small, well-qualified team that supports the institution's worldwide investment activities, areas of responsibility will include . . . *Times*[17]

It is not 'areas' but the unmentioned appointee who will work as a member of the team: *Working as a member of a . . . team, the appointee will be responsible for . . .*

Reporting to the General Manager Marketing, the responsibilities will encompass marketing programmes . . . *Times*[18]

It is not the 'responsibilities' that will report. *Reporting to the General Manager Marketing, the appointee will have responsibilities which encompass marketing programmes.*

5 The genitive trap

You can say 'Groping in the dark, the intruder suddenly lost his bearings', where the participle 'groping' qualifies 'the intruder'. But you cannot say 'Groping in the dark, the intruder's bearings were suddenly lost', because the 'bearings' were not 'groping' and 'groping' cannot qualify the genitive possessive 'intruder's'.

Suffering appalling conditions and preyed upon by traffickers in human cargo, the family's journey of hope eventually becomes a bitter struggle for survival . . . *Daily Express*[19]

In strict grammatical terms the sentence tells you that the journey suffered appalling conditions and was preyed upon by traffickers. 'The family's' is a genitive case and the participle 'suffering' cannot qualify it. *Suffering appalling conditions and preyed upon by traffickers in human cargo, the family found its journey of hope transformed into a struggle for survival.*

Self-effacing to a fault, West-Taylor's influence lay in a combination of administrative skill, personal warmth and a persuasive enthusiasm. *Guardian*[20]

Here you are told that West-Taylor's influence was self-effacing to a fault. Again, 'West-Taylor's' is a genitive case and 'self-effacing' cannot qualify it: *Self-effacing to a fault, West-Taylor exercised his influence through a combination of administrative skill.*

Quickly attaining cult status in Europe and America, the new work's success owed much to the true story of the brave, but doomed attempt of a Munich student group which distributed subversive literature during the Second World War. *Opera Now*[21]

It was the work, not its success that attained cult status: *Quickly attaining cult status in Europe, the new work had a success which owed much to the true story.*

Currently doing a year's course in shamanism, his studies involve not only a whole series of Sweat Lodges . . . *Times*[22]

His studies are not doing a year's course: *Currently doing a year's course in shamanism, he is pursuing studies which involve.*

In the last two sections the sentences have been corrected in such a way as to preserve the participle construction. Some of them could be more felicitously corrected by abandoning the participle construction, eg: *He is currently doing a year's course in shamanism, and his studies involve. . . .*

6 Participle following the subject

We turn now to cases where the detached participle appears *after* the noun or pronoun on which it has an improper dependence.

Every material used has been thoroughly researched, concentrating on recycling and being as green as can be. *Green Magazine*[23]

Here it appears to be the 'material' that has concentrated on recycling, because there is no other word for 'concentrating' to be dependent upon. Whoever has concentrated must be cited: *We/They have thoroughly researched every material used, concentrating on recycling and being as green as can be.*

Each bait was carefully prepared, skinning the squid so that the white flesh looked more appealing. *Sea Angler*[24]

The bait did not skin the squid. *We prepared each bait carefully, skinning the squid so that the white flesh looked more appealing.*

The journey took three days, avoiding the autoroutes, picnicking in fields at lunchtime, drowning ourselves in wine at night. *Good Housekeeping*[25]

This is an interesting case. It would be allowable to write 'The journey took three days, avoiding the autoroutes'. But, although the journey could avoid autoroutes, it could not picnic in the fields or drown itself in wine. *We took three days over the journey, avoiding the autoroutes, picnicking in fields at lunchtime, drowning ourselves in wine at night.*

The great natural beauty of the surrounding countryside has been taken into account, developing the site with native woodland trees and shrubs . . . *Caravan Magazine*[26]

Here the natural beauty of the countryside is said to have developed the site. It would be clumsy to try to preserve the active participle 'developing'; so preserve the passive voice of the first clause. *The great natural beauty of the surrounding countryside has been taken into account, and the site developed with native woodland trees and shrubs.*

The Society's constitution contains five specific aims; these remain the same as they were in 1975, showing remarkable foresight. *Traditional Homes*[27]

The 'aims' do not 'show' foresight. Only living beings can do that. In this case the verb is the wrong one: . . . *giving evidence of remarkable foresight.*

Although the participle is generally dependent upon a single noun or pronoun ('The wall collapsed, falling into the road', where the wall is what falls), it is sometimes made dependent upon a clause as a whole ('The stock market collapsed, causing havoc among investors', where it is the market's collapsing that causes havoc). Care should be taken not to abuse the freedom represented by this usage.

Listeria is commonly found in soil, water and our own digestive systems, again reinforcing the need for thorough washing of fresh fruit and vegetables, and especially our own hands. *Annabel*[28]

It is not the noun 'Listeria' on which 'reinforcing' is dependent but the whole susbstance of what has been said so far. There is a good case here for use of that neglected construction, the noun clause as subject: *That Listeria is commonly found in soil, water and our own digestive systems further reinforces the need for thorough washing of fruit and vegetables, and especially our own hands.*

> Kiki Camarena is found murdered, spurring on his colleagues to bring down the Mexican drug barons responsible. *Times*[29]

If Kiki Camarena is dead he clearly cannot spur anyone on to do anything at all. Better get rid of the participle: *When Kiki Camarene is found murdered, his colleagues are spurred on to bring . . .* Alternatively change the subject of the sentence: *The discovery that Kiki Camarena has been murdered spurs on his colleagues.*

> It also soothes, heals, softens and nourishes the skin, making it a really effective ingredient. *19*[30]

'It soothes . . . making it': You would not write 'He also soothes, helps and comforts people, making him an effective counsellor'. The participle must go: *It also soothes, heals, softens and nourishes the skin, and is thus a really effective ingredient.*

7 Participle after 'when'

A participle does not cease to be a participle if it follows the word 'when'. The sentence 'He always shook my hand when leaving the house' is the equivalent of 'He always shook my hand when he was leaving the house' and of 'Leaving the house, he always shook my hand'. For theoretical purposes, the use of the participle here should be differentiated from the use of the gerund in 'He always shook my hand on leaving the house', where the preposition 'on' governs the gerund 'leaving'. In practical terms, however, the two constructions have the same rules (the need for a subject) and present the same dangers of error.

> When leaving Teignmouth via the road bridge (A379) which spans Teignmouth's broad, sandy estuary, the quality of light and the vistas are unforgettable. *In Britain*[31]

The quality of light does not leave Teignmouth, nor do the vistas. Yet they supply the only subjects for 'leaving'. *When you are leaving Teignmouth via the road bridge (A379) . . . the quality of light and the vistas are unforgettable.*

> When looking at the new crop of Cape wines, a number of factors must be taken into account. *Decanter*[32]

It appears that 'a number of factors' will be 'looking' at the wines. Either supply a fit subject – *When looking at the new crop of Cape wines, we must take a number of factors into account* – or change the construction: *When the new crop of Cape wines is looked at, a number of factors must be taken into account.*

> When looking for a flat, Neil Ware's most pressing consideration was enough room for his 18th-century doors salvaged from a Georgian House in Regent's Park . . . *The World of Interiors*[33]

This sentence exemplifies what we have called the 'genitive trap' into which users of the participle fall. There is no doubt that Neil Ware is meant to be the subject of 'looking'; but 'Neil Ware' is not cited, only 'Neil Ware's most pressing consideration'. If the genitive case is kept the participle must go: *When he was looking for a flat, Neil Ware's most pressing consideration was enough room for his 18th-century doors.*

The detached participle can jar sharply when the subject to which it leans is 'it'.

> It is a wonderful tool, especially when embarking on a long-term project. *The Artist*[34]

In this case 'it' is clearly the tool, but it is not embarking on a project. *You will find it a wonderful tool, especially when embarking on a long-term project.*

> When striking the firing plunger, it will only require a slight but sharp tap if the mechanism is in good order. *Old Glory*[35]

'It' is the firing plunger and cannot govern 'striking'. Better scrap the participle: *When the firing plunger is struck, it will only require a slight but sharp tap if the mechanism is in good order.*

> If helping at an accident, it is a priority to ensure that an unconscious rider can maintain an airway, and to presume that there is a neck injury. *The Field*[36]

For our purposes 'if' is the equivalent of 'when' here. *If helping at an accident, you should first ensure that an unconscious rider can maintain an airway, and presume that there is a neck injury.*

2 THE CHANGING PARTICIPLE

There are certain participle constructions which, over the years, have established a kind of independence and come to be used without adjectival attachment.

And there is also the old tradition, speaking generally, of reacting against parental wishes. *Daily Telegraph*[1]

Clearly 'speaking generally' does not depend on the noun 'tradition'. It is one of those participle constructions which have acquired idiomatic independence by a process of natural development. Some of these are too well-established to question: 'Considering the circumstances' for instance, and 'roughly speaking'. 'Speaking generally' (or 'generally speaking') has acquired a similar degree of respectability. So has 'assuming'. In 'Assuming that is true, I shall resign' the participle 'assuming' agrees with 'I'. In 'Assuming that is true, the whole case collapses' the word 'assuming' has ceased to be a participle and become a pseudo-conjunction.

1 'using'

The participle 'using' seems to be in the process of claiming independence, through it should be dependent on a noun or pronoun. In 'I repaired the crack, using a little plaster', 'using' is quite properly attached to the pronoun 'I'.

A simple yet elegant scheme has been created using a limited palette of yellow and white with touches of green. *House Beautiful*[2]

Far better than to risk the awkward seeming dependence of 'using' on 'scheme' would be to eliminate the participle: *A simple yet elegant scheme has been created by the use of a limited palette of yellow and white with touches of green.*

A better texture will be obtained using an electric mixer . . . *My Weekly*[3]

The texture does not use the mixer, so apply the same remedy here. *A better texture will be obtained by the use of an electric mixer.*

Athens is little more than an hour away using a combination of taxi and hydrofoil. *Go Greek*[4]

Either supply the participle with a subject – *Athens is little more than an hour away for a passenger using a combination of taxi and hydrofoil* – or scrap the participle: *Athens is little more than an hour away by taxi and hydrofoil combined.*

. . . Manufacturers such as Sympa-Tex and Gore-Tex actually set standards for any garment produced using their material. *Outdoors Illustrated*[5]

The two participles 'produced' and 'using' seem grammatically to depend on the same noun 'garment', and this makes the laxity of 'using' worse. Either change again to 'by the use of' – *any garment produced by the use of their material* – or, better still simplify: *any garment produced from their material.*

2 'looking'

A habit has also the developed of using the participle constructions 'looking', 'looking back', and 'looking at' as though they required no anchorage to a noun.

> Looking about us, the headland was unprepossessing, covered with an acre of empty, rutted car park. *Independent*[6]

Here the headland is said to be 'looking about us'. The participle must go. *The headland before us was unprepossessing, covered with an acre of empty, rutted car park.*

> Looking further back, prior to the latest round of sales, however, it is not quite so obvious that there has been such irresponsibility . . . *Guardian*[7]

'Looking back' can here only agree with 'it'. If the participle 'looking' is to be kept, a subject must be found for it: *Looking further back . . . we find it not quite so obvious that there has been such irresponsibility.* It might be better to scrap the participle: *If we look further back . . . it is not quite so obvious.*

> Looking to the longer term, this strategy has not always proved successful. *Guardian*[8]

This sentence follows the previous one. Here 'this strategy' is said to be 'looking', but in any case 'looking to' adds nothing. *In the longer term this strategy has not always proved successful.*

> *Wierdstone* was my first book and, looking back, the gap between what I envisaged and what I actually got down on paper was enormous. *Country Living*[9]

There is a simple way to avoid risking an unanchored 'looking back': *Wierdstone was my first book and, to hindsight, the gap between what I envisaged and what I actually got down on paper was enormous.*

3 'following'

'Following' is the present participle of the verb 'to follow' and functions as an adjective. There is no case for trying to make it do the work of 'after' or 'since' or 'as a result of'.

> A visit to some Lancashire museums is now cheaper following the introduction of season tickets. *Lancashire Life*[10]

As a participle 'following' must depend on the subject 'visit'. In fact nothing is 'following' anything and so the word is inappropriate. *A visit to some Lancashire museums is now cheaper since the introduction of season tickets.*

> Cross-border services on the Belfast-Dublin railway resumed yesterday after the army finished searching the track following the IRA bombing of Newry station, Co Down, on Friday. *Times*[11]

If someone wrote 'I searched the track leading to Dublin', everyone would understand that the participle 'leading' agreed with 'track'. To write 'I searched the track following the IRA bombing' is to use the participle for a purpose it cannot serve. No doubt the journalist, having already used the word 'after' ('after the army finished searching'), did not wish to repeat it. But there was no need for 'following'. *Cross-border services on the Belfast-Dublin railway line resumed yesterday as the army finished searching the track after the IRA bombing of Newry station, Co Down, on Friday.*

> The local press reports were substantial and the matter filled virtually three pages of the evening paper following the demonstration at County Hall . . . *Horse & Hound*[12]

The paper did not 'follow' the demonstration: . . . *the matter filled virtually three pages of the evening paper published after the demonstration.* And does 'virtually' mean 'almost' or 'approximately'?

> Those fine views carried the disadvantage that the house was very exposed, and, following recent storm damage, the entire roof was in course of replacement . . . *Traditional Homes*[13]

The 'entire roof' ought not to be said to be 'following' the storm damage. In any case 'following' here means something more than 'after'. It is not just that the the storm damage *preceded* the replacing of the roof; it also *caused* that replacement. *Those fine views carried the disadvantage that the house was very exposed, and, as a result of recent storm damage, the entire roof was in course of replacement.*

4 'including'

'Including', like 'following', is a participle and must function as such. You can say 'I purchased several articles, including a shirt and a tie', because 'including' there depends on the noun 'articles' and introduces specimens. You cannot say 'I travelled widely, including Greece and Italy', because there is no noun for 'including' to depend upon. Whereas 'articles' could be said to include a tie and a shirt, there is no comparable word in the sentence above which could be said to include Greece and Italy. You would have to say 'I visited many countries, including Greece and Italy', where 'including' depends on the noun 'countries'.

Meanwhile Serb militants have frequently attacked and killed in recent months, including ambushes on Croatian police. *Independent*[14]

It would be grammatically satisfactory to say 'Meanwhile Serb militants have frequently attacked in recent months, including January and February', where 'including' would depend on the noun 'months'. Some noun must be inserted on which 'including' could thus depend: *Meanwhile Serb militants have made frequent murderous attacks in recent months, including ambushes on Croatian police.*

The South African Defence Force (SADF) has deliberately fanned the township violence of recent months, including funding and supplying weapons to Mangosuthu Buthelezi's Inkatha Freedom Party, as part of a comprehensive 'dirty tricks' strategy . . . *Independent*[15]

Once more the participle 'including' is used without anchorage. Why not omit it? *The South African Defence Force (SADF) has deliberately fanned the township violence of recent months, funding and supplying weapons to Mangosuthu Buthelezi's Inkatha Freedom Party.*

Seals have been seen in the Bristol Channel after many years – including Clevedon pier. *Sea Angler*[16]

Since 'Clevedon pier' is obviously not a specimen year, the reader naturally wonders whether it is a rare species of seal. What else, other than 'seals' or 'years', can the participle 'including' relate to? If 'including' is to be kept, a noun must be provided for it: *After many years seals have been seen in the Bristol Channel from various points, including Clevedon pier.* But 'including' is rarely worth the effort of preservation. *Seals have been seen in the Bristol Channel after many years – indeed even from Clevedon pier.*

The three-abreast steam-driven Gallopers will be in action, and four steam railway systems will be running, including footplate trips on a standard-gauge locomotive. *Old Glory*[17]

Steam railway systems obviously cannot 'include' footplate trips. There is no such system. The effort to keep 'including' here would be scarcely worth-while. *The three-abreast steam-driven Gallopers will be in action, and four steam railway systems will be running, one of them offering footplate trips on a standard-gauge locomotive.*

5 'depending on'
Before we turn to faulty use of the expression 'depending on', it is best to look first at the use of 'depend on'.

54

The one you opt for will depend largely on how serious a cook you are and the sort of cooking that you typically do at home. *Money-wise*[18]

This piece examines the range of food-processors available, and exemplifies a common faulty use of 'depend on'. The food-processor will *not* 'depend on' how serious a cook you are. It is the *choice* which will depend on how serious a cook you are. *Which you opt for will depend on how serious a cook you are.*

The flooring is also something which will depend on the way you work. *The Artist*[19]

The piece is about setting up a studio. Once more it is not the 'flooring' which 'depends' but the choice of flooring: *What kind of flooring you choose will depend on how you work.*

Of course, the one you choose will depend on your circumstances but I suspect a high yielding plan would suit the bill . . . *Money-wise*[20]

Here again it is not the 'one' you choose which will 'depend on' the circumstances but 'which' you choose: *Of course, which you choose will depend on your circumstances.* Even so, 'depend on' is not the best verb for the purpose served here: *Of course, which you choose will be determined by your circumstances.* Strictly, the verb 'to depend on' means 'to be contingent upon' rather than 'to be determined by'. These two meanings often overlap in a given context, but 'to be determined by' will often prove safer than 'to depend on'.

'Depending' is the present participle of the verb 'depend' and it must function accordingly. It is adjectival and must itself depend on a noun. But the adjective 'dependent' meets the need for adjectival use. In fact, looking for a satisfactory use of 'depending on' is like looking for a needle in a haystack.

Depending on how many other boy friends you have had, you may already have some experience of how it feels to be unceremoniously dumped. *Catch*[21]

There is no noun or pronoun here for 'depending' to relate to. You might write 'Depending on a daily supply of food and drink, the prisoner was at the mercy of his captors'. That is the correct use of 'depending on', where the participle 'depending' hangs on the noun 'prisoner'. The *Catch* sentence tries to make 'depending on' do the work of a conjunction. Better use a proper conjunction: *If you have had a number of boy friends, you may already have some experience of being unceremoniously dumped.*

Depending on how busy the court is, this should be within a month of two. *Company*[22]

Why have recourse to this awkward expression 'depending on' when the meaning could be simply put? *If the court is not too busy, this should be within a month or two.*

Depending on how recently you bought your shares, you may not receive interim dividends. *Investors Chronicle*[23]

Put this straightforwardly: *Whether you receive interim dividends will depend on how recently you bought your shares.*

If you convert your loft, you may or may not get some of your investment back, depending on how well it suits your property. *Traditional Homes*[24]

Apply the same treatment here. *If you convert your loft, whether you get some of your investment back will depend on how well the change suits your property.*

Kenwood table mixers can also be used with the full range of food processing accesories, which means you can custom-build your system depending on which attachments you use most often. *Moneywise*[25]

As so often, the issue of 'dependence' does not really arise here at all. Replace 'depending on' by 'according to': . . . *you can custom-build your system according to which attachments you use most often.*

6 'providing'

'Provided' or 'provided that' introduces a stipulation from which something else follows. 'Provided that the weather is good, we shall go for a picnic.' By some peculiar perversity a habit has grown of using 'providing' instead of 'provided'. There is no justification for this at all. 'Providing' is the present participle of the verb 'provide' and would, like all such participles, require a noun or pronoun to depend on. 'Provided' is the past participle and it can be used as short-hand for 'it being provided that', thus acting as a kind of conjunction.

Ponds with shallow, moist areas make ideal sites for *Osmunda regalis* (the royal fern), which will grow in full sunshine providing the roots are always wet. *Practical Gardening*[26]

Use the word 'provided' here: Osmunda regalis *(the royal fern), which will grow in full sunshine provided that the roots are always wet.*

Robert Gifford, the National Union of Teachers' principal secondary education officer, says he considers bans on dissection 'perfectly reasonable' providing teachers' organisations are consulted beforehand. *Green Magazine*[27]

Make the same change here: ... *he considers bans on dissection 'perfectly reasonable' provided that teacher's organisations are consulted.*

7 Ill-timed participles

Although the 'ill-timed' present participle represents an error of a different character from those examined above, it is nevertheless convenient to treat it alongside other ill uses of the participle. In 'Lifting his hands, he surrendered', the participle 'lifting' represents a process that is contemporaneous with the act of surrendering. If this element of the contemporary is lacking, the present participle cannot be well-used.

> Luny, a prolific marine artist spent his last years here, dying in 1837. *In Britain*[28]

The act of dying was not contemporaneous with spending his last years here (in Teignmouth). There is no point in not putting the facts naturally. *Luny, a prolific marine artist, spent his last years here and died in 1837.*

> A live hand grenade fell from her pocket, which then rolled down the aisle. Searight was injured in the explosion that followed, spending the next month in hospital. *Independent*[29]

The spending of a month is hospital was subsequent to being injured and not contemporaneous with it. It is illogical to use the present participle here. *Searight was injured in the explosion that followed, and spent the next month in hospital.*

> This engine was built in 1895 for Lutterworth based showman, G. Twigdon, being exhibited at Smithfield in December before delivery. *Old Glory*[30]

Here the present participle is in the passive voice ('being exhibited'). The engine was certainly not in the process of 'being exhibited' at the time when it was being built. Again the participle lures a writer away from simple directness. *This engine was built in 1895 for Lutterworth-based showman, G. Twigdon, and was exhibited at Smithfield in December before delivery.*

> Successful flotation on The London Stock Exchange was achieved on 12 March this year despite coming in a difficult period for the UK economy and during the Gulf War. *National Power*[31]

Gammatically, 'coming' must agree with 'successful flotation', but in fact 'coming' should refer only to 'flotation'. It was the flotation that came in a difficult period and, in spite of that, proved successful. *Flotation on The London Stock Exchange was successfully achieved on 12 March this year despite coming in a difficult period.*

3 DETACHED PAST PARTICIPLE

Descriptive additions can be formed by the use of the past participle as well as by the use of the present participle. 'Quickly recognised as a powerful novelist, Charlotte Brontë became widely known.' There the words 'quickly recognised as a powerful novelist' hinge on the words 'Charlotte Brontë'. The word 'recognised', a past participle which functions like an adjective, is properly attached to the words 'Charlotte Brontë'. Again it is important to ensure that the past participle is thus properly attached. All too often it is allowed to float away from its proper anchorage and then to produce an absurd impression of being attached elsewhere.

1 Crude mismatch

Made in brass and copper, prices start at £165. *The World of Interiors*[1]

We have to look back two sentences to discover that it is not the 'prices' but certain artefacts, namely pens, that are made in brass and copper. *Made in brass and copper, the pens are priced from £165.*

Sent away to boarding school from the age of seven, the regiment and their father came to mean holidays, skiing and sailing. *Times*[2]

It was not the regiment and the father who were sent away to boarding school. *Sent away to boarding school from the age of seven, they found that the regiment and their father came to be associated with holidays, skiing and sailing.*

Sold mainly in tea bags, the method of decaffeination sometimes appears on the packaging, i.e. by water, carbon dioxide or chemical solvents. *Cosmopolitan*[3]

Here is a pretty mess. We are told that the 'method of decaffeination' is sold mainly in tea bags, for there is no other term for the participle 'sold' to depend upon. We are then told that this 'method' appears on the packaging, but it is a *description* of the method that there appears. *Decaffeinated tea is sold mainly in tea-bags, and details of the method of decaffeination used – whether by water, carbon dioxide, or chemical solvents – are printed on the packaging.*

> The temptation to stray close to the main coverts was enormous, but if caught the punishment would almost certainly have been to miss an organised day. *The Field*[4]

This piece, on educating young guns, seemingly tells us what would happen to the punishment if it were caught. The culprits must be mentioned: *. . . but if we were caught, the punishment would almost certainly have been to miss an organised day.*

> Married to artist and film-maker, Gerald Scarfe, they have three children . . . *Gateway*[5]

Who are 'they' who are 'married to Gerald Scarfe'? Remove the suggestion of polygamy. *She is married to artist and film-maker Gerald Scarfe, and they have three children.*

> Accustomed to the fierce thin smells of Araby, Muscat seemed deodorised *Times*[6]

Either give 'accustomed' a subject – *Accustomed to the fierce thin smells of Araby, I found Muscat deodorised* – or scrap the participle: *After the fierce thin smells of Araby, Muscat seemed deodorised.*

> Forced into keeping them in a large barn, lack of food became a dire problem and, in an emergency evacuation, seven mares and a stallion went to a Shropshire stud. *Wild About Animals*[7]

'Lack of food' is, in strict grammatical terms, 'forced into keeping' the animals. Some person or persons will have to be introduced if the participle is to remain. *Forced into keeping them in a large barn, we found that lack of food became a dire problem.*

> My wife will never forget his kindness when, persuaded no doubt unwillingly that their ladies should be shown some hospitality, she found herself seated at his right hand at a ladies' night *Times*[8]

In this tribute to John Sparrow we must assume that it was Sparrow who was 'persuaded' to show hospitality to the ladies, but the only word that 'persuaded' could grammatically depend on is 'she'. *My wife will never forget his kindness when, persuaded no doubt unwillingly that their ladies should be shown some hospitality, he seated her at his right hand at a ladies' night.* (We overlook the question of whom 'their' refers to.)

2 The genitive trap
The last example is from a an obituary tribute. In biographical accounts of all kinds the temptation to mismatch past participles seems to be

especially strong. And the error very often involves what we have called the 'genitive trap'. The sentence 'Brought up in Liverpool, John became a world-famous musician' is satisfactory because 'John' was brought up in Liverpool. But the sentence 'Brought up in Liverpool, John's music soon became world-famous' will not do because John's music was not brought up in Liverpool. Nevertheless, this error is widely perpetrated in the press.

> Exiled from her native Czechoslovakia since 1985, Magdalena Jetelova's sculptures are a visual testament to the brutality of a totalitarian regime. *Artists & Illustrators Magazine*[9]

The participle 'exiled' cannot depend upon the genitive 'Magdalena Jetelova's', and the sculptures were not 'exiled', as is suggested here: *Exiled from her native Czechoslovakia since 1985, Magdalena Jetelova has produced sculptures which are a visual testament.*

> Born and bred in County Wexford, his accent mysteriously reverberates with the rich texture of English privilege . . . *Elle*[10]

But his accent was not born in Wexford: *Born and bred in County Wexford, he has an accent which mysteriously reverberates.*

> Tipped in his early days as a future PM, his political career was cut short . . . *British Book News*[11]

This is a review of a biography of Robert Boothby and implies that his political career was 'tipped' as a future PM. *Tipped in his early days as a future PM, he found his political career cut short.*

> Forced out of office after the IRA gun-running scandal, acquitted in court but nevertheless disgraced, his career was one long fightback against the odds. *Times*[12]

This account of Charles Haughey implies that his career was forced out of office and then acquitted in court. *Forced out of office after the IRA gun-running scandal, acquitted in court but nevertheless disgraced, he made his career one long fight-back against the odds.*

> Born in a smart Paris suburb, her father was a top civil servant and her upbringing was entrusted to an English nanny. *Options*[13]

This piece about Edith Cresson might leave one wondering who was born in Paris. Was it the father, as the grammatical construction suggests? The context makes clear that it was Edith herself, and the grammar is at fault. *Born in a smart Paris suburb to a father who was a top civil servant, she was entrusted for her upbringing to an English nanny.*

Born in 1912 in Krokees, near Sparta, Vrettakos's first collection, *Under Shadows and Lights*, was published in 1929, and contained many poems composed while still at school. *Independent*[14]

The first collection, we gather, was born in Krokees, and the poems were still at school when composed. *Born in 1912 in Krokees, near Sparta, Vrettakos published his first collection,* Under Shadows and Lights*, in 1929: it contained many poems composed while he was still at school.*

3 'Having said that' etc.

So far we have considered past participles that are passive. 'Forsaken by my husband, I settled down to the single life.' 'Forsaken' is passive there. 'Having forsaken my husband, I settled down to the single life.' 'Having forsaken' is an active past participle there. There are one or two active past participle constructions which are overused and badly used. 'Having said' is a participle construction that must obey the rules of such constructions. If you begin a sentence with 'Having said', then the person who has spoken must be cited. 'Having said that, I feel a lot better' is correct. 'Having said that, the rain seems to be clearing' is nonsense because the rain has said nothing. Yet the press abounds in such usages.

Having said all that, this is a book to gladden the hearts of Euro-enthusiasts and jolt the rest of us out of our parochialism. *Spectator*[15]

But 'this' has not 'said that' or anything else. The irony is that there is a perfectly good English construction to meet the need here: *That being said, this is a book to gladden the heart.*

Having said that, it is true that even if you followed all the rules, the coup might well have failed. *Sunday Times*[16]

But it is not 'it' that has 'said that', it is the writer, here Barbara Amiel, and she ought not to be so modest. *Having said that, I believe that even if you followed all the rules, the coup might well have failed.* Another option remains available: *That being said, it is true that even if you followed all the rules the coup might well have failed.*

Having said that, you can take some tax-free cash out of a fund before drawing the pension. *Moneywise*[17]

At last we have a personal subject for 'having said that' to depend on, for 'you' are declared to have said it. Unfortunately you didn't. The journalist said it. *That being said, you can take some tax-free cash out of a fund before drawing the pension.*

Making love is, after all, something that should come naturally, unadulterated by a checklist of dos and don'ts. Having acknowledged that, it is also about give and take – and inevitably there will be those who do more taking than giving. *Options*[18]

Writing sentences, unlike making love, does require some reference to a checklist of dos and don'ts. Had the writer consulted one, he would have learned that 'Having acknowledged' requires a subject to make it meaningful, and 'it' will not do. Again why not use the neglected absolute construction? *That being acknowledged, it is also about give and take.*

Having read yesterday's speech and most of tonight's speech, it is full of falsehoods – in ordinary English: lies. *Independent*[19]

This is Edward Heath on Mrs Thatcher. In the heat of the moment he fails to make the grammatically necessary reference to the reader of the two speeches, and then refers to them as 'it'. *I have read yesterday's speech and most of tonight's, and they are full of falsehoods.*

Press night of Troilus and Cressida. It is even better than at Stratford. Having brought in Sam to repair the fortunes of our cricket team (he was a Cambridge blue) there is a certain relief in the reminder of his brilliance as a director. *Weekend Guardian*[20]

It would be natural and easy to match 'Having brought in' here with the appropriate subject. *Having brought in Sam to repair the fortunes of our cricket team (he was a Cambridge blue) we feel a certain relief in the reminder of his brilliance as a director.*

4 Participles following their subject
The examples above all involved participles which precede the nouns they are mismatched with. Though less frequently, detached participles may occur later in the sentence.

The highspot was Pringle's dismissal, athletically thrown out by Moody . . . *Times*[21]

In this record of a cricket match it appears that Pringle's dismissal was 'thrown out'. The remedy is easy: *The highspot was the dismissal of Pringle, athletically thrown out by Moody.*

There were no more dismal, empty evenings in my room, slumped in front of the television . . . *My Weekly*[22]

Get rid of the picture of the empty evenings slumped in front of the television: *There were no more dismal, empty evenings in my room for me, slumped in front of the television.*

. . . and after a pre-match party excessive by even Zimbabwean standards, the margin of defeat was again only six runs, having been confronted on the morning of the match with a three-figure temperature and a large scoreboard displaying 'Wankie v Sussex'. *The Cricketer*[23]

In a long sentence we never do learn *who* was 'confronted' with this and that on the morning of the match: . . . *and after a pre-match party excessive by even Zimbabwean standards, the margin of defeat was again only six runs, our team having been confronted on the morning of the match with a three-figure temperature.*

While the walks are not terrifically arduous, the sense of achievement, having found your way hobbit-like across the wilderness, is immense. *Elle*[24]

The participle construction 'having found your way' must have a noun to depend on. Better remove it: *While the walks are not terrifically arduous, the sense of achievement at finding your way hobbit-like across the wilderness, is immense.*

The struggle to produce a painting is three-quarters won when painted with confidence. *The Artist*[25]

It sounds as though the struggle has to be painted with confidence. *The struggle to produce a painting is three-quarters won when the painting is done with confidence.*

5 'followed by'
'Followed', like 'following' is a participle, a past participle instead of a present one, and is subject to the rules governing participles. It cannot function independently of attachment to a noun or pronoun. Just as we must resist the temptation to abuse 'following', so we must not free 'followed' from proper anchorage.

It was a luxury we relished after wandering round the leather and wicker stalls of the street markets, followed by the 414 steps up Giotto's campanile in the nearby Piazza del Duomo. *Homes & Gardens*[26]

(The 'luxury' was a Jacuzzi.) If you try to picture these people wandering round street markets followed by 414 steps, you will see how absurd grammatical laxity can be. 'Followed' must go. *It was a luxury we relished after wandering round the leather and wicker stalls of the street markets and climbing the 414 steps up Giotto's campanile in the nearby Piazza del Duomo.*

> At the age of 18 she was duly presented to George V at court, followed soon afterwards by her coming-out ball at the Ritz. *Times*[27]

It is as entertaining to picture a girl followed by a ball as it is to picture tourists followed by a flight of steps. There is nothing for the word 'followed' to attach to. *She was duly presented to George V at court, and soon afterwards had a coming-out ball at the Ritz.*

> We were soon learning to duck dive and submerse ourselves in the unwelcoming waters, followed by a 5-metre pier-side jump (holding masks and snorkel correctly). *Outdoors Illustrated*[28]

Here are athletic swimmers apparently being 'followed' by a huge jump. No participle can do the job that 'followed' is made to attempt here. *We were soon learning to duck dive and submerse ourselves in the unwelcoming waters, then to do a 5-metre pier-side jump.*

> Here much darker and richer colours are used, particularly reds and browns, to develop the shadow areas, using the pencils dry, followed by some careful work with a wet brush to darken even more, if necessary. *Artists & Illustrators Magazine*[29]

Both participles, 'using' and 'followed', lack a noun to be attached to. 'Using' could relate only to the artist, who is not mentioned, and nothing is mentioned that can be 'followed'. *Here much darker and richer colours are used, particularly reds and browns, to develop the shadow areas: use the pencils dry and then do some careful work with a wet brush to darken even more.*

6 Distortion of past participle

There is a temptation to try to make the past participle do jobs it is quite unfitted for.

> The Equitable . . . could have reaped an extra 69% of pension fund for retiring holders of an Equitable with-profits personal pension plan, having paid regular contributions for 10 years. *Moneywise*[30]

The participle 'having paid' is quite unsatisfactory if, as it seems, it is a substitute for a relative clause. *The Equitable . . . could have reaped an extra 69% of pension fund for retiring holders of an Equitable with-profits personal pension plan who have paid regular contributions for 10 years.*

> If this is Walkinshaw's strategy, then it will not be the first time that a F1 newcomer has infiltrated an existing grand prix team to dramatically improved effect. *Guardian*[31]

You would not write 'She washed her baby to dramatically improved effect' for you would recognise that it is the baby and not the effect that is 'improved' by the cleansing. Similarly here it is the grand prix team that is improved by the infiltration: *it will be not be the first time that a F1 newcomer has infiltrated an existing grand prix team and thereby dramatically improved it.*

> The surprise saving of Rosyth, after months of leaked documents that suggested the base would close, came after six months of negotiations between Mr King and Ian Lang, the Scottish secretary. *Times*[32]

One could perhaps picture yards of leaked documents but not months of them. Why be so tortuous? What is wrong with saying what is meant directly? *The surprise saving of Rosyth, after documents have been leaked for months suggesting that the base would close, came after six months of negotiations.*

> A suspected villa lies in the vicinity . . . *History Today*[33]

It is not the villa that is suspected, but its existence. *It is suspected that a villa lies in the vicinity.*

> As such we see NEDs at their most independent and I don't believe that Noel Falconer's suggestion of NEDs elected on an individual shareholder rather than size of stake basis would achieve his purpose of broader input to board decisions. *Times*[34]

To use 'shareholder' and 'size of stake' as pseudo-adjectives is bad. More immediately, the participle 'elected' will not do. Noel Falconer's suggestion for electing NEDs on this or that basis is the issue, and 'electing NEDs' is not the same as 'elected NEDs'. If 'suggestion' were altered to, say, 'concept' ('Noel Falconer's concept of NEDs elected on this or that basis') the sentence might be rescued. However, it is not the 'suggestion' that 'would achieve his purpose' but its execution: *I don't believe that Noel Falconer's plan for electing NEDs by the votes of shareholders without reference to the size of their holdings would achieve his purpose.*

4 THE GERUND

The gerund is the part of a verb which functions as a noun. In form it is identical with the present participle. In 'I heard him singing in the bath', the word 'singing' is a present participle. In 'His singing is too noisy', the word 'singing' is a gerund, and acts like a noun as subject of the sentence. There are usages in which the gerund acts independently, seemingly as a pure noun. 'Seeing is believing' we say, and the question '*Who* is seeing?' does not arise. The same may be said of the sentences 'Hunting is a respectable sport' (of which 'hunting' is the subject) and 'I detest hunting' (of which 'hunting' is the object). But in most usages the gerund, like other parts of the verb, requires a subject. 'He rushed to help without hesitating for a moment' makes sense because the subject of the sentence ('He') also supplies a subject for 'hesitating'.

Sometimes the subject of the gerund is understood. In the sentence above, 'His singing is too noisy', there can be no doubt about who is singing. Similarly, in 'Do stop banging that drum' the gerund 'banging' has as its 'subject' the implicit 'you' which is the subject of all imperatives. (It would be quite natural and proper to say 'For heaven's sake, stop *your* banging'.)

Because the subject of the gerund can be implicit instead of explicit, the construction has to be used with the utmost care. There is clearly for some people a difficulty in appreciating the distinction between having a subject that is implicit and not having a subject at all, and this is where the main difficulty arises. Just as in careless writing the participle can become detached from any appropriate noun or pronoun and seemingly attached to an inappropriate noun or pronoun, so the gerund, if not properly anchored to a subject, whether explicit or implicit, can float away into detachment, or attach itself seemingly to the wrong subject.

1 The detached gerund after 'by'
You can say 'By setting off early he caught the first train', where 'he' is the person who set off. But you cannot say 'By setting off early, his toast was left uneaten', because the toast did not set off.

> The central tenet is that by getting children to do things for themselves, their confidence – and ability to take the next step – will grow. *She*[1]

You can say 'By getting children to do things for themselves we increase their confidence', because 'by getting' relates to the subject 'we'. But in the sentence above, 'by getting' floats free of any proper anchorage and therefore attaches itself improperly to 'their confidence'. *The central tenet is that by getting children to do things for themselves, we ensure that their confidence – and their ability to take the next step – will grow.*

> The Baccarat sconce in the bedroom is one such flea-market find. By hanging it next to a mirror, its own reflection gives the illusion of a pair. *Homes & Gardens*[2]

The gerund 'hanging' is bereft of a subject and is therefore attracted grammatically to the subject of the sentence, 'reflection'. This makes

66

nonsense. To preserve the gerund would be clumsy ('By hanging it next to a mirror, they enable its reflection'). Better scrap the gerund. *As it is hung next to a mirror, its own reflection gives the illusion of a pair.*

> Jackson believes that by putting '50s designs into an international context, people might be persuaded to rethink their assumptions that much of it belongs at a jumble sale. *Viva*[3]

The 'people' are not the ones who are putting the designs into an international context, as the grammatical construction implies. To preserve the gerund insert a subject for it. *Jackson believes that by putting 50's designs into an international context, he might persuade people to rethink their assumptions that much of it belongs at a jumble sale.* The alternative is to scrap the gerund: *Jackson believes that, if the '50s designs are put into an international context, people might be persuaded to rethink.*

> By building these layers of pencil on the paper (through a slow process of trial and error) they gradually seem to become as solid and opaque as a layer of oil paint or gouache. *The Artist*[4]

'By building these layers . . . they gradually seem . . .' They seem to be building themselves. *If these layers of pencil are built on the paper (through a slow process of trial and error), they gradually seem to become as solid and opaque as a layer of oil paint.*

> By dropping the saddle as low as it will go and leaning back with your weight entirely over the rear wheel, a mountain bike becomes the cycling world's equivalent of a four-wheel-drive jeep. *Independent*[5]

The bike cannot drop the saddle and lean back. Supply a subject that can. *By dropping the saddle as low as it will go and leaning back with your weight entirely over the rear wheel, you can turn your mountain bike into the equivalent of a four-wheel-drive jeep.*

We have used the word 'subject' for the noun or pronoun which provides anchorage for the gerund. Fowler uses the word 'agent' so as to allow for those cases where the subject of the sentence is distinct from the 'agent' implicitly governing the gerund. For instance, we can allow the sentence, 'The risks of loss can be reduced by insuring the property', even though the risks do not do the insuring. The passive verb 'can be reduced' implicitly introduces a reducer (an 'agent') who can do the insuring.

> The snood can be made to stand off from the main trace by tying a further overhand knot in the loop. *Sea Angler*[6]

This is correct even though the subject of the sentence, 'snood', cannot tie knots. Implicit in 'can be made' is a maker (an 'agent') who can do the tying.

2 Detached gerund after 'without'

The same freedom is allowed in the use of 'without' followed by a gerund. We say 'The door can be opened without turning the key' as well as the more logically defensible 'You can open the door without turning the key'.

> The seat can be made to face forward or back without removing the seat cover, and it has adjustable suspension. *Parents*[7]

Thus this is an acceptable variant of the more strictly defensible 'You can make the seat face forward or backward without removing the seat cover'. But commonsense sets limits to such variants.

> One cylinder at £1.20 lasts six hours and can be changed in a few seconds without getting covered in fuel. *Sea Angler*[8]

Here good taste seems to call for an explicit subject for 'getting covered with fuel'. *One cylinder at £1.20 lasts six hours and you can change it in a few seconds without getting covered in fuel.*
Subtleties of this kind do not arise where the main verb of the sentence is in the active voice.

> Without arguing for the rehabilitation of the narrow canals there are waterways for which minimal investment in channel improvement and interchange facilities could provide high capacity freight arteries . . . *Times*[9]

Who is refraining from arguing? *Without arguing for the rehabilitation of the narrow canals, we submit that there are waterways for which minimal investment in channel improvement . . .*

> . . . but the lush wooded scenery, wild flowers and exotic bird-life make for some excellent walking without having to reach for the oxygen cylinder. *Chat*[10]

The scenery, the flora and the fauna perform their function without reaching for the oxygen cylinder, we are told: . . . *but the lush wooded scenery, wild flowers and exotic birdlife make for some excellent walking without our having to reach for the oxygen cylinder.*

> Travelling conditions are bad enough without adding to the problem. *Prima*[11]

Here a question arises. Strictly 'without adding' needs attachment to a subject ('You will find travelling conditions bad enough without adding to the problem'), but has changing usage perhaps given 'without adding to the problem' idiomatic independence of such rules?

3 Detached gerund: other cases

> Sadly and reluctantly we have accepted his resignation after being on the committee for 30 years. *Yorkshire Evening Press*[12]

Clearly it is the unmentioned 'he' and not 'we' who has been on the committee for 30 years. Here is a version of the genitive trap again, for the sentence proceeds as though 'he' has been mentioned when only the genitive 'his' has been used. It would be correct but clumsy to write 'Sadly and reluctantly we have accepted his resignation after his being on the committee for 30 years'. Better change the construction. *Sadly and reluctantly we have accepted his resignation after he has been on the committee for 30 years.*

> In spite of having some brains, Isabel's view of life and love derives from the 391 romantic novels of one Babs Cartwheel, and she thinks in passionate one-sentence paragraphs in the approved Mills & Boon fashion. *Times*[13]

Here is another genitive trap. It is not Isabel's 'view of life' but Isabel herself who must be allowed to have some brains. *In spite of having some brains, Isabel derives her view of life from the 391 romantic novels of one Babs Cartwheel.*

> After filling and rubbing down, the cars are primed three times before having several coats of paint baked on. *Meridian*[14]

No one is mentioned who does the 'filling and rubbing down'. It sounds as though the cars fill themselves. The passive voice must be used: *After being filled and rubbed down, the cars are primed three times before having several coats of paint baked on.*

> It is proving a high-spirited week, playing in cramped conditions to a larger and livelier audience than the usual New Music camp followers. *Independent*[15]

Perhaps we are dealing here with a detached participle rather than a detached gerund. In any case, however high-spirited the week, it surely did not play in cramped conditions: *It is proving a high-spirited week for the performers, playing in cramped conditions to a larger and livelier audience.*

> Those with a taste for sampling the life-styles of England's 'natural rulers' before our own more democratic age, could do worse than

taking up one of the Hilton National weekends at *Haddon Hall* and *Knebworth House. History Today*[16]

This is not so much a 'detached' as a misplaced gerund: . . . *could do worse than take up one of the Hilton National weekends.*

4 Gerund or infinitive?

There are occasions when the infinitive is used where the gerund would be more acceptable (see Chapter IV, 1). We are concerned here with sentences in which the gerund is used where the infinitive would be more acceptable.

Psychologists agree that the most important function of autobiographical memory is in providing people with a shared past. *New Woman*[17]

This is surely a straightforward case. We say of the postman 'His function is to deliver letters', not 'his function is in delivering letters'. *Psychologists agree that the most important function of autobiographical memory is to provide people with a shared past.*

But, when work commenced it was discovered that much of the brickwork was in a rotten condition and that the besemer beam had been badly burnt and was so weakened that it needed replacing. *Old House Journal*[18]

The beam needed 'to be replaced' (in the passive). But the passive gerund is an awkward form in English. 'Being awakened in the middle of the night upsets me' is fine, as is 'He dislikes being awakened in the middle of the night'. But 'It was so weakened that it badly needed being replaced' is not. Use the infinitive: . . . *that the besemer beam had been badly burnt and was so weakened that it needed to be replaced.* Alternatively use the abstract noun: . . . *was so weakened that it badly needed replacement.*

State of the art that bike might be but it still needed wheeling back and the inner tube shoving into a bowl of water. *Annabel*[19]

What the bike needed was 'to be wheeled back' (in the passive), and what the inner tube needed was 'to be shoved' (in the passive) into a bowl of water. Colloquially we might say 'The bike needs mending' but precision in writing demands the passive. *State of the art that bike might be but it still needed to be wheeled back and the inner tube to be shoved into a bowl of water.*

. . . The dedicated wireless-loving oldie . . . often finds it difficult getting to grips with the rash of new stations on tricky medium wave. *Oldie*[20]

The more literate oldie recognises that 'finds it difficult' must be followed by an infinitive: *finds it difficult to get to grips.*

> However, as extensive research has proved, protecting your skin against the harmful effects of UVA and UVB rays is a wise decision. *Cosmopolitan*[21]

'Protecting' is an act, not a 'decision'. Although the substitution of the infinitive would be correct ('to protect your skin . . . is a wise decision'), it would be less than felicitous. Better remove 'decision': *protecting your skin against the harmful effects of UVA and UVB is a wise precaution.*

> And the hardest part is what I call 'The Final Exam' – how to cope with finishing being the protective guiding mum of a teenager and let go to become the friend of a mature and responsible adult. *Essentials*[22]

The double gerund 'finishing being' jars. Why not 'ceasing to be'? It is incorrect to say 'finishing being . . . and let go' instead of 'finishing being . . . and letting go': *how to cope with ceasing to be the protective guiding mum of a teenager and letting go to become the friend of a mature and responsible adult.*

> For 1992 the company proposes developing that principle into a 33ft × 10ft cruiser that can still be towed behind a family car. *Waterways World*[23]

Replacing the gerund 'developing' by the infinitive ('proposes to develop that principle') would still leave a problem, as you cannot develop a principle into a cruiser. *For 1992 the company proposes, on that principle, to develop a 33ft × 10ft cruiser.*

5 The 'gerciple' attached to a noun

The gerund is a part of the verb which functions as a noun. The participle is a part of the verb which functions as an adjective. Since the gerund has the same form as the present participle it is easy to confuse the two. As a result of confusion between the two an illegitimate form has established itself which is neither properly a gerund nor properly a participle but a strange mixture of both. Fowler called this form the 'fused participle'. I am calling it the 'gerciple'. It appears everywhere in the daily press, and to that extent it might be argued that usage makes the form respectable. However, it is rarely found in the work of good writers, so to that extent it is to be avoided. Moreover, logic is against it.

If I say 'I found my mother peeling potatoes', the participle 'peeling' is clearly adjectival. The words 'I found my mother' have a validity even without the adjectival expression that follows. But if I say 'My mother hates her children bringing muddy boots into the house', the words 'My mother hates her children' have no validity on their own and would totally misrepresent my meaning. 'Bringing' is not a participle, nor is it adjectival. 'Bringing muddy boots into the house' is in fact the object of my mother's hatred. Thus the sentence as it stands is incorrect, and should read 'My mother hates her children's bringing muddy boots into the house'. This, you will say, is an awkward, stilted sentence. Agreed. But it is logical. Do not take refuge from awkwardness and stiltedness in illogicality. If the gerund cannot be used neatly, then use some other construction. 'My mother hates her children to bring muddy boots into the house.'

Use of the gerciple marks a writer as less than expert. Writers who wish to avoid it should take note of how and why other writers slip into it. An attempt is made here to exemplify various contexts in which recourse to the gerciple is all too popular.

1 Cause and result

We are often tempted to use gerciples when causes are explored or results are defined. Use of the verb 'result', or of comparable verbs, is especially dangerous in this respect. There is a tendency to say 'The accident resulted in the driver losing a leg', where 'losing' is a gerciple. The correct version would be 'The accident resulted in the driver's losing a leg', where 'losing' is a proper gerund. But a more sensible version would be 'The accident caused the driver to lose a leg', or 'As a result of the accident the driver lost a leg'. Thus in the following examples the construction should be changed as shown.

> . . . the prospect of gradual reductions in base rates will undoubtedly result in many institutional investors increasing their exposure to gilts . . . *Times*[1]

The word 'increasing' is a gerciple: *will undoubtedly lead many institutional investors to increase their exposure to gilts.*

> A recurrence of vacuum brake problems . . . resulted in Driver Callum MacRaild calling for diesel assistance . . . *Steam Railway*[2]

The word 'calling' is a gerciple: *led/caused Driver Callum MacRaild to call for diesel assistance.*

> The reversal of the housing market, the introduction of TESSAs . . . and the encouragement of personal pensions have all contributed to people saving more. *Investors Chronicle*[3]

'Saving' is a gerciple: *have all encouraged people to save more.*

Where sequences are expressed in terms of cause rather than result, the gerciple creeps in just as insidiously.

> The changes have come about because of industry lobbying, and a growing awareness in the Commission that advertising policy is non-existent and needs co-ordinating. *Marketing Week*[4]

The word 'lobbying' is here a gerciple. Either make it a genuine gerund – *The changes have come about because of industry's lobbying* – or change the construction: *The changes have come about because industry has lobbied the Commission, and the Commission has become increasingly aware that advertising policy is non-existent.*

> It is estimated that 40 hospital incidents a day stem from people swallowing household chemicals. *Good Housekeeping*[5]

It would be clumsy to turn the gerciple into a gerund ('40 incidents a day stem from people's swallowing household chemicals'), unless the sentence is re-shaped. *It is estimated that people cause 40 hospital incidents a day by swallowing household chemicals.*

> The RCN has reported an increase in cases of hardship among nurses, caused by rents doubling and trebling. *Nursing Standard*[6]

'Doubling' and 'trebling' are both gerciples. Turn them into proper gerunds: *The RCN has reported an increase in cases of hardship among nurses, caused by the doubling and trebling of rents.*

> It was based on building societies agreeing loans to housing associations at interest rates of both six and eight per cent. *Times*[7]

Here 'agreeing' can become a proper gerund if 'building societies' is turned into a genitive: *based on building societies' agreeing loans.* Better change the construction: *It was based on agreement by the building societies to give loans to housing associations.*

> Because inclusion is based on the veterinary surgeon reading about the list and sending off notification of his willingness to be included, there are some well respected equine practitioners not included . . . *Horse & Hound*[8]

This piece concerns the *British Equine Directory.* Let us translate it into English: *Because veterinary surgeons are included only if they have read the list and indicated their willingness.*

In the sentences we have been examining, the gerciple was attached to a noun ('people swallowing', 'rents doubling'). Even greater grammatical disasters occur when the subject of the gerciple is not a single word but a collection of words.

If so, the Conservative recovery could have to do with the controversies over the reform of the NHS receding from the headlines. *Independent*[9]

Here the gerciple 'receding' is attached to the words 'the controversies over the reform of the NHS'. In such a case use the expression 'the fact that'. *If so, the Conservative recovery could have to do with the fact that the controversies over the reform of the NHS have receded from the headlines.*

Health ministers fear the loss of talented women from all levels of the NHS, due to inadequate or non-existent child care provision and inflexible employment patterns threatening to undermine the Government's equal opportunities policies. *Independent*[10]

Here the gerciple ('threatening') is attached to a phrase of enormous length ('inadequate or non-existent child care provision and inflexible employment patterns'). The ungrammatical 'due to' is, as so often, the root of subsequent error (see Chapter V, 3), and must go. *Health ministers fear that talented women will be lost from all levels of the NHS because inadequate or non-existent child care provision and inflexible employment patterns are threatening to undermine the Government's equal opportunities policies.*

2 After 'despite'

'Despite' is a word to be used only with the utmost care. It readily traps writers into use of the gerciple.

Despite money being a constant headache, reconstruction of Churchward Collett 2885 class 2-8-0 No3802 is now pushing ahead at a cracking pace. *Steam Classic*[11]

It would be awkward to change the gerciple 'being' into a proper gerund ('Despite money's being a constant headache'). Substitute 'although' which, unlike 'despite', does not attract the gerciple: *Although money is a constant headache, reconstruction of Churchward Collett . . . is now pushing ahead.*

Despite Bergevin having little direct experience in advertising and marketing, and Bruhann being the mastermind behind the data protection directive, Europe's advertising professionals are optimistic about working with them. *Marketing Week*[12]

Again to make the gerciples genuine gerunds would be awkward ('Despite Bergevin's having little direct experience . . . and Bruhann's being the mastermind'). Replace 'despite' by 'although': *Although Bergevin has little direct experience in advertising and Bruhann is the mastermind behind the data protection directive.*

Despite all promotions of stockmarket-based investments having to contain a caveat about fluctuating prices, the message does not always appear to be appreciated. *Moneywise*[13]

It is not a question of *them* having to contain but of *their* having to contain, and 'promotions of stockmarket-based investments' cannot be neatly turned into a genitive. It would be correct to use 'the fact that' – *Despite the fact that all promotions of stockmarket-based investments have to contain a caveat* – but more acceptable to replace 'despite' by 'although': *Although all promotions of stockmarket-based investments have to contain a caveat about fluctuating prices.*

The imprisonment does not affect his right to sit in Parliament or to take the Labour whip, despite Labour officially opposing nonpayment. *Independent*[14]

The simplest correction here – *despite Labour's official opposition to non-payment* – is probably preferable to use of 'although': *although Labour officially opposes non-payment.*

Last year, income of about £40,000 was marginally exceeded by expenditure, despite the association not paying its central office quota. *Times*[15]

This account of the affairs of the Newbury Tory party combines 'despite' excruciatingly with a negative gerciple: *even though the association did not pay its central office quota.*

3 After certain nouns and prepositions

There are certain nouns, followed by prepositions, which naturally attract gerunds and gerciples: the 'importance of', 'desirability of', 'risk of', 'danger of', 'protection against', 'obstacle to', and many others. It is correct to speak of 'the importance of being earnest' or 'of being Ernest'; it is incorrect to speak of 'the importance of Jack Worthing being earnest/Ernest'.

. . . and one of the book's concerns is the importance of the press bearing witness to apartheid's horrors. *Times*[16]

Turning 'bearing' into a proper gerund would be awkward ('the importance of the press's bearing witness'). As often, the trouble stems from overuse of nouns such as 'concerns' and 'importance': *and the book shows how important it is for the press to bear witness.*

Arrangements for roof drainage needed to be improved to eliminate the risk of water spilling from the roof and down the walls. *Traditional Homes*[17]

The corrected gerund would again be awkward ('the risk of water's spilling from the roof'). Use 'that' after 'risk': *Arrangements for roof drainage needed to be improved to eliminate the risk that water would spill from the roof and down the walls.*

> But water-safety experts at RoSPA are scathing about parents who rely on armbands as sole protection against children drowning. *Woman*[18]

The use of noun 'protection' instead of the verb 'protect' lures the writer to the gerciple, 'children drowning'. *Water-safety experts at RoSPA are scathing about parents who rely solely on armbands to protect their children from drowning.*

> Banque Worms, the French private bank, was last night the only obstacle to Brent Walker gaining approval from its bankers for its refinancing proposals. *Independent*[19]

'Brent Walker's gaining approval' would be both correct and acceptable here. Alternatively use the verb 'prevent': *was last night the only obstacle to prevent Brent Walker from gaining approval.*

> M. N. Roy . . . argued with Lenin in the Comintern about the correctness or otherwise of the working class forging political alliances with the colonial bourgeoisie. *History Today*[20]

Omit 'or otherwise' as redundant. Arguing about correctness must involve arguing about incorrectness or there would be no argument: *argued . . . whether it was correct for the working class to forge political alliances with the colonial bourgeoisie.*

> The only threat to Britain achieving this 'inflation miracle' comes either from sterling being withdrawn from the ERM or the Bundesbank going down with the old English disease. *Times*[21]

There are here three gerciples in a sentence ('Britain achieving this', 'sterling being withdrawn', 'the Bundesbank going down'). *The only threat to Britain's achievement of this 'inflation miracle' comes either from the withdrawal of sterling from the ERM or from the collapse of the Bundesbank with the old English disease.*

There are certain prepositional phrases which attract gerciples. They include 'in return for', 'in exchange for', and 'prior to'.

> The plot revolves around a medical student who, in return for the government paying for his training, has agreed to work for four years in the tiny Alaskan town of Cicely. *More*[22]

The plot revolves around a medical student who, in return for his training at the government's expense, has agreed to work for four years in the tiny Alaskan town of Cicely.

> For nine years prior to Soviet spy Geoffrey Prime confessing to stealing thousands of secret documents from GCHQ, I went through all the 'proper channels', stating that hundreds of secret documents had vanished from that department . . . *Oldie*[23]

This is what comes of using a fancy word like 'prior' instead of 'before': *For nine years before Soviet spy Geoffrey Prime confessed to stealing thousands of secret documents from GCHQ.*

> America will lift $165m in sanctions in exchange for Japan (possibly) raising the foreign share of its market to 20% . . . *Economist*[24]

The simplest correction ('in exchange for Japan's raising') may not be the best. *America will lift $165m in sanctions if Japan will raise the foreign share of its market to 20%.*

4 Other usages

> She doesn't resent Rob not being around on her birthday. *Woman*[25]

Use a proper gerund ('Rob's not being around') since 'the fact that' ('doesn't resent the fact that Rob is not around') is clumsy, or re-word: *She doesn't resent Rob's absence on her birthday.*

> Some wives grow to like their men being away for long periods. Stacey, who lives in Eastbourne, is now anxious about her husband James coming back. *Me*[26]

Here are two gerciples. They won't stand direct change to gerunds ('their men's being away', 'James's coming back'). *Some wives grow to like their men's absence for long periods. Stacey . . . is now anxious about her husband James's return.* It would appear that absent husbands breed gerciples.

> I cannot recall my father ever arriving or departing from the town's LM&SR station . . . *Steam Railway*[27]

Either make the gerciples gerunds – *I cannot recall my father's ever arriving or departing*– or change the construction: *I cannot recall that my father ever arrived or departed from the town's LM&SR station.*

> One can only hope that an opera company owning its own opera house will prove to be less disastrous than what has happened as a consequence of most football clubs owning a stadium. *Times*[28]

Poor marks must be awarded for these two crude gerciples in a sentence. *One can only hope than an opera company's ownership of its own opera house will prove to be less disastrous than what has happened in many cases where football clubs have gained ownership of their stadia.*

This decision coincided with an Australian friend moving into a new apartment in New York and hiring Sandra to decorate it. *Homes & Gardens*[29]

It would be adequate to change the gerciple ('friend moving') into a genuine gerund – *coincided with an Australian friend's moving* – but better perhaps to re-cast: *This decision was made at the same time as an Australian friend moved into a new apartment in New York and hired Sandra to decorate.*

5 Passive gerciples

The passive gerciple may be rarer than the active gerciple, but it is no less offensive. There is a quite proper passive gerund in 'He hated being bullied at school'. There is a passive gerciple in 'He hated his son being bullied at school', which should be either 'He hated his son's being bullied at school' or 'He hated his son to be bullied at school'.

The Major initiative called for some $18 billion (£10.9 billion) being written off the outstanding debt of the poorer nations of the world, nearly $1 of which is owed to Britain. *Times*[30]

The infinitive is so natural here that one marvels at the determination to evade it: *The Major initiative called for some $18 billion (£10.9 billion) to be written off the outstanding debt.*

The regulator denied he had known Mr Frost had three times 'put off' a new firm of solicitors being brought in. The exchange followed Mr Jones criticising NatWest's own enquiry into the Blue Arrow saga as whitewash. *Times*[31]

While the two gerciples ('new firm of solicitors being brought in' and 'Mr Jones criticising') must go, it would help to introduce a genuine gerund instead of 'he had known'. *The regulator denied knowing that Mr Frost had three times 'put off' the involvement of a new firm of solicitors. The exchange followed Mr Jones's claim that NatWest's own enquiry into the Blue Arrow saga was a whitewash.*

Terry Steel . . . said Boots will gain by Manoplax being distributed by Warner-Lambert's American sales force. *Times*[32]

Terry Street . . . said that Boots will gain when (if) Manpoplax is distributed by Warner-Lambert's American sales force.

At present estimates, 17 per cent of the market in 1998 would mean about 2.5 million Japanese cars being sold in Europe . . . *Times*[33]

Change 'at' to 'on', correct the loose use of 'mean' (see Chapter VIII, 1) and the gerciple: *On present estimates, 17 per cent of the market in*

1998 would represent the sale of about 2.5 million Japanese cars in Europe.

> This case again, like the Hungerford massacre, brings into public question the whole procedure of men being permitted to hold firearms and ammunition. *Times*[34]

'Procedure' is the wrong word and the gerciple must go: *brings into question the whole practice of permitting men to hold firearms and ammunition.*

6 THE 'GERCIPLE' ATTACHED TO A PRONOUN

The use of the gerciple after a pronoun is not uncommon in lax conversation. 'You don't mind me asking', we say, making 'asking' into a gerciple where it should be a genuine gerund, 'You don't mind my asking'. In the same way we say 'I hated him going away' instead of 'I hated his going away'. The habit sounds bad in public speaking and looks bad in print. It can generally be corrected without changing the construction but by making the pronoun a possessive ('my' instead of 'me', 'his' instead of 'him'). Sometimes a change of construction is better. (It will be observed that the word 'without' attracts gerciples dangerously.)

1 After 'me'

> He said he wasn't too worried about me going . . . *Essentials*[1]

He said he wasn't too worried about my going . . .

> Without me telling him what to do he would be absolutely useless. *Private Eye*[2]

Without my telling him what to do he would be absolutely useless.

> My parents don't mind me living at home . . . *More*[3]

My parents don't mind my living at home . . .

> He doesn't like me going out, even in the day . . . *Parents*[4]

He doesn't like my going out, even in the day . . .

> It is all very well me pontificating . . . *Cumbria Life*[5]

Though correct, 'my pontificating' could be improved upon: *all very well for me to pontificate.*

> When we argue it usually starts with me accusing him of being like any other man . . . *New Woman*[6]

Turning the gerciple into a proper gerund ('with my accusing him') would be correct, but not felicitous: *starts when I accuse him.*

2 After 'him'

I think it would be a mistake, though, to start fantasising that you and he might get back together somehow through him keeping in touch with your child . . . *Catch*[7]

. . . *through his keeping in touch with your child* . . .

Forget the fairytale stuff about him leaving his wife and living with you happily ever after. *Catch*[8]

. . . *about his leaving his wife and living with you* . . .

It's going to be hard getting used to him coming home again when the contract's finished. *Me*[9]

. . . *It's going to be hard getting used to his coming home again* . . .

After one such session, one of their number, a former Lt-Colonel, had an altercation with the head of the typing pool which ended with him dumping her typewriter in the wastepaper basket. *Meridian*[10]

If the straightforward correction does not satisfy – *which ended with his dumping her typewriter* – change the construction: *which ended when he dumped her typewriter in the wastepaper basket.*

In the end I think the immaturity of the salesman has led to him not getting on with the customer . . . *Times*[11]

Either correct the pronoun – *led to his not getting on* – or change the construction: *led to his failure to get on with the customer.*

This has coincided with him being kicked out of university and his beginning to drink a lot. *Company*[12]

The gerciple must go – *This has coincided with his being kicked out of university* – while the subsequent gerund *his beginning* stays.

3 After 'them'

But I am afraid that the chance of them succeeding is not very high . . . *Times*[13]

This is Bernard Levin himself. *But I am afraid that the chance of their succeeding is not very high* . . .

. . . Maxwell took the banks for yet another few hundred millions in loans without them bothering with anything like sufficient security for the money. *Times*[14]

And this, alas, is Bernard Levin too: *without their bothering.*

> To prevent them becoming lifeless museums, we are beguiled into maintaining their owners in the style to which they have become accustomed. *Times*[15]

And this is Janet Daley. There are two ways in which the gerciple ('them becoming') could be dealt with. Either change the pronoun – *To prevent their becoming lifeless museums* or insert 'from': *To prevent them from becoming lifeless museums.*

> 'There's only a slight tendency towards them having a drinking problem themselves or towards them marrying someone with a drinking problem,' says Dr Orford. *Company*[16]

If corrected gerunds do not satisfy – *towards their having a drinking problem themselves or towards their marrying someone with a drinking problem* – change the construction: *There's only a slight tendency for them to have a drinking problem themselves or to marry someone with a drinking problem.*

4 After 'you'

> Nothing annoys a bank manager more than you running into the red with him knowing nothing about it until he is forced to bounce your cheques. *House Beautiful*[17]

Here are two gerciples ('you running' and 'him knowing'). While the first can be turned into a correct gerund – *Nothing annoys a bank manager more than your running into the red* – the second must give way to another construction: *while he knows nothing about it.*

> She's having a bad enough time with that new front tooth without you annoying her, too. *My Weekly*[18]

She's having a bad enough time . . . without your annoying her too.

> . . . a blood-curdling ride that hurtles you through a futuristic landscape without you moving an inch. *Vivid*[19]

. . . without your moving an inch.

> In lieu of the most unlikely event of you seeing the *Steam Railway* sticker displayed on the porthole of my cabin, can I please lay claim to 'the furthest North'. *Steam Railway*[20]

Although the gerciple could be easily corrected – *In lieu of the most unlikely event of your seeing the* Steam Railway *sticker* – it would be better to start again and forget 'in lieu': *Since it is highly unlikely that you will see the* Steam Railway *sticker displayed.*

5 After 'us'

> . . . I did wonder if there was still any reason for us being together. *New Woman*[21]

Making the gerciple a proper gerund – *reason for our being together* – could be improved upon: *any reason for us to remain together.*

> Despite us being on the brink of what's been dubbed the caring, sharing decade, we're not about to witness another baby boom in the Nineties. *New Woman*[22]

Either correct this as it stands – *Despite our being on the brink* – or get rid of 'despite': *Although we are on the brink of what has been dubbed the caring, sharing decade, we're not about to witness.*

> I'm looking towards us doing *Romeo and Juliet* together, actually. *Meridian*[23]

I'm looking forward to our doing Romeo and Juliet *together.*

6 After 'it'

The gerciple after 'it' jars excruciatingly.

> You need to buy what you like and not worry about it being an investment. *Viva*[24]

Either use a correct gerund – *and not worry about its being an investment* – or change the construction: *You need to buy what you like without worrying whether it is an investment.*

> Its relative ease of access has resulted in it becoming extremely popular. *The Great Outdoors*[25]

Either correct as usual – *has resulted in its becoming extremely popular* – or get rid of the generally unnecessary 'has resulted in'. *The relative ease of access has made it extremely popular.*

> Some countries actually require certificates of vaccination against certain diseases such as cholera and yellow fever, while others recommend vaccination without it being a requirement. *Money-wise*[26]

As often, straightforward correction – *without its being a requirement* – is not felicitous. There are better ways of solving the problem: *recommend vaccination without making it compulsory.*

– IV –

USING VERBS CORRECTLY

1 THE INFINITIVE

The infinitive is most often governed by another verb. 'I helped him to move house', we say. There are many verbs like 'help' which make use of this construction (for instance 'advise', 'persuade', 'decide', 'teach', and 'allow'). Sometimes the infinitive can stand alone and function like a gerund as a noun ('To know her is to admire her'). There are certain idiomatic usages in which an infinitive hinges upon a noun ('time to go', 'reason to believe', 'room to manoeuvre') but such usages remain exceptional. Many of the current misuses of the infinitive derive from relating it directly to a noun instead of to a verb.

1 Infinitive or gerund?
It is ironical that the infinitive is widely used where a gerund would be better, for in correcting misuse of the gerund we often found it advisable to use an infinitive in its place.

> New machines usually come with a small indicator strip to measure your water hardness. *Good Housekeeping*[1]

You can say 'The postman comes with a van to deliver letters', because the infinitive construction 'to deliver letters' is related to the verb 'come'. But new machines do not come 'to measure your water hardness', and the infinitive cannot hinge on the noun 'indicator strip'. A gerund is needed: *a small indicator strip for measuring your water hardness.*

> If you can spare a few hours on any day between September 23rd and October 6th, Coastwatch UK would be interested in your help to survey a 5km stretch of local coastline. *Outdoors Illustrated*[2]

You can help someone 'to survey' where 'help' is a verb, but the noun 'help' calls for a gerund. *Coastwatch would like your help in surveying a 5km stretch of local coastline.*

> Courses are available in 1992 to decorate your own plates and tiles or block print your own fabric. *Country Living*[3]

You could say 'Porters are available to carry your luggage', but courses do not decorate plates and tiles. *Courses in decorating your own plates and tiles or block printing your own fabrics are available in 1992.*

Midsummer is undoubtedly the most popular period to experience the outdoors . . . *Outdoors Illustrated*[4]

You might say 'He was the last man to experience depression', but there is no possibility that midsummer will experience anything: *the most popular period for experiencing the outdoors.*

Helpful tips are interspersed with advice to simplify the job . . . *Best*[5]

The subject is how to make an attractive shirt. Giving someone 'advice to simplify the job' would mean telling them to simplify it, which is very different from supplying guidance on how to simplify it: *with guidance for simplifying the job.*

There is a danger for any established organisation to rest on tradition and not want to move forward. *Church Army Report*[6]

The writer, Archbishiop Carey, has confused two constructions here. Either change the infinitives to gerunds – *There is a danger for any established organisation in resting on tradition and not wanting to move forward* – or get rid of the noun 'danger': *It is dangerous for any established organisation to rest on tradition.*

To achieve all this will require a considerable effort both to produce the information that is needed and to present and disseminate it in ways that can easily be understood by anyone. *Independent*[7]

You would not write 'To win the match will require effort both to bat well and to field well'. The infinitives 'to produce', 'to present and disseminate' have nothing to hinge upon but the noun 'effort'. Rewriting is necessary. *To achieve all this will require a considerable effort, effort directed both at producing the information that is needed and at presenting and disseminating it in ways that can easily be understood by anyone.* The pedant would add that it is not the 'ways' that have to be understood but the 'information': *presenting and disseminating it so that it can easily be understood by anyone.*

2 The 'adjectival' infinitive

We have seen infinitives attached to nouns where gerunds are needed. It is common also to find infinitives attached to nouns where adjectival constructions are called for.

New businesses like telecommunications and reinvestments to increase income and the value of our assets will ensure that we are building up a more solid business base for the future. *Waterways World*[8]

Here 'to increase income and the value of our assets' explains the nature of the 'reinvestments'. It is not the function of the infinitive to introduce a qualification adjectival in character. Insert a participle to agree with 'reinvestments' and the infinitive can hinge on it: *New businesses like telecommunications and reinvestments designed to increase income and the value of our assets.*

> The award acknowledges the considerable investment at Merley Court Touring Park to provide excellent indoor and outdoor facilities. *Caravan Magazine*[9]

The infinitive 'to provide' hinges upon the noun 'investment'. Either use the verb 'to invest' on which the infinitive can justly hinge – *considerable sums have been invested at Merley Court Touring Park to provide excellent indoor and outdoor facilities* – or insert a participle for the same purpose: *the considerable investment at Merley Court Touring park undertaken to provide . . .*

> Included will be information to help resolve problems with smoking or troublesome chimneys. *Old-House Journal*[10]

Substitute a relative clause for the infinitive. *Included will be information that will help to resolve problems with smoking or troublesome chimneys.*

> I am not for a minute suggesting that museums should avoid commercial techniques to help raise money. *Viva*[11]

If I said 'I suggest that you should avoid over-eating to help you to keep slim', the meaning would be obvious. The infinitive ('to help') is out of place above. *I am not for a moment suggesting that museums should avoid commercial techniques in trying to raise money.*

> Limpets, barnacles and winkles all have devices to survive prolonged periods of immersion. *Outdoors Illustrated*[12]

If I offered you some new door-locks and said 'Here are some devices to make you safe', it would be clear that the devices were going to make you safe. But in 'devices to survive prolonged periods' it is not the devices that are going to survive. This is a tortuous abuse of the infinitive. *Limpets, barnacles and winkles all have devices which enable them to survive prolonged periods of immersion.*

3 Misconnected infinitives

> Mr Major is not going to rush into a decision. The Tory lead is not large enough to take the risk. *Times*[13]

If I say 'Smith is not big enough to jump the pond' it is quite clear that the jumping has to do with Smith. If I say 'The Tory lead is not large enough to take the risk', it appears that the risk-taking has to do with the lead. The context does not justify the liberty taken here. *The Tory lead is not large enough for him to take the risk.*

> Odense, Denmark's third largest city, is only 4.5 miles away and has much to see. *Caravan Magazine* [14]

Odense is not going to see anything. *Odense . . . is only 4.5 miles away and has much for the visitor to see.*

> Anti-drugs investigators use freight data to construct detailed 'profiles' of the way traffickers transport drugs, but often the information arrives too late to make seizures. *Times* [15]

In 'the policeman arrived too late to make an arrest' the meaning is clear enough. But in 'the information arrives too late to make an arrest' nonsense seems to prevail: *but often the information arrives too late for seizures to be made.*

> It is a piece of highly competent planting, with a seat placed under the shelter of a purple-leaved cotinus bush to survey the scene and catch reflections in the pond. *Homes & Gardens* [16]

The seat is not put there 'to survey' anything, but in order that anyone sitting on it can do so: *with a seat placed under the shelter of a purple-leaved bush from which you can survey the scene.*

> Malcolm Rifkind wants a 'cultural change' on British Rail. To presume that state ownership is the total cause of customer dissatisfaction is belied by the facts of life around the world. *Oldie* [17]

Here is a pretty piece of illogicality. It is not the act of presuming that is 'belied' by the facts but the substance of the presumption. There is all the difference between telling a man that he has lied and denying that he has said anything at all. In this case the facts belie what someone presumed, not that he presumed something. *The presumption that state ownership is the total cause of customer dissatisfaction is belied by the facts of life around the world.*

> The number of guests is small enough to be friendly but large enough to find your own particular brand of soulmate. *Meridian* [18]

It is not the 'number' but the guests who are friendly, and it is neither the number nor the guests who are going to find a soulmate. *The number of guests is small enough for the atmosphere to be friendly but large enough for you to be able to find your own particular brand of soulmate.*

As a consumer of both art and burgers (usually on the same night because the end of a play and the departure of the last bus are too close to eat anything else) I can well appreciate that the citizens of Hampstead need McDonald's as well as Waterstone's. *Independent*[19]

We must not say that the end of the play and the departure of the bus are too close to eat. The ambiguity – whether the end and the departure are eating or being eaten – taxes the reader: *because the end of the play and the departure of the last bus are too close to allow of eating anything else.*

4 Various forms of misuse

Sometimes we find the infinitive used for no apparent reason.

The reconstruction of the station, which *The Railway Fly* deals with so amusingly, was complete at the end of 1874, to give four island platforms. *British Railways Illustrated*[20]

Remove the infinitive. *The reconstruction of the station ... was complete at the end of 1874, and gave four island platforms.*

Miss Hepburn was served with a summons for harassment, which carries a $250 fine, and to pay the parking ticket. *Hello*[21]

The infinitive 'to pay' appears to be governed by some absent verb. *Miss Hepburn was served with a summons for harassment, which carries a $250 fine, and ordered to pay for the parking ticket.*

To explore the area you need a car to tootle along country roads, staying overnight at small hotels ... *Options*[22]

It seems to be suggested that the car stays overnight at small hotels. *You can explore the area by tootling along country roads in a car, staying overnight at small hotels ...*

MIPIM is an outstanding environment to pursue commercial interests ... *Investors Chronicle*[23]

This is one of the most frequent of all misuses of the infinitive. *MIPIM is an outstanding environment in which to pursue commercial interests.*

The Clarins Studio offers the ultimate Clarins treatment service in a soothing, relaxing environment to escape the hustle and bustle of everyday life. *Harpers & Queen*[24]

Surely 'treatment' makes 'service' redundant, and 'soothing' makes 'relaxing' redundant. The infinitive 'to escape' floats in the air. The job it seems to be trying to do can be done only by some construction such as a relative clause. *The Clarins Studio offers the ultimate Clarins treatment in a relaxing environment which enables you to escape the hustle and bustle of everyday life.*

> A visit to Maison is highly recommended to appreciate a selection which is wholly modern, yet never too serious nor too extreme. *Harpers & Queen*[25]

'A visit is recommended to appreciate' is nonsense. The infinitive 'to appreciate' is asked to carry a burden beyond its range. A clause is needed to save the construction: *A visit . . . is highly recommended if you are to appreciate a selection.* But the construction would be better changed: *You are firmly recommended to visit Maison so that you can appreciate a selection which is wholly modern.*

> He said his stance was that as the Bank had been assured by NatWest there was a 'solid story' behind the affair, the full facts should be known to defuse criticism. *Times*[26]

If I said 'Jones is known to defuse criticism', it would characterise Jones in a definite way. That is patently not the construction here. Clearly by 'should be known' the writer intends 'should be made known'. Equally clearly by 'to defuse' the writer intends 'in order to defuse'. Thirdly, of course, he should have inserted 'that' after 'NatWest'. Were it not for these three errors the sentence could stand. *He said his stance was that as the Bank had been assured by NatWest that there was a 'solid story' behind the affair, the full facts should be made known in order to defuse criticism.*

> Elections are not supposedly to punish past behaviour, but they are opportunities to review, preview and perhaps *encourager les autres. Times*[27]

You could say 'The intention/purpose is not to punish' but not 'The election is not to punish' or 'Elections are not to punish'. This Leader could easily be corrected in that respect: *Elections are not supposed to punish past behaviour.* Moreover, 'to review, preview and perhaps *encourager les autres*' involves '*les autres*' as object of three infinitives, 'review', 'preview' and 'encourager', for all three are transitive verbs. But *les autres* are not going to be reviewed or previewed: *review performance, preview developments and perhaps* encourager les autres.

> . . . Stephen Oliver, whose newly-commissioned harpsichord recitatives to replace Sussmayer's hark further back to the more turbulent progressions of the Baroque than Mozart might have done. *Independent*[28]

There are two ways out of the error here. Either change the word-order so that 'to replace' hinges on 'newly-commissioned' – *Stephen Oliver,*

*whose harpsichord recitatives, newly-commissioned to replace Sus-
smayer's, hark further back* – or scrap the infinitive: *whose newly-
commissioned harpsichord recitatives, replacing Sussmayer's . . .*

The excitement of opera from a singer's point of view is to bring life
and your own emotion to the part you are creating. *Viva*[29]

*The excitement of opera from a singer's point of view lies in bringing
life and your own emotion to the part you are playing.*

2 SINGULAR/PLURAL

The rule that a singular noun must be followed by a singular verb and a
plural noun by a plural verb is an elementary one. In taking up our pens
we assume that we shall not slip up in that respect. Yet in fact it is not
hard to find examples of the error in the publications we are surveying.

1 Plural subject with singular verb
Mistakes often seem to result from sheer forgetfulness.

Ultimately the entire education and training service must be
developed as a whole, in the knowledge that changes at one level
necessarily affects every other level. *Independent*[1]

'Changes . . . affects' will not do. Presumably the writer forgets that he
has written 'changes at one level' and continues as though his message
is 'one level affects every other level': *changes at one level necessarily
affect every other level.*

The Belgrade daily newspaper *Borba* has decided that the intricate
enmities of Yugoslav politics is beyond the comprehension of its
usual journalists and commentators and has called in the services of
Charles Harvey and Nick Campion, the *Daily Mail* astrologer.
Times[2]

'The intricate enmities . . . is beyond the comprehension' must be
corrected: Borba *has decided that the intricate enmities of Yugoslav
politics are beyond the comprehension of its usual journalists.*

The effects of 1992 and the liberalising of trade across boundaries is
not being addressed with sufficient rigour. *Horse & Hound*[3]

The effects . . . and the liberalising . . . is not being addressed'. The verb
must be plural: *The effects of 1992 and the liberalising of trade across
boundaries are not being addressed.*

> Major areas of research interest within the Department includes Development Economics, Industrial Economics, Macroeconomics and Regional Economics . . . *Times*[4]

This is advertising a post at a university. *Major areas of research interest within the Department include* . . .

> Uplighters throwing light up on to the ceiling makes the room seem more spacious, but don't do this if the plasterwork is poor. *Annabel*[5]

If 'Uplighters-throwing-light' is supposed to be the subject of 'makes', it won't do, because 'throwing' is a gerciple. Choose a plural subject and verb – *Uplighters which throw light up on to the ceiling make the room seem more spacious* – or a singular subject and verb: *Light thrown up on to the ceiling from uplighters makes the room seem more spacious.* The words 'don't do this' won't do because 'this' (actually fixing up such lights) has not been mentioned: *but don't use these if the plasterwork is poor.*

> Stephen Howe, principal of the Outward Bound centre at Ullswater, said that the ages of those on courses was rising. *Independent*[6]

Better than just correcting the verb ('the ages of those on the course were rising') would be to re-write: *the courses were attracting older participants year by year.*

> Of course the media loves a scientific and technological sensation. *Meridian*[7]

'Media' is the plural form of the word 'medium'. *Of course the media love a scientific and technological sensation.*

> Ahead lies the natural stones of Carn Kenidjack which may have some spiritual significance . . . *The Great Outdoors*[8]

Ahead lie the natural stones of Carn Kenidjack.

> Super-Hack Dennis MacShane's subtle attempts to win the Labour Party's nomination for Dave Nellist's Coventry East seat has been tragically curtailed. *Private Eye*[9]

The subject ('attempts') is plural: *have been tragically curtailed* (By 'curtailed' does the writer mean 'frustrated'?).

In the case of the verb 'to be' the complement that follows it may by 'attraction' make it singular where the subject is plural. The biblical axiom 'The wages of sin is death' is sometimes quoted in defence of this practice.

> Visits, especially during summer months, to gardens where conducted tours are sometimes arranged, is another added bonus. *Money-Maker*[10]

The use of 'is' after 'visits' cannot be defended here. *Visits, especially during summer months . . . are another added bonus.*

> Mountains, fellsides, woodlands, river, lake and waterfalls is the environment. *The Artist*[11]

This is an advertisement for Lake District holidays. *Mountains, fellsides, woodlands, river, lake and waterfalls are the environment.*

2 Singular subject with plural verb

> The outcome of these meetings invariably show large gaps in our knowledge of animals in the field. *BBC Wildlife*[12]

Here a totally illegitimate force of 'attraction' is at work. The writer forgets that she began with 'outcome' and adjusts the verb as though its subject were 'meetings'. This is a common error. *The outcome of these meetings invariably shows large gaps.*

> The beauty of many corals lead to their being ripped from their natural reef habitats for sale in the world's tourist shops . . . *Wild about Animals*[13]

Here the writer forgets that he began with 'beauty' and adjusts the verb as though its subject were 'many corals'. *The beauty of many corals leads to their being ripped from their natural reef habitats.*

> There are no shortage of books to act as *vademecums* to those seeking out historic places in Britain. *History Today*[14]

There is no shortage of books to act as vademecums.

> The purchase of unit trusts alleviates such problems and are also an inexpensive way for investors to spread their risk. *Meridian*[15]

'The purchase alleviates . . . and are also' will not do. The writer forgets after the first verb ('alleviates') that his subject was 'purchase' and adjusts the second verb ('are') as though it were 'unit trusts'. *The purchase of unit trusts alleviates such problems and is an inexpensive way for investors to spread their risk.*

> Radio 1 is still dull, patronising and moronic. The tawdriness of its perpetual phone-ins and insulting jokes have to be heard to be believed. *Times*[16]

'The tawdriness . . . have to be heard to be believed' Janet Daley writes, and the editorial staff are so proud of the sentence that they headline it: 'The tawdriness of its phone-ins and jokes have to be heard to be believed'. *The tawdriness of its phone-ins and jokes has to be heard to be believed.*

> . . . Sandown's superb provision of disabled facilities – including
> ramps and viewing patios overlooking the course, winners' enclo-
> sure and parade ring – further attract the public. *The Field*[17]

It is easy to forget that the subject 'provision' was singular when you
exemplify it immediately afterwards with so many instances. *Sandown's superb provision of disabled facilities . . . further attracts the
public.*

> Most of the growth in jobs over this period have been based on self-
> employment and new small business start-ups. *Money-Maker*[18]

How quickly the writer forgets that his subject was 'growth' and not
'jobs': *Most of the growth in jobs over this period has been based on self-
employment.*

In the examples so far quoted in this section there is a singular
subject followed by a second noun in the plural ('outcome of meetings',
'shortage of books', 'growth in jobs') and the writer forgot that the real
subject was singular. Thus the subsequent noun ('meetings', 'books',
'jobs') was treated as the subject and was given a plural verb. This is the
pitfall to be avoided. Other versions of the error are less easy to find.

> The surest sign that water voles are still in residence along a stretch
> of canal are the little well trodden platforms that the voles habitually
> use as a feeding and grooming site. *Waterways World*[19]

The main verb is the verb 'to be' ('are'), and here is the 'wages of sin'
kind of attraction in reverse. The 'surest sign' is denied its singular verb
because the plural complement ('the little well trodden platforms')
attracts a plural verb in anticipation. To get rid of the awkwardness of
'The surest sign . . . is the little well-trodden platforms' make the subject
'sign' plural. *The surest signs that water voles are still in residence along
a stretch of canal are the little well trodden platforms.*

> Mary McGinley riding Charlie Brown had the same mark as Tessa in
> the Medium 30, but were just pipped into second place by one
> point on the bottom marks. *Horse & Hound*[20]

'Mary . . . had the same marks . . . but were just pipped' will not do. I am
not sure why the writer gave us the plural verb 'were'. Is it because 'Mary
McGinley riding Charlie Brown' has become the equivalent of 'Mary
McGinley and Charlie Brown'? Has the writer treated horse and rider as
the subject of 'were pipped'? It seems the likeliest explanation: *but was
just pipped into second place.*

3 Verbs after collective nouns

Collective nouns are singular and generally take a singular verb. There is a degree of freedom, however. We say 'The audience is large and enthusiastic', but we should say 'The audience are now clapping their hands and stamping their feet' where the emphasis is on what individual members are doing, for 'clappinng its hands and stamping its feet' would sound wrong. But the singular verb is the norm, and the habit of using it needs to be cultivated.

> The Sudbury silk firm soon became a member of Wardle's Silk Association, and in 1912 a selection of its hand-woven upholstery fabrics were displayed in the Association's London exhibition. *Traditional Homes*[21]

'Selection' is singular. Here it refers to the exhibits as a whole. There is no case for a plural verb: *and in 1912 a selection of its hand-woven upholstery fabrics was displayed in the Association's London exhibition.*

> The firm's range of services include re-building any size lean-to or plant house, designing new glasshouses and re-creating traditional Victorian geenhouses. *Old-House Journal*[22]

'Range' is singular: *The firm's range of services includes re-building any size lean-to or plant house.*

> Our range of separates are designed to bring you an infinite repertoire of sound. *The World of Interiors*[23]

'Infinite' is surely an extravagant term for what is on offer in this advertisement for Technics. *Our range of separates is designed to bring you an extensive repertoire of sound.*

> Gallons of shampoo are needed to get the horses squeaky clean and a large supply of crisp white trousers and shirts are essential. *Daily Telegraph*[24]

'Supply' is singular: *A large supply of crisp white trousers and shirts is essential.*

> A flight of steps assist a purposeful ascent of the slipped cliff-end. *Cumbria Life*[25]

'Flight' is singular. *A flight of steps assists a purposeful ascent.*

> His vast array of trophies, displayed in his parents' home, also include mementos from squash tournaments he's won . . . *Cumbria Life*[26]

There is no excuse for the plural verb 'include' after 'array of trophies' or 'collection of trophies' or any other such subject. *His vast array of trophies . . . includes mementos.*

We add some examples in which insistence on a singular verb after the collective noun might be regarded as over-pedantic. What is recommended below is recommended with varying degrees of conviction and doubt.

> An inner core of favoured clients queue for hot loaves in the only bakery that is still working. *Oldie*[27]

An inner core of favoured clients queues for hot loaves . . .

> Our team of expert correspondents have been briefed to supply our computer with up-to-date catch information . . . *Sea Angler*[28]

Our team of expert correspondents has been briefed . . .

> A whole variety of proposals have been put forward . . . *Daily Mail*[29]

A whole variety of proposals has been put forward . . .

> . . . a substantial number of handlooms were set up in purpose built garrets above the workers' dwellings. *Traditional Homes*[30]

Here is a case where the collective noun ('number') does not really 'collect' the individuals concerned. Indeed 'a substantial number' becomes a mere euphemism for 'many'. *Many handlooms were set up in purpose-built garrets.*

> In some of the rooms the top row of border tiles have been cut into a sort of castellated effect round the pattern. *The World of Interiors*[31]

Here neither singular nor plural verb would be elegant after 'the top row of border tiles'. Change the subject of the sentence: *The border tiles along the top* or *The topmost border tiles.*

Finally, here are four instances of what we may now call the 'institutional plural', the plural verb used for a given institution such as a firm or a school. Usage seems to be establishing it.

> Large blue chip telecommunications company seek a polished professional for high profile role . . . *Times*[32]

'Company' is singular: *Large blue chip telecommunications company seeks a polished professional.*

> The London Business School carry this information on all sorts of companies and operate an information service. *Company*[33]

'School' is singular: *The London Business School carries this information on all sorts of companies and operates an information service.*

A busy licensed and centrally located Glasgow Chinese Restaurant urgently require an experienced and talented head chef. *Guardian*[34]

A busy . . . Glasgow Chinese Restaurant urgently requires an experienced and talented head chef.

One of Britain's oldest football clubs are celebrating a victory over financial adversity . . . *Times*[35]

The subject 'one' cannot be followed by 'are': *is celebrating.*

4 Singular pronouns with plural verbs

The liberties taken with singular pronouns cannot be excused as the liberties taken with certain collective nouns may be excused. Nevertheless examples of plural verbs misused with singular pronouns are not hard to find.

None of the old arguments trundled out by ministers against elected police authorities hold water. *Guardian*[36]

'None' (the equivalent of 'not one') is singular. *None of the old arguments trundled out by ministers against elected police authorities holds water.*

I scanned the surface for the tell-tale V's of departing mullet, but none were visible. *Sea Angler*[37]

'None' is singular, and 'V's' should be 'Vs'. *I scanned the surface for the tell-tale Vs of departing mullet, but none was visible.*

Everybody in British Waterways believes in the importance of the inland waterways and are determined to develop the potential for the network to become one of the most valuable environmental assets in the country. *Waterways World*[38]

'Everybody' is singular and is rightly given a singular verb ('believes'), but then, inexplicably, a plural verb ('are') to follow. *Everybody in British Waterways believes in the importance of the inland waterways and is determined to develop the potential . . .*

Sculpture proved more difficult to sell than last year. Whereas everything by Dame Elizabeth Frink and Lynn Chadwick were snapped up at the previous sale, a number of their sculptures failed to find buyers. *Independent*[39]

'Everything' is singular. *Whereas everything by Dame Elizabeth Frink and Lynn Chadwick was snapped up at the previous sale . . .*

Each of the bedrooms have full facilities, most enjoying delightful seaviews . . . *Daily Mail*[40]

'Each' is singular. *Each of the bedrooms has full facilities.*

Neither are quite like the other young people of their age. *Independent*[41]

'Neither' is singular. *Neither of them is like the other young people of their age.*

Neither of us were born to this, were we? *Times*[42]

(Neil Kinnock, at the Cenotaph, has just prevented John Major from making a gaffe.) The use of 'were we?' makes the simple correction rather awkward, but if the singular verb had been properly used, 'were we?' would not have sprung to Mr Kinnock's lips: *Neither of us was born to this.*

3 TRANSITIVE/INTRANSITIVE

A transitive verb is one which is followed by a direct object. In the sentences 'He caught a fish', 'He cleaned his gun', 'She likes tomatoes' and 'They trust their solicitor', the verbs 'caught', 'cleaned', 'likes' and 'trust' are all transitive. The meaning conveyed would be incomplete were they not followed by the nouns which form the direct objects. When a subject is followed by an intransitive verb, however, no direct object is required to complete the meaning. In the sentences 'He departed', 'She remained', 'They quarrelled' and 'We hesitated' the verbs 'departed', 'remained', 'quarrelled' and 'hesitated' are all intransitive. In the English language many transitive verbs also have an intransitive form. We mostly use the verb 'to read' transitively ('He is reading a book'), but we also use it intransitively ('He is reading'). This flexibility in the language can easily be overstrained. Care must be taken not to manufacture intransitive forms for verbs which are invariably transitive.

1 Transitive verbs used intransitively

The music has simplified since the Led Zeppelin album . . . *Oldie*[1]

There is no intransitive form of the verb 'to simplify'. You can simplify an issue and thereby the issue will be simplified, but it would be absurd to pretend that the issue 'has simplified'. It is no more logical to treat the verb 'simplify' like that than it would be to treat the word 'eat' similarly. You eat a sausage and thereby the sausage 'is eaten'. No one would think of saying 'The sausage has eaten'. *The music has got simpler since the Led Zeppelin album.*

Foxes are giving birth now, too, but the vixens are more secretive about the locations of their nursery earths than badgers – you won't find soil or bedding scattered outside, and it is only later, when the cubs begin to wean, that bones and feathers betray their presence. *BBC Wildlife*[2]

A mother weans her baby and the baby is thereby weaned. As the music does not simplify and the sausage does not eat, so the cub does not wean: *it is only later, when the cubs begin to be weaned, that bones and feathers betray their presence.*

But there are occasions when I would prescribe an antibiotic before giving acupuncture, for instance if the ear drum was about to perforate. *Independent*[3]

When you 'perforate' a piece of paper you make a hole in it, and the paper is thereby 'perforated'. As with paper, so with ear drums: *for instance, if the ear drum was about to be perforated.*

New cells are pushed up from the basal layer and gradually compress as they reach the surface to form the very outer layer of your skin. *Company*[4]

You can 'compress' (press together) your clothes into the smallest possible space in packing a suitcase, and the clothes are thereby compressed. But the clothes themselves do not 'compress'. *New cells are pushed up from the basal layer and are gradually compressed as they reach the surface.*

So you need to be careful about where you display your miniatures. Too close to a fire and the ivory may buckle and distort; exposed to direct sunlight and the watercolours will lose their brilliance. *Moneywise*[5]

There is no intransitive form of the verb 'distort'. *Too close to the fire and the ivory may buckle and be distorted.*

His wood is chosen carefully so as to create an object that will not deform. *Cumbria Life*[6]

Like 'distort', 'deform' cannot be used intransitively. *His wood is chosen carefully so as to create an object that will not lose shape.*

. . . . as the ball diverted into the net, it was Ray Houghton who rose to take the acclaim. *Sunday Times*[7]

The ball did not 'divert' but 'was diverted': . . . *as the ball was diverted into the net.*

You may be required to pay a deposit or the whole sum there and then, although you cannot remove the piece until your cheque has

cleared, unless you are known to the auctioneer. *Homes &
Gardens*[8]

The sky can 'clear' of its own accord, but not a cheque: *although you
cannot remove the piece until your cheque has been cleared.*

Your fund also escapes tax while it is building up – so your money
grows faster. *Moneywise*[9]

You can build a house or even a fund, but neither house nor fund can
build. We allow a passage of music to 'build up' to a climax or pressure
of water to 'build up' to bursting point, but there is an inner force in
music and torrent that justifies the usage. Money is inert. *Your fund also
escapes tax while it is being built up.*

2 False intransitives

The examples above illustrate the kind of misuse of transitive verbs
which could generally have been avoided if the verb had been put in the
passive voice (e.g. 'begin to wean' becoming 'begin to be weaned'). But
what goes wrong is not always as straightforward as that.

Lastly *Triumphs and Tragedy* . . . traces back to before the Aztecs
to look at the achievements of the Mestizo peoples, the Olmecs and
the Mayas . . . *History Today*[10]

The obvious question to arise is 'traces what back?'. Nothing can be said
simply 'to trace', let alone 'to trace back'. Lastly Triumphs and Tragedy
. . . *takes us back to before the Aztecs to look at the achievements of the
Mestizo peoples.*

But Britain's libel laws hampered more than oblique warnings in
print. *The Field*[11]

(The topic is the BCCI.) Though 'hinder' can be used intransitively,
'hamper' is always transitive. *But Britain's libel laws were more of an
obstacle than oblique warnings in print.*

Keeping in cover I scanned across, but not a bird in sight. *Dalesman*[12]

To scan something is to look at it searchingly. The only thing that can
just 'scan' (without an object) is a piece of verse. *Keeping in cover, I
looked across, but not a bird in sight.*

The virtue of the reasonably diverse conglomerate is that businesses doing well should protect against those doing badly.
Investor's Chronicle[13]

You can protect a person from danger, but there is no mention here of
who is being protected. There is no justification for an intransitive use

of the verb 'protect'. Protection is not the issue anyway. *The virtue of the reasonably diverse conglomeration is that businesses doing well should compensate for those doing badly.*

> There's no need to be 'careful' when you use Vanderbilt – its affordable price means that you can lavish on this luxury fragrance and really enjoy wearing it. *Prima*[14]

The verb 'means' here signifies 'allows' (see Chapter VIII, 1). The verb 'lavish' requires an object. You can lavish money on something, but you cannot just 'lavish': *its affordable price permits you to use this luxury fragrance lavishly.*

> Not only will we have saved ourselves money, but we shall be using an outfit that has proved. *Caravan Magazine*[15]

Proved what? You can use the verb transitively with an object ('prove a theory') or intransitively with a complement ('prove succesful'). Use the one – *an outfit that has proved itself* – or the other: *an outfit that has proved effective.*

3 Improper use of intransitive verbs

There seems to be less temptation to misuse intransitive verbs as though they were transitive, but when it happens the effect is bad.

> That is all the charisma that will ever matter: does a politician's nature impinge itself upon the citizens and draw their affections and sympathy? *Guardian* (quoted in *Private Eye*[16])

To 'impinge' cannot have an object ('itself'). And it is not the best word here. The idiomatic 'come across' would be better.

> 'Sometimes,' Cash says, as the carousels disappear his billboarded Yonex luggage and the passenger announcements bing-bong monotonously around him . . . *Esquire*[17]

Surely even 'fun' journalism must stop short of distortions such as this. 'Disappear' can never be transitive: . . . *as the carousels remove his billboarded Yonex luggage from sight.*

> Bring into warmth only when the flower shoots – not the leaves – are well emerged from the neck of the bulb. *Prima*[18]

A flower shoot might be well watered or well tended, but it cannot be 'well emerged', for 'emerge' is an intransitive verb. *Bring into warmth only when the flower shoots – not the leaves – have fully emerged from the neck of the bulb.*

> If the aim is to decline the level of terrorism . . . *Radio 4*[19]

You can decline a proposal of marriage and you may be able to decline a Latin noun, but you cannot decline the level of anything: *If the aim is to lower the level of terrorism.*

4 TENSES AND FORMS

1 Past, present, future

Keeping one's head in using the past, present and future tenses of verbs is a matter of commonsense. We may slip up, however, if our concentration lapses in the middle of a sentence. This is obviously most likely to happen in involved sentences.

> Twenty years later, as I sat in the guard's compartment of a restored vintage IoW train hauled by W8 *Freshwater* steaming towards Smallbrook Junction, I feel that the wait has been worthwhile. *Steam Railway*[1]

Concentration lapsed here between 'as I sat' and 'I feel'. Either 'sat' must go – *as I sit in the guard's compartment . . . I feel* – or 'feel' must go: *as I sat in the guard's compartment . . . I felt.*

> Riding horses or ponies on the road has always been a dangerous pastime, even more so nowadays because of increased traffic. *Daily Mail*[2]

'Even more so nowadays', a reference to the present, cannot be made to hang on the past verb 'has always been'. A verb in the present tense must be provided. *Riding horses or ponies on the road has always been a dangerous pastime; it is even more so nowadays.*

> To exploit his difficulties Labour is stepping up its campaign criticising Mr Major's handling of the economy, particularly when the latest jump in unemployment figures are published on Thursday. *Times*[3]

There is a curious illogicality here. 'The temperature is rising, especially when the sun comes out next Friday' would be regarded as absurd. And what about the 'jump' which 'are published' soon? *To exploit his difficulties Labour is stepping up its campaign criticising Mr Major's handling of the economy, and will make a special target of the increase in unemployment figures to be announced on Thursday.*

> Tarmac, one of Britain's biggest construction groups, has warned that first-half profits would show a 'very severe' shortfall and market conditions had continued to worsen in the second. *Independent*[4]

The sequence of tenses here should be either: 'has warned that first-half profits *will* show . . . and that market conditions *have* continued to worsen', or 'warned that first-half profits *would* show. . . and that market conditions *had* continued to worsen'. Moreover, 'first-half' is a composite adjective applying to 'profits' and there is no noun for 'second' to qualify. *Tarmac, one of Britain's biggest construction groups, has warned that profits in the first half will show a 'very severe' shortfall and that market conditions have continued to worsen in the second.*

Most of us had never even glimpsed such luxury, let alone be part of it. *Cumbria*[5]

Although 'let alone been part of it' would correct the bad grammar, it would be better to change the verb: *let alone experienced it.*

What you have done is face the inequality and change the way the relationship works. *Chat*[6]

You would not say 'What you have done is lose a friend'. The past tense ('have done') must be sustained. *What you have done is faced the inequality and changed the way the relationship works.*

But such aircraft would never have shown their full value unless they were flown with real precision and total dedication. *Independent*[7]

The words 'would never have shown' take us back into the past for something that actually happened. 'Unless' generally postulates a future condition on which what the main clause postulates is dependent. It is not the best usage here. *But such aircraft would never have shown their full value had they not been flown with real precision and total dedication.*

The Neanderthal inhabitants deliberately travelled many miles to obtain suitable stone for tools, as the flint used to make the implements in the cave is not available locally. *Independent*[8]

They deliberately travelled many miles because the flint *was* not available. If 'is' is kept, use 'must have travelled': *They must have deliberately travelled many miles . . . as the flint used to make the implements in the cave is not available locally.*

2 'may/might, would'
We say 'I may go today' but 'I might have gone yesterday'. 'May' goes with present and future, 'might' with past.

Many of the plants available today may have been lost for ever had it not been for the enthusiasts who formed the Hardy Plant Society (HPS) in 1957. *Traditional Homes*[9]

Many of the plants available today might have been lost for ever had it not been for the enthusiasts who formed the Hardy Plant Society (HPS) in 1957.

> Despite unhappiness with the stance taken by the OFT, and by the industry regulator Ofgas, British Gas chose not to risk asking for an MMC enquiry which may have led to it being broken up. *Investors Chronicle*[10]

'May' cannot follow the past tense, 'chose'. There is also an inadmissible gerciple, 'led to it being broken up' (see Chapter III, 6). *British Gas chose not to risk asking for an MMC enquiry which might have led to its being broken up.*

> In many cases a few treatments turn out to be the most cost-effective way of solving those specific beauty problems that they might have been struggling with for many years. *New Woman*[11]

Here we have the converse situation, a verb in the present tense ('turn out') followed by 'might' instead of 'may'. *In many cases a few treatments turn out to be the most cost-effective way of solving those specific beauty problems that they may have been struggling with for many years.*

> As far as ICI is concerned, the company is keen that employees are already committed to the group's ethos before they are promoted to sensitive areas . . . *Green Magazine*[12]

The words 'is keen' express desire, not knowledge. 'I know that you are committed' represents knowledge (and therefore 'are' is right). 'I am keen that you should be committed' represents desire (and therefore 'should be' is used). *The company is keen that employees should be committed to the group's ethos before they are promoted.*

> The view of industry as a whole is that it wants a single currency. It facilitates their activities and will give them welcome opportunities and lower costs. *Times*[13]

The topic, of course, is the plan for European common currency. It remains a plan, at least at the time of writing, and therefore the indicative 'facilitates' and 'will give' are out of place. *It would facilitate their activities and (would) give them welcome opportunities and lower costs.*

> Even those who concentrated on the more lucrative theatres of war will have realised that they were playing a high-risk game in which only a few could hope to be really lucky. *History Today*[14]

Again we are dealing with conjecture and possibility, this time in the past. *Even those who concentrated on the more lucrative theatres of war would have realised that they were playing a high-risk game.*

> The small rocky knoll upon which it shelters forms the watershed between the Naddle and St John's beck valleys, a division created by the last Ice Age, prior to which Thirlmere waters will have flowed due north. *Cumbria Life*[15]

Surely never could the future verb 'will' have been more out of place: *a division created by the last Ice Age, prior to which Thirlmere waters would have flowed due north.*

3 'shall/will'

For normal plain utterance 'shall' is used in the future tense with the first person singular ('I shall') and the first person plural ('We shall'). For the other persons ('he', 'she', 'it', 'they', 'you') the normal form is 'will'. There are exceptions to this practice whereby 'will' is allowed for the first person and 'shall' for the second and third persons. (For instance, a very emphatic intention could be 'I will' and a very emphatic order could be 'You shall'.) Entering upon the complexities of such variations is not necessary here. We are concerned with the proper practice for plain statement.

> Hundreds of you have responded to our orienteering competition and we will be announcing our winners in our October/November issue. *Outdoors Illustrated*[16]

There is no justification at all for 'will' here: *we shall be announcing our winners in our October/November issue.*

> We will need to consider carefully the wider question of policy which will arise from this important innovation. We will be studying how we can build on this breakthrough to reduce congestion on the trunk road network. *Independent*[17]

This quite improper use of 'will' sounds stilted and awkward. *We shall need to consider carefully the wider question . . . We shall be studying how we can build on this breakthrough.*

> We intend to ensure that National Power secures its position as the leading power Company in the country. We will be professional, running the business in a cost-effective way to keep ahead of competition. We will be enterprising and profit-orientated, but will pursue financially prudent policies at all times. We will provide quality services. *National Power Review*[18]

And so the Chief Executive goes on in his review. Replace 'will' by 'shall' on each occasion.

4 Irregular verb forms

English has verbs which take their various forms for the past tenses by simply adding *-d* or *-ed* ('live – lived', 'fill – filled'). English also has verbs which change their vowels for the past tenses ('sing', 'sang', 'sung'). Then again there are verbs which form their past participle in *-en* ('speak', 'spoke', 'spoken'). Certain verbs have both irregular forms and irregular forms in the past tense.

> But Mr Maxwell, a larger-than-life character, thrived on adversity. *Times*[19]

This is quite correct. It would be equally correct to write 'Mr Maxwell, a larger-than-life character, throve on adversity'. However, this same piece continues later with:

> . . . Mr Maxwell had been under mounting pressure from his bankers and shareholders to sell off many of the assets he had strived so hard to acquire.

Here the situation is different. The verb 'strive' has the past tense 'strove' and the past participle 'striven': *many of the assets he had striven so hard to acquire.*

> But while Vanity Fair has always strived to be very international in its outlook, it remains an exciting challenge to seek to find an editorial voice that speaks as strongly to readers in Southend as in San Francisco. *Vanity Fair*[20]

Whatever may be correct in San Francisco it remains true that 'has strived' is incorrect in Southend: *But while Vanity Fair has always striven to be very international in its outlook.*

> Goodbye to all that rollicking fun when Mr Major hoves to with his classless steam-roller. *Oldie*[21]

The past tense of 'heave' is 'hove'. The present tense is wanted here: *when Mr Major heaves to.*

> Council-house sales were popular, because people felt that a lifetime spent caring for a home earnt them the right to pass it on to their descendants. *Times*[22]

The verb 'learn' has 'learnt' as an alternative to 'learned' in the past tense and past participle. The writer has mistakenly assumed that the verb 'earn' has the same variations, but it does not: *because people felt that a lifetime spent caring for a home earned them the right to pass it on.*

> They're a lily-livered bunch if ever I knew one. Either that, or they're being lent on. *Daily Telegraph*[23]

The verb 'to lend' has the past tense 'lent', misused here for the past tense of 'to lean': *they're being leant on.*

> Although it leant much character to the uneven exterior render was in such poor condition that there was no option but to replace it. *Old-House Journal*[24]

Here is the error in reverse. 'Leant' is the past tense of the verb 'to lean', and the past tense of the verb 'to lend' is required: *Although it lent much character to the uneven exterior, the render was in such poor condition.*

> These workshops, lead by an experienced mental health nurse and counsellor, went well. *Nursing Standard*[25]

The past tense and past participle of the verb 'to lead' are 'led': *led by an experienced mental health nurse.*

One might here arouse controversy by airing prejudices in favour of 'sown' rather than 'sowed', 'swollen' rather than 'swelled' and 'wrought' rather than 'wreaked', but there would be no controversy over the award of wooden spoons for the following:

> Steve . . . wràpped [*rapped*] briskly on the window. *Outdoors Illustrated*[26]
>
> . . . the Rother Valley Company . . . sòrt [*sought*] permission . . . *British Railways Illustrated*[27]
>
> Others could hardly bare [*bear*] to mouth its name . . . *British Railways Illustrated*[28]
>
> With the rod absolutely taught [*taut*], the line was hard to fish . . . *Sea Angler*[29]

5 MISUSED VERBS

The simple verbs, 'to be', 'to do' and 'to have', are needed so frequently that we get careless in using them.

1 'to be'

> There are two ways of making potpourri. The original method is the moist type, less common today because, although it smells wonderful, it is not particularly good to look at. *Ideal Home*[1]

The 'original method' is certainly not the 'moist type'. *The original method produces the moist type of potpourri, less common today.*

We were unable to stretch to that sort of price, but the most important factor was in the increase in weight of such a caravan. *Caravan Magazine*[2]

The writer is citing the pros and cons of exchanging one model of caravan for another. The word 'factor' is used as of a persuasive consideration to be taken into account. If 'factor' is kept, 'in' must go from 'in the increase': *but the most important factor was the increase in weight.* Otherwise change the construction: *the most important deterrent lay in the increase in weight.*

Decisions must be made in the national interest, which in this case is not increasing food production but protecting wildlife. *Outdoors Illustrated*[3]

You cannot say 'the national interest is not increasing food production' when you mean 'it is not in the national interest to increase food production'. Use the verb 'to lie'. *Decisions must be made in the national interest, which in this case lies, not in increasing food production, but in protecting wildlife.*

... I do not think the relative charging structures should be a reason for choosing one investment over another. *Moneywise*[4]

The verb 'to be' is here a somewhat lax and colloquial substitute for a verb such as 'provide' or 'constitute'. *I do not think the relative charging structures should constitute a reason for choosing one investment over another.*

Whipsnade was the first attempt in this country to provide animals with a natural environment ... *My Weekly*[5]

A zoo cannot be an 'attempt'. *Whipsnade represented the first attempt in this country to provide animals with a natural environment.*

The now annual Scottish Railway preservation Society excursion south from Fort William is a month earlier than in previous years ... *Steam Railway*[6]

For 'is' substitute 'takes place' or 'occurs'. *The ... excursion ... takes place a month earlier ...*

He was one of the first leaders of the Chartered Institute of Patent Agents to be from an industrial company rather than from a private practice ... *Times*[7]

He was one of the first leaders of the Chartered Institute of Patent Agents to come from an industrial company. An alternative to 'to come from' would be 'to be drawn from'.

While he is small enough to sit on your lap, use the 'cuddle position' to clean his teeth. Later on, choose whichever position is easiest for you to see what you're doing and to get an effective brushing action going. *Parents*[8]

Can you 'use a cuddle position' to clean someone's teeth? Is it not more effective to use a toothbrush and toothpaste? And it is not the 'position' which is 'easiest' but the act of cleaning which is easiest *from* a given position. *While he is still small enough to sit on your lap, use the cuddle position when cleaning his teeth. Later on, choose whichever position makes it easiest for you to see what you're doing.*

It is not until the traveller reaches Sarasota that the prospect changes and you look out from the car at a place you think you might want to be. *Times*[9]

'You look up to the stage at an actor you might like to be' would make sense. Wanting to be a certain actor is one thing, but wanting to be a certain place is another. It would be clumsy to add the word 'at' ('you look out from the window at a place you think you might want to be at'). Better use 'where': *you look out from the car at a place where you think you might like to be.*

Most of my shooting at this age was either walking up hedgerows with the keepers or pigeon shooting over decoys. *The Field*[10]

We cannot allow that a young boy's shooting was walking up hedgerows. *I did most of my shooting at this age either walking up hedgerows or aiming at pigeons over decoys.*

The best bit of the day was watching everyone be transformed from the way we normally look in school uniform to our new 'made up' look. *Catch*[11]

Both the verbs here are incorrect. You cannot say that a bit of the day was 'watching' something. Nor can you speak of watching everyone 'be' transformed. *The best experience of the day was seeing everyone transformed from the way we normally look in school uniform.*

Unless he truly believes that the private sector is the way forward . . . *Times*[12]

The private sector is not a way of going anywhere. *Unless he truly believes that the right policy is to develop the private sector.*

. . . many of those modern works which are indubitably novels are not a very powerful argument for the traditional form of story-telling. *Independent*[13]

The writer, Mark Lawson, does not really mean to suggest that a novel can *be* an 'argument' for a particular kind of fiction, but that it can by its effectiveness provide support for such an argument: *do not strengthen the case for the traditional form of story-telling.*

2 'to do'

'It is that section of the market that we do very well at Kempton but not so well here' says Timothy Neligan. *The Field*[14]

What does it mean to 'do a section' of a market? The verb must be changed. *It is that section of the market that we serve very well.*

Do this step extremely carefully or you'll start to remove the layers of paint. *Me*[15]

Either change the verb 'do' – *Take this step extremely carefully* – or omit 'step': *Do this extremely carefully or you'll start to remove the layers of paint.*

Our policy is total integration. Recognising that we cannot do that immediately, we have to do it in stages. *Times Educational Supplement*[16]

'Integration' is not something that you 'do' so both usages of the verb are incorrect. *Our policy is total integration. Recognising that we cannot achieve that immediately, we have to work for it in stages.*

. . . there are others who want to climb the social ladder and see preparatory schools for their children as the right thing to do. *Independent*[17]

Preparatory schools may or may not be the right places to attend, but they certainly cannot be the 'right thing to do'. *There are others who want to climb the social ladder and see preparatory schools as the right schools for their children.*

When you do this stage you need to be as accurate as possible. To help you do this, use orienteering lines which are the parallel lines on the base of the housing. *Country Walking*[18]

Both usages of 'do' are bad. You cannot 'do a stage' and 'do this' cannot refer back to 'be as accurate as possible'. *When you reach this stage you need to be as accurate as possible. To this end use orienteering lines.*

Few women in public life have suffered as she has suffered and done it with such grace. *Times*[19]

Billy Graham is paying a tribute to Mrs Pat Nixon. Suffering is not something that any one can 'do'. *Few women in public life have suffered as she has suffered, and suffered with such grace.*

3 'to have'

We should avoid the tendency to overwork the verb 'to have', trying to make it do a job it is unfitted for.

> . . . there is still a buoyant market among professional people who want 'a place in the country', and who are more interested in the house and the opportunity for shooting and fishing than in the farmland itself, which they will probably have a manager run . . . *The Field*[20]

Here is a typical example of the use of 'have' where any one of a number of verbs would be better – 'order', 'allow', 'arrange for': *who are more interested in the house . . . than in the farmland, which they will probably arrange for a manager to run.*

> And the connection impressed the Sunday Telegraph enough to have him write an article on the martial law that had just been introduced in Poland. *Daily Mail*[21]

It is lax to write 'to have him write'. Moreover, you would not write 'He impressed me enough to like him', but 'He impressed me enough for me to like him'. *And the connection impressed the Sunday Telegraph enough for them to invite him to write an article on the martial law that had just been introduced in Poland.*

> I'll have my solicitor take this to the European Court of Human Rights. *Moneywise*[22]

I'll instruct my solicitor to take this to the European Court.

> And I had him be a very violent Hamlet. *Guardian*[23]

This is Anthony Hopkins, actor–producer, talking. *And I persuaded him to be a very violent Hamlet.*

> We have to repair a caravan which had a car collide with it on the Continent . . . *Caravan Magazine*[24]

The producer ordered ('had') the actor to be a violent Hamlet, but the caravan did not arrange for the car to collide with it. *We have to repair a caravan with which a car collided on the Continent.*

> Eastern Province had the better of Natal, who were unlucky to have both their strike bowlers, Rod McCurdy and Trevor Packer, break down with injury. *The Cricketer*[25]

The verb 'to have' is peculiarly out of place here: . . . *who were unlucky in that both their strike bowlers, Rod McCurdy and Trevor Packer, broke down with injury.*

. . . the Pakistani version of a cricketing upbringing compares favourably; the informal games have more opportunity inherently . . . *The Cricketer* [26]

It is not the games that 'have' more opportunities, but the players: *the informal games offer more opportunities.*

4 Nouns used as verbs

A correspondent to *The Times* complained of what he called 'BR-speak' and quoted an example.

Passengers in coaches A to D should alight from coach E, as only the front four carriages will be platformed. *Times* [27]

The use of the noun 'platform' as a verb amused the correspondent. We cannot condemn this practice in all circumstances. Poets have used it. It can produce vivid expressions. Even in this case it has to be admitted that the usage produces a clear and economic statement. The most that can be said is that the practice is to be deplored when it does not 'come off', and that whether in a given instance it does 'come off' must remain to some extent a matter of taste.

The celebrations will climax at midnight with Taylor cutting a giant birthday cake . . . *Daily Mail* [28]

This very doubtful case results from evading the slightly cumbersome expression 'reach a climax'. There is a precedent in that the expression 'reached a peak' has already been converted into 'peaked'.

The tale of a Beverly Hills-bound plastic surgeon (Michael J. Fox) detoured by love in a sleepy southern hamlet seemed an odd choice . . . *Vanity Fair* [29]

The conversion of the noun 'detour' (a deviation from a direct route) into a verb here achieves nothing. Since the surgeon is 'Beverly Hills-bound' the verb 'detained' would say all that is needed.

You may even luck out and find a dry crossing: stable stepping-stones, a dry downed tree to walk on, or a chasm narrow enough to leap. *Outdoors Illustrated* [30]

Surely 'luck out', which turns 'luck' into a verb, is a misplaced innovation. Since what is clearly meant is 'Your luck may be in', what is the point of 'luck *out*'? *You may be lucky and find a dry crossing.* And why a 'downed tree' instead of a 'fallen tree'?

After suffering long hours trying to orgasm with my boyfriend I was close to forgetting about sex altogether. *Company* [31]

She decided apparently to forget about grammar instead. 'Orgasm' is a noun and not any number of long hours of trying can turn it into a verb. *After suffering long hours trying to achieve an orgasm with my boyfriend.*

> The kit is designed to help concerned individuals, groups and organisations network and become informed about the significance of 1992 from Indian perspectives . . . *Spare Rib*[32]

There is no need to turn the noun 'network' into a verb. *The kit is designed to help concerned individuals, groups and organisations to interconnect and become informed.*

> My daughter, who's 14, is very naive for her age. She still wants to be babied and does things like refuse to boil the kettle because she's afraid of its heat. *Bella*[33]

Turning 'baby' into a verb might be defended here. 'Babied' could be said to be more economical than 'treated as a baby', and the usage has slight links with a respectable tradition ('Don't woman me!'). But 'does things like refuse' will not do: *does things like refusing.*

> Colin, our 'reserve' internal checker was at work on the boats so the only person left to pump out, diesel, gas and water the Middlewich boats was myself. *Waterways World*[34]

The three nouns, 'diesel', 'gas' and 'water', are here used as verbs meaning to supply with diesel, gas and water. The effect is lax and clumsy. *The only person left to pump out the Middlewich boats and supply them with diesel, gas and water was myself.*

5 'lie/lay'

The verb 'to lie' is intransitive. Its past tense is 'lay' and its past participle in 'lain'. (Only the verb 'to lie', meaning to speak untruthfully, has the form 'lied'.) The verb 'to lay' is transitive. Its past tense is 'laid' and its past participle is also 'laid'. Perhaps some difficulties arise from the fact that the past tense of 'lie' ('lay') matches the present tense of 'lay' ('lay').

> At the foot of the high rise, she could just about make out a bundle of black and white fur laying motionless on the grass. *Today*[35]

The verb 'to lie' is required here: *she could just about make out a bundle of black and white fur lying motionless on the grass.*

> My writing day starts at 1.30 when I lay on the sofa and dictate 6,500 words, as I did today and will tomorrow. *Times*[36]

This is Barbara Cartland being quoted, one hopes, incorrectly. *My writing day starts at 1.30 when I lie on the sofa and dictate.*

Laying Lion and Base. *Advertisement for garden statuary*[37]

'Lying Lion' would be more satisfactory grammatically but would suggest dishonesty rather than posture. *Lion couchant and base.*

Previously we laid in bed on Saturday . . . *Essentials*[38]

Previously we lay in bed on Saturday . . .

So far we have considered cases where the verb 'lay' is erroneously used in place of the verb 'lie'. Cases where the converse misuse occurs are perhaps slightly less common.

Once patients are calm, lie them on their side with some form of cushion under their head. *Me*[39]

This is advice on dealing with a person in a fit. *Once patients are calm, lay them on their side.*

'Has anyone fallen sick yet?' I asked the Red Cross lady waiting to one side of the Royal Tea Tent. 'Oh yes,' she said. 'They keep keeling over. We take their hats off and lie them down in a tent, and usually they come round quite quickly and go out again.' *Independent*[40]

It appears that garden party guests at Buckingham Palace get the same treatment. *We take their hats off and lay them down in a tent.*

Mothers, fathers and carers will be advised to lie young babies on their backs or sides when putting them to sleep in tonight's 30-second slot. *Evening News & Star* (W. Cumbria)[41]

Word order needs attention here. It ought to be made clear that babies are not going to be put to sleep in a very short slot. *Mothers, fathers and carers will be advised in tonight's 30-second slot to lay young babies on their backs or sides when putting them to sleep.*

– V –

AVOIDING FALSE CONNECTIONS

Much of this book may be said to be about avoiding improper connections. Good writing relies for its clarity and smoothness (as well as for its correctness) upon the ease and sureness with which word is connected to word, phrase to phrase, and clause to clause. We turn in this chapter to a few of the crucial grammatical elements in the making of sound connections. It is not just a question of correctly managing link-words such as prepositions ('to', 'in', 'for' etc.) and conjunctions ('but', 'if', 'because' etc.). It is also a matter of maintaining exactness of reference in the use of pronouns.

1 PRONOUNS

Pronouns do the work of nouns. They are used as a kind of shorthand, and the reader must be left in no doubt about what they refer to.

1 'it'

> The painter's identity is unknown, though its mastery has impressed some into assuming the hand of Holbein and Dürer. *Independent*[1]

The only possible noun that 'its' could refer back to is 'identity'. By the time the writer wrote 'its' she was assuming that she had mentioned the painting as well as the painter, but you would have to go back another three lines into the previous sentence to find the word 'painting'. There is no place for 'its'. *The painter's identity is unknown, though the mastery revealed in the work has impressed some into assuming the hands of Holbein and Dürer.*

> The consistency was good – it didn't 'drip' off the end of the brush when I applied it. *Catch*[2]

We are told that the consistency didn't drip off the brush. *The consistency was good – the paint didn't drip off the end of the brush.*

> He is standing at his writing desk (he wrote standing up), his pen in one hand, his ink-bottle in the other; there are three or four handsome folios beside his table; his mouth is set, but softly; there is a little pot of flowers and ferns on it. *Times*[3]

Here Bernard Levin is picturing Erasmus. We have all heard the joke about the man who opened his mouth and put his foot in it. The picture here is of a man with a pot of flowers and ferns on his mouth.

> This is a job that needs to be done as soon as possible before it becomes a safety risk. *Good Housekeeping*[4]

'Job' is the only possible word for 'it' to refer back to. But the job (replacing a pane of glass) will never become a safety risk. On the contrary: *This is a job that needs to be done as soon as possible before failure to do it presents a safety risk.*

> Section your hair (at least five sections). Spray the first section (if you're using spray), and comb it through to make sure it's evenly distributed. *My Weekly*[5]

'It' appears twice. The 'it' which you have to comb is obviously hair, or rather 'section'. The writer might properly have said 'Comb it through until it is evenly moistened' because then the second 'it' would equate with the first. But the 'it' which has to be evenly distributed can only be the 'spray'. This you discover by a game of grammatical hunt the slipper. *Spray the first section . . . and comb it through to make sure the spray is evenly distributed.*

> Paper could provide more detailed gauging: when the paper turned dark brown it was suitable for pastry; when light brown, it did pies; when dark yellow, for cakes; and when light yellow, for puddings and biscuits. *Old House Journal*[6]

This piece on baking with an old-fashioned oven would seemingly suggest that pastry and pies can be made from paper. But the 'it' is presumably the unmentioned temperature of the oven. The change of construction represented by 'it did' must go. *Paper could provide more detailed gauging; when the paper turned dark brown the heat was suitable for pastry, when light brown it was suitable for pies, and when light yellow for puddings and biscuits.*

> In appearance she was not a beauty and did not play roles that required it. *Independent*[7]

(Obituary of Peggy Ashcroft.) 'In appearance' is redundant. 'A beauty' is not the same thing as 'beauty'. Having said that Peggy Ashcroft was not 'a beauty', the writer cannot continue his sentence as though he had mentioned 'beauty' in the abstract. *She was not a beauty and did not play roles that required her to be.*

> To me, you don't just miss someone you love when they're not with you. You can actually miss them when they're there, in the flesh, before your very eyes. Such is its power. *More*[8]

There is a similar grammatical crossover here. The word 'love' is used as a verb ('someone you love') and the writer then uses 'it' as though she has used the noun 'love'. The pronoun 'its' floats in a verbal vacuum. *Such is the power of love.*

> What is the perfect tawny? Perhaps it is subjective. Having blended a few myself, I know that it is difficult. *Decanter*[9]

The reference of 'it' here on both occasions is wildly imprecise. The first 'it' appears to mean something like 'deciding this matter', and the second 'it' appears to mean something like 'blending a good tawny'. We are in a world where 'it' can be used as a substitute for both thought and utterance. *What is a good tawny? Perhaps the answer to the question will be subjective. Having blended a few myself, I know how difficult it is to make (define?) the perfect tawny.*

> Such systems are cumbersome and costly and offer imperfect clues as to how a deaf person might learn to speak properly because it studies only how the tongue and palate interact. *Times*[10]

'Such systems . . . offer imperfect clues . . . because it studies only' will not do. Either 'systems' must become singular – *Such a system is cumbersome . . . because it studies only* – or 'it studies' must become 'they study': *Such systems are cumbersome and costly and offer imperfect clues . . . because they study only . . .*

> What is this Citizen's Charter? If the intention is to offer quality services to all citizens then goals must be different. Standards in education will be raised when parents are encouraged to feel at ease in schools. It is not about power, but partnership. *Times Educational Supplement*[11]

What must goals be different from? And what is 'it'? Is it the 'Citizen's Charter' or is it 'education'? Grammatically, it cannot be either. *Education is not about about power, but partnership.*

> If, by chance, you have sown a wild flower patch in your garden, many of them can be turned into scented and coloured sugars for use in confectionery, particularly the violets, primroses and cowslips. *Times*[12]

What happens with 'it' in the singular happens also with the plural impersonal 'they' and 'them'. Here is the familiar error of assuming that you have mentioned 'flowers' (as a noun) when in fact you have merely used 'flower' adjectivally ('wild flower patch'). Therefore 'many of them' is totally ungrammatical. Mention 'flowers': *If, by any chance, you have sown a patch of wild flowers in your garden, many of them can be turned into scented and coloured sugars.*

'These are a good set of results,' Alan Curtis, an analyst at stock-broker Barclays de Zoete Wedd, said: 'They are going in the right direction and eventually they will be a much leaner ship when they have restructured.' *Daily Telegraph*[13]

The 'results' are 'going in the right direction' and will eventually be 'a much leaner ship'. That won't do. 'They' and 'they' scarcely match with 'these'. A change of subject is needed: *This is a good set of results . . . The firm is making progress.* As for the 'leaner ship', one doubts whether the strength and durability of a ship necessarily benefit from structural slimming.

2 'this/that, these/those'

You may say 'Jack damaged his new Porsche; this was a gift from his father', and 'this' clearly refers back to the noun 'Porsche'. Or you may say 'Jack damaged his new Porsche; this was a great pity', where 'this' refers back to the previous clause as a whole ('Jack damaged his new Porsche'). Mistakes tend to occur when 'this' is used without clear reference of either kind.

> Egg donors are badly needed to help infertile women. This is a procedure which is regulated by law and has a 30% success rate. *Parents*[14]

What does 'this' refer to? Eggs being needed is not a 'procedure'. No procedure of any kind is directly mentioned. So 'this' must go. *Egg donors are badly needed to help infertile women.* In vitro *fertilisation is regulated by law and has a 30% success rate.*

> Vitality is usually the ingredient which gives a picture its appeal. This can be helped by painting as quickly as you are able – always assuming that you are in control. *The Artist*[15]

There is no word here to which 'this' can refer, nothing mentioned which could 'be helped'. Nor can 'this' refer back to the previous sentence as a whole. Replace 'helped' by a verb which 'this' (meaning 'vitality') can govern: *This can be conveyed by painting as quickly as you are able.*

> You'll find Fimo easier to work with if it's slightly warm; this occurs naturally as you knead the pieces into shape. *Prima*[16]

Again there is no word for 'this' to refer back to, no word by which the verb 'occurs' could be governed. Being warm does not 'occur'. *You'll find Fimo easier to work with when it gets slightly warm: this occurs naturally as you knead the pieces into shape.*

> But a bully's power is only real if it is accepted. If we do this, then that is how they will always behave. *Chat*[17]

You might say 'It is important to get up early: if we do this our health will benefit', because getting up early is something that one may 'do'. But you cannot say 'It is important to be awakened early: if we do this our health will benefit', because *being awakened* is not something that anyone can 'do'. So being accepted cannot be 'done'. Change the passive verb ('is accepted') into an active verb. *But a bully's power is only real if people accept it. If we do this* . . . There remains the problem of 'that' which is grammatically unanchored, and of the plural 'they' which goes back to the singular 'a bully'. *If we do this the bully will always remain a bully.*

> In Britain, a further decline in confidence at this point could be an economic disaster. But this assumes no countervailing action from the government. *Times*[18]

The effect of 'this' here is, virtually, to put the previous sentence within quotation marks. It is the statement as a 'view' of things to which 'this' refers. Make the point clearly: *But this view assumes no countervailing action* or *But this view presupposes that the government will take no countervailing action.*

> We finished a long day grateful that despite extreme difficulties we managed to do all that was necessary and keep the customers satisfied, though this turned out to be a little premature. *Waterways World*[19]

This piece calls for comparable treatment in that 'this' refers back to nothing in what has been said but to the state of mind represented by what has just been said: *though our assumption proved premature.*

> I have always taken composition for granted but having spent some years conducting painting courses I realise that this is certainly not the case. *The Artist*[20]

What is 'not the case'? The writer is not denying that he always 'took composition for granted'. He is trying to say that he has changed his mind: *I realise that this attitude was mistaken.*

> The very fact that you get people together does not mean that support will happen: if this is the case then probably it is happening outside the group . . . *Nursing Standard*[21]

If I said 'The fact that we eat a meal does not mean that we are hungry', and then went on 'if this is the case . . .', you would naturally ask 'If *what* is the case?' So what is the above sentence saying?

> Mr Major's failure to confront the small minority of Tory MPs who do not share his pragmatic approach has made the Conservatives' disunity seem worse than it is. This he must now do. *Times*[22]

What must he do? *Mr Major has not confronted the small minority of Tory MPs . . . This he must now do.*

> The festival's main platform is the arts, but other aspects of modern Japan – science, technology, sports, food, lifestyle and education – are also featured. This includes those men who make Pavarotti look like the slimmer of the year – sumo wrestlers. *Viva*[23]

'Other aspects are featured . . . This includes': here is a good example of the rogue 'this' thoughtlessly flung on to the page. 'Aspects' must be followed by 'these': *These include (those) men who make Pavarotti look like the slimmer of the year.*

We turn to misuse of the plural pronouns, 'these' and 'those'.

> A 50 per cent reduction in waste will be achieved by 1995 – with particular emphasis on those regarded as harmful to the environment. *Meridian*[24]

The pronoun 'those' is totally at sea. There is no plural noun for it to refer back to. It must go and the meaning be made clear. *A 50 per cent reduction in waste will be achieved by 1995 – with particular emphasis on the wasteful practices regarded as harmful to the environment.*

> The beginnings of dewponds go back probably to prehistory, and these are found mainly on limestone or chalk hills. *Country-Side*[25]

As it stands this can only mean that 'beginnings of dewponds' can be found on limestone hills, for so the use of the word 'these' implies. *Dewponds probably originated in prehistory; they are found mainly on limestone or chalk hills.*

> Times were when all ladies rode side-saddle. These were changes which in due course became tradition; today more 'tradition' is evolving. *Horse & Hound*[26]

Nothing to which the words 'these changes' could apply has been mentioned. Riding side-saddle does not constitute a change. Nor could a 'change' become a 'tradition', though the result of the change might. Get rid of 'these' and 'tradition'. *Times were when all ladies rode side-saddle. The abandonment of that practice became an established convention as such innovations do.*

3 Personal pronoun: misconnection
There is a noticeable tendency to misconnect the pronoun 'they'.

> Many teachers of musical instruments opt not to put their pupils into every single examination between grades one and eight: instead they skip a grade, passing grade four, say, and not sitting

another examination until the teacher decides they are ready for grade six. *Independent*[27]

The opening subject is 'Many teachers', which 'they' of the second clause would naturally refer back to. When we get to 'skip a grade' the writer may still, we assume, be talking about the 'teachers'. When we reach 'passing grade four' and 'not sitting', we realise that the writer has ceased to tell us what the teachers do and turned his attention to the pupils. *Many teachers . . . opt not to put their pupils into every single examination . . . instead their pupils skip a grade, passing grade four, say, and not sitting another . . .*

The role of an artist's wife is not the simplest one to play, blamed as they are for either jealous indifference or tiresomely excessive concern for the welfare and reputation of their mate. *Independent*[28]

The single 'wife' cannot become 'they': *The role of an artist's wife is not the simplest one to play, blamed as she is for either jealous indifference or tiresomely excessive concern.*

My client is an established 5 Partner firm who is now ready to boost its Commercial expertise. They have a small unit that deals with Company and Commercial matters, but because of intended growth, they now wish to expand the team. *Times*[29]

If the 'firm' is to be personalised by 'who' ('an established 5 Partner firm who is now ready'), it cannot thereafter be neuterised ('ready to boost its Commercial expertise'). Nor can it start as singular ('who is now ready') and continue as plural ('They have a small unit'). It is safest to stick to the neuter: *My client represents a 5 Partner firm which is now ready to boost its Commercial expertise. It has a small unit that deals with Commercial matters.*

GCSE's can embody the same parental projection. One chivvies the child to study, to put her or his all into the exam, to perform as one has performed or would have wished to have performed. Their child's result becomes their result, their stamp of approval or disapproval. *Weekend Guardian*[30]

First error: 'GCSEs' is a plural and requires no apostrophe. Second error: you would not say 'One must listen to their child', but 'to one's child'. Why not use the straightforward 'parents'? *Parents chivvy their children to study, to put their all into the exam, to perform as they themselves have performed or would have wished to have performed. Their children's results become their own results.* Third error: 'their stamp of approval' is good English, but it means what it says – the stamp

119

of approval *they* have given, not the stamp of approval they have received. *Their children's results become their own results, a stamp of approval or disapproval for themselves.*

> Recognising their obligation to provide food and shelter to these small travelling groups, and to encourage more pilgrims to make the otherwise difficult journeys, the Church set up a small number of hospices connecting the various monasteries. *Heritage*[31]

'Recognising their obligation' anticipates a plural subject, but 'the Church' is singular: *Recognising her/its obligation.* The preposition 'to' after 'provide food and shelter' should be 'for' (the writer's mind was still dwelling on the noun 'obligation').

> Remain cheerful and positive when showing a potential buyer around the house – and don't dwell on why it is being sold or tell the would-be buyer what a scoundrel/slag their spouse is (people don't want to buy a battleground). *Harpers & Queen*[32]

Only a fool would try to interest a possible purchaser in a house by insulting the purchaser's spouse. This piece gives advice to divorcees who have to sell their homes. 'Don't dwell on why it is being sold' is no doubt sensible advice. The imperative 'Don't' is, as always, a variation of the second person 'You don't' ('Don't you sell the house!', we say colloquially). But the writer continues as though he has lost sight of whom he is addressing. *Don't dwell on why it is being sold or tell the would-be buyer what a scoundrel/slag your spouse is.*

> Browse through ancient mythological accounts of the origin of the world and one is cocooned in completeness. *Times*[33]

Here is a misconnected pronoun that is neither 'they' nor 'their'. The imperative form of the verb 'go' or 'browse' is addressed to a second not a third person. 'You' (not 'one') are the person who must go or browse. *Browse through ancient mythological accounts of the origin of the world and you are cocooned in completeness.*

4 Personal pronoun: case

The most common error to be dealt with here is the confusion between 'I' and 'me'. 'I' is the subject form ('I like her') and 'me' is the object form ('She likes me'). An extraordinary idea is abroad that you must at all costs avoid saying 'and me'. Here are a series of sentences in which 'and I' should be replaced by 'and me'.

> The prospect of living in such an environment appealed to my wife and I, and we moved into an old cottage six years ago. *Dalesman*[34]

People who would never contemplate writing 'The prospect appealed to I' are nevertheless capable of writing 'The prospect appealed to my wife and I'. The error is equally culpable in both cases: *appealed to my wife and me*.

> My mother took my twin sister and I away from school a year early so we could be presented to the Queen. *Daily Mail*[35]

Again the speaker would never have said 'My mother took I away from school early', yet she makes that error here. *My mother took my twin sister and me away from school early.*

> In terms of Graham and I having separate careers in the force, I've always made it clear that I married my husband to be with him, not apart from him. *Essentials*[36]

The error is compounded here. Though 'I' is wrong, 'me' would not be right (see Chapter III, 6). *As for our having separate careers in the forces, I've always made it clear that I married my husband Graham to be with him, not apart from him.*

Errors of case with other personal pronouns are rarer.

> I often go to see her statue on the Embankment opposite Big Ben and fantasise that I am her – she stands there in her chariot with two little handmaidens. *New Woman*[37]

Lindi St Clair finds Boadicea a fit role model, but the verb 'to be' is not followed by an object. *I often go to see her statue on the Embankment opposite Big Ben and fantasise that I am she.*

> Criticised by a boy about your sexual attitudes? It's him who needs to rethink and when he has, he'll be very apologetic. Make him grovel. *19*[38]

No journalist would write 'Him needs to rethink', yet this one makes that kind of error. *It's he who needs to rethink.*

> It's the agenda of we Liberal Democrats. *Radio 4*[39]

So the Chairman was reported from the party conference. 'You mustn't do that to us' or 'for us' (not 'to we'), we say, and the pronoun 'of' works in the same way, even though 'of us Liberal Democrats' may not be all that elegant.

5 *'its/it's'*

'It's' is an abbreviation of 'it is' or of 'it has'. Unless you can substitute 'it is' or 'it has' for the abbreviation then 'it's' is wrong.

> If that introduction to this comment comes across as foreboding then it has served it's purpose. *Cumbria Life*[40]

Since you cannot say 'has served it is purpose' (or 'it has purpose'), the form 'it's' is wrong: *it has served its purpose.*

> They are not afraid of being vain or fickle, always showing their personality at it's utmost, and their naked egos. *Gentlemen's Quarterly*[41]

And you cannot say 'personality at it is utmost' (or 'at it has utmost'): *always showing their personality at its utmost.*

> The Moray Steiner School has a considerable intake of local children, as parents feel that their siblings will benefit from it's [*its*] 'natural' teaching methods. *Green Magazine*[42]

> It's [*its*] uses throughout history have been varied . . . *Wild about Animals*[43]

> Entertainment Xpress . . . has got off to a flying start, signing up more than 20 thousand members in it's [*its*] first four months of operation. *Money-Maker*[44]

> This little animal does not live underground, preferring instead the malted cover formed by fallen grasses, where it's [*its*] favourite food . . . is freely available. *Cumbria Life*[45]

2 ILL-CONNECTED CLAUSES AND PHRASES

You might say 'He ran swiftly', but you would not say 'He was a swiftly runner'. The adverb 'swiftly' can modify the verb 'ran' but it cannot qualify the noun 'runner'. What applies to the adverb applies to those clauses and phrases whose proper function is adverbial. It is not permissible to try to make such constructions hang on a noun instead of a verb.

1 Clauses beginning with 'when' etc.

In Chapter II, 3 we set the limits for the legitimate use of 'when' to introduce a relative clause ('the day when I fainted'). We saw how 'when' clauses improperly attached to nouns could sometimes be turned into proper relative clauses. Misuse of 'when' clauses is widespread and creates more problems than those already examined.

> They mark the Dent fault, when the earth moved and limestone that should have been thousands of feet above the fell now lies hundreds of feet below . . . *Country Walking*[1]

The 'when' clause ('when the earth moved') is here hung directly on the noun 'fault'. It must hinge on a verb. Use the participle 'caused': *They mark the Dent fault, caused when the earth moved.*

> If and when these are resumed, to whom are back dividends paid, the current holder or the holder when the dividend was passed? *Investors Chronicle*[2]

You cannot define a person as 'the holder when the dividend was passed', for the clause beginning with 'when' must be linked either to a noun of time ('the day when the dividend was passed') or to a verb: *the current holder or the one holding them when the dividend was passed.*

> The reason for the survival of this particular house from the middle ages when so many others have vanished is difficult to say with any authority. *Old-House Journal*[3]

The clause 'when so many others have vanished' could hang on a verb ('survived'), but not on the noun 'survival'. And you cannot declare a reason 'difficult to say'. *That this particular house has survived from the middle ages when so many others have vanished is difficult to account for.*

> The predicted growth in consumer spending when recessionary pressures lift is likely to be led by growth in the sale of electrical goods, clothing, footwear, wine and a significant rise in leisure spending. *Money-Maker*[4]

The 'when' clause cannot be left hanging on 'growth': *The growth in consumer spending expected when recessionary pressures lift.*

> The recent success of diving boat owner Keith Roberts in the High Court, when the court upheld his 'not guilty' verdict in the magistrates court when he was charged with breaking DTI rules, undoubtedly hastened the publication of these proposals. *Sea Angler*[5]

The first 'when' clause is made to hang on the noun 'success', the second 'when' on the noun 'verdict'. The first 'when' can go, and the second can be hung on a participle. *The recent success of diving boat owner Keith Roberts in the High Court, which upheld the 'not guilty' verdict, returned in the magistrates court when he was charged with breaking DTI rules.*

> Following a period as house surgeon at the General Infirmary at Leeds he returned to Archie Durward's anatomy department as a lecturer, when a fruitful period of research helped him to acquire both a reputation as a researcher . . . and a Ph D. *Independent*[6]

You would not write 'He returned to Wigan, when he worked hard'. Why not 'where'? . . . *he returned to Archie Durward's anatomy department, where a fruitful period of research helped him to acquire* . . .

Other words which, like 'when', introduce temporal clauses (e.g. 'while' and 'before') are sometimes similarly misconnected.

> In America the deregulation of savings and loan companies (building societies) while government guaranteed their deposits triggered a boom of irresponsible lending and fraud . . . *Times*[7]

Provide a verb for 'while' to hinge on. *In America deregulating savings and loan companies (building societies) while government guaranteed their deposits triggered a boom.* The gerund (here 'deregulating') replacing the noun (here 'deregulation') will often rescue one from the error in question.

> When Alison moved into her flat she had to pay her new landlord two months' rent, £600, as a deposit to cover any damage to the flat while she lived there. *Company*[8]

One cannot speak of 'damage while she lived there'. The 'while' clause must hinge on a verb: *as a deposit to cover any damage the flat might suffer while she lived there.*

> Four months ago I wrote about the Oliver Stone movie *JFK* and the attack on it even before it was completed. *New Statesman*[9]

. . . and the attack made on it even before it was completed.

2 Other misconnected clauses

We turn to clauses introduced by other conjunctions.

> Are there any more engines waiting to be found? I do not mean that literally, but there may be some laying neglected where a bit of pressure could be put on the owner to get them into preservation. *Old Glory*[10]

The places where the engines may be lying (not 'laying', which is what hens do to eggs) are not the places where pressure could be exerted, so 'where' must go: *but there may be some lying neglected in circumstances such that a bit of pressure could be put on the owner to get them into preservation.*

> One day in 1990 Jackson broke into the flat where his wife had moved to and found her in bed with Mr Gibbs. *Daily Telegraph*[11]

It does not sound well to say either 'where she had moved to' or 'to where she had moved'. There is a perfectly good word which ought not to be allowed to fall into disuse: *Jackson broke into the flat whither his wife had moved and found her in bed.*

Clauses introduce by 'as' are often misconnected.

> . . . provision for Gypsy children. Their complete integration, as is now the practice in many schools, will give to future generations of travellers the tools to participate fully in the life of this country . . . *Times*[12]

You can say 'At Eton the gypsy children are completely integrated, as is now the practice in many schools' because the clause 'as is now the practice in many schools' hinges on the verb 'are integrated', but the clause cannot hang on the noun 'integration'. *To integrate Gypsy children completely, as is now the practice in many schools, will give to future generations of travellers the tools to participate fully in the life of this country.*

> The loss of talent and expertise as people gave up in despair was painful to watch . . . *Green Magazine*[13]

Provide a verb for 'as people gave up in despair' to modify: *It was painful to watch how talent and expertise were lost as people gave up in despair.*

> As a result their work now seems new and fresh, with an exciting sense of discovery as paintings which have hung ignored in old houses are brought out, recognised, restored to glory and sold abroad. *Spectator*[14]

The clause 'as paintings . . . are brought out' cannot hang on 'sense of discovery'. It must hinge on a verb. The word 'with' is ill-used (see Chapter V, 4). *As a result their work now seems new and fresh, producing an exciting sense of discovery as paintings which have long hung ignored in old houses are brought out.*

Perhaps the worst errors of the kind we are investigating here occur when clauses introduced by 'if' or 'because' are misconnected.

> The high cost to Britain if Labour gained power was spelled out by the Government yesterday. *Daily Mail*[15]

Provide a verb for the 'if' clause to qualify. It cannot depend on the noun 'cost'. *The high cost Britain would pay if Labour gained power was spelled out by the Government yesterday.*

> This is a reflection of the key importance of vigilance if we are to achieve a cure for the patient. *Independent*[16]

Provide a verb for the clause 'if we are . . .' to hinge on: *This shows how important it is to be vigilant if we are to achieve a cure.*

By the time Mrs Thatcher resigned last November, only five ministers had been in her cabinet since the mid-1980s. In most cases their departures were because they had nothing much further to contribute. *Times*[17]

You can say 'I am going because I want to', but not 'My departure is because I want to'. The 'because' clause cannot hang on the noun 'departure'. *In most cases they departed because they had nothing much further to contribute.*

3 Misconnected phrases

As is the case with adverbial clauses, there is a tendency to hang adverbial phrases on to nouns instead of on to verbs.

International law is an intensely political creation, with a not conspicuously creditable history – a history which . . . is also replete with violations in order to score political points. *Times*[18]

You can say 'He violated the law in order to score political points'. But you cannot hang the phrase beginning 'in order' on to the noun 'violation'. A verb is needed: *a history which . . . is also replete with violations committed in order to score political points.*

The attendance of 7,000, despite thick fog, was overwhelming and far exceeded the expectations of the organiser . . . *Horse & Hound*[19]

You can say '7,000 people attended despite thick fog' where the phrase 'despite thick fog' hinges on the verb 'attended'. It cannot hang on the noun 'attendance'. *The attendance, which reached 7,000 in spite of thick fog, was overwhelming.*

There are 100,000 prostitutes in the Falkland Road red-light area of Bombay, about half of whom are Nepalis because of their popular oriental looks. *Times*[20]

You cannot say that the girls are Nepalis because of their looks. That is not what makes them Nepalis: *Nepalis chosen for their popular looks.*

The improvements which the other companies foresaw were increased turnover, financial benefits because of reduced costs, less time needing to be spent on administration, better transport and the ability to standardise products. *Marketing Week*[21]

Likewise we cannot allow 'financial benefits because of' (*financial benefits due to*). And 'less time needing to be spent' is a barbaric gerciple (see Chapter III). *The improvements which other companies foresaw were an increase in turnover, financial benefits caused by reduced costs, a reduction in time spent on administration, better transport and the ability to standardise products.*

> Mr Kunzlick is convinced that environmental problems are now on such a scale that only national action orchestrated through legislative bodies such as the European Parliament can be successful. *Times*[22]

You can speak of problems having developed 'on such a scale' that action is needed. You cannot say the problem *is* 'on such a scale' that action is needed. 'The problem is' requires to be followed by a complement ('The problem is grave'). Why not use an adjective therefore? *Mr Kunzlick is convinced that environmental problems are now so vast that only national action . . . can be successful.*

> A Gecko, a small lizard whose species I am still not sure of was on our apartment wall as we arrived and was duly photographed before retiring to bed after our long journey. *Country-Side*[23]

Here the phrase 'before retiring to bed' hangs on the verb 'was photographed', making it appear that the lizard was on the point of retiring. It must qualify the active voice of the verb 'to photograph'. *A Gecko, a small lizard whose species I am still not sure of, was on our apartment wall as we arrived and we duly photographed it before retiring to bed after our long journey.*

> On arrival at his house, he was loping round the garden in a floral brocade waistcoat and the kind of vagrant's trousers that would look better in the cat's basket. *Elle*[24]

From the context we gather that it is the writer's arrival at the house and not (as the grammar suggests) the waistcoated interviewee's: *On my arrival at his house, he was loping round the garden.*

> Earlier in the day finds her caring for eight B&B bedrooms, some ground floor, some family and some ensuite. *In Britain*[25]

It is good idiomatic English to say 'Morning finds her hard at work'. But you cannot make the adverbial phrase 'earlier in the day' do the work of a noun like 'morning'. Why use the fancy word 'finds' anyway? *Earlier in the day she cares for eight B&B bedrooms.*

> The Booker Prize is one way that we recognise outstanding ability and reward excellence. Another is through our search from time to time externally for exceptional business people from a variety of backgrounds and industries. *Times*[26]

We have already dealt with the first sentence here (see Chapter II, 3). In the second sentence the phrase 'from time to time' is bound, not to a verb, but to the noun 'search'. An adjective should be used to do what is an adjective's job ('our periodical search'). But 'externally', itself an adverb, appears likewise to do an adjective's job in relation to 'search'. *The Booker Prize is one device by which we recognise outstanding ability and excellence. Another is our periodical external search for exceptional business people from a variety of backgrounds and industries.*

4 'if/whether'

Among the conjunctions, or link-words, which establish connections between other words or groups of words, 'if' seems to present writers with special difficulties. A most common fault is to use 'if' where 'whether' should be used, that is to say in indirect speech.

The spokesman did not know if [*whether*] Mr Baker had studied the officials' report . . . *Daily Mail*[27]

Occasionally, I catch myself wondering if [*whether*] I'll ever regret not having children . . . *New Woman*[28]

It is not known if [*whether*] the hearing could take place before the summer recess. *Independent*[29]

They tell the bank or the building society if [*whether*] the property is worth the money that they're lending. *Me*[30]

A close look at the feathers may confirm if [*whether*] the kill was made by a fox or a bird of prey . . . *Waterways World*[31]

Other misuses of 'if' are less easy to find.

Former GER coach No1266 also stood in the platform, if supported by a farm trailer due to its lack of an underframe. *Steam Classic*[32]

There is no condition here. It is a fact that the coach stood by the platform, and there is no 'if' about it. Moreover, 'due to' is misused. *Former GER coach No1266 also stood in the platform, though supported by a farm trailer because it lacked an underframe.*

On Monday, Post Office management will open a new round of negotiations with the Post Office Users' National Council to examine the present system of complaints and obtaining redress, including compensation levels if service standards fail to meet customers' reasonable expectations. *Times*[33]

Adjust the balance by inserting 'making' before 'complaints'. You can say 'Compensation will be awarded if service standards fail . . .' because the conjunction 'if' hinges on the verb 'be awarded' (see Chapter V, 2), but here there is no such verb for 'if' to hinge on: *to examine the present system of making complaints and obtaining redress, including compensation appropriate in cases where service standards fail.*

> To get a better picture of what goes on at The Art Materials Exhibition and you belong to an art club, then ask your club secretary to write to us to hire the exhibition video . . . *Artists & Illustrators Magazine*[34]

Here there is no 'if', but there should be. The writer tries to make the word 'and' do the work of 'if'. Better substitute 'if' for the opening infinitive: *If you want a better picture of what goes on at The Art Materials Exhibition and you belong to an art club, then ask your club secretary to write to us.*

3 MISUSE OF ADJECTIVES

There are certain adjectives which are used, not simply to qualify a noun but to make a connection between one noun (or pronoun) and another. The adjective 'due' is one such. When followed by 'to' it establishes a link causal in character. The adjective 'like' is another one that establishes linkages, as we saw in Chapter I, 1. In the use of these adjectives it is always necessary to guard against making misconnections. The temptation is to try to make these adjectives do a job they are unfitted for.

1 'due to': general
You can say 'His death was due to an accident' where the adjective 'due' hangs on the noun 'death', but you cannot say 'He died due to an accident', because 'due' cannot act adverbially upon the verb 'died'. Nevertheless, the misuse of this construction, as illustrated below, is now so widespread that the question arises: Is it too late to halt the misuse? The reply must be that good writers do not commit the error. It grates on the literate ear whenever it is heard or read. Fowler rightly recommended greater use of 'owing to', because while 'owing to' can be either adjectival or adverbial, 'due to' can only be adjectival. When misused, 'due to' can usually be replaced by 'owing to' or by 'because of'.

> Despite this increase, the risk of dying from testicular cancer has dropped dramatically due to advances in treatment. *Gentlemen's Quarterly*[1]

You could say 'The dramatic drop in deaths was due to advances in treatment', where 'due' hangs on the noun 'drop'. But you cannot make 'due' hang on the verb 'dropped'. *The risk . . . has dropped dramatically owing to advances in treatment.*

> Latest figures show that about 4 per cent of days were lost due to sickness absence in the non-industrial civil service . . . *Times*[2]

Again you could speak of a 'loss due to sickness', but you cannot say 'days were lost due to sickness'. What is wrong with 'through'? *4 per cent of days were lost through sickness absence.*

> It was being said that industry backed the Conservatives due to their belief in free enterprise. *Times*[3]

. . . backed the Conservatives because of their belief in free enterprise.

> Though this bird was once common, it is now increasingly rare in the British Isles due to a loss of habitat caused by modern farming methods. *Out & About*[4]

The bird is the corncrake. Although it would be correct to say 'it is now increasingly rare because of the loss of habitat caused by modern farming methods' the causal duplication ('because of', and 'caused by') is not felicitous. Better start again: *it is now increasingly rare in the British Isles because modern farming methods have destroyed its habitat.*

> If we are unable to offer you a place due to oversubscription we will return your cheque. *Options*[5]

There is only one thing that 'a place due to oversubscription' can mean, and that is – a place produced by oversubscription. But oversubscription prevents places from arising. Change the word order here as well as the use of 'due to'. *If we are unable because of oversubscription to offer you a place, we shall* (sic) *return your cheque.*

> The Government doesn't really like self-employed people, due to the difficulty of collecting taxes . . . *Moneywise*[6]

Self-employed people are not, of course, 'due to the difficulty of collecting taxes'. *The Government doesn't really like self-employed people because of the difficulty of collecting taxes.*

> Ever since Sir Gordon Borrie announced last August that he might revoke Eurocopy's licences due to dubious sales practices, the threat has hung over its head like a sword of Damocles. *Investors Chronicle*[7]

It must not be suggested, as here, that Eurocopy's licences are 'due to dubious sales practices'. Word order is again at issue: *Ever since Sir Gordon Borrie announced that, owing to dubious sales practices, he might revoke Eurocopy's licence.*

2 'due to': opening of sentence

We must think of the words 'due to' as being properly employed in such statements as 'This payment is due to you', 'The 9.45 train is due to depart', in which the dependence of the adjective 'due' on the nouns 'payment' and 'train' is clear. The only satisfactory way of using 'due to' at the opening of a sentence would maintain such a dependence: 'Due to depart at 9.45, the train is standing at platform 3.' The need for such usages is very rare. It seems to be a safe rule that if you open a sentence with the words 'Due to' you are almost certainly going to get into a grammatical mess.

> Due to my aforementioned disability, I am unable to carry out this research myself, but I offer my theory, free of charge, to her future biographers. *Independent*[8]

Lucy Ellmann is exercising her sarcasm unfortunately at the expense of the novelist Barbara Cartland. She provides no noun for the adjective 'due' to qualify. *Owing to my aforementioned disability, I am unable to carry out this research myself.*

> Due to the forced emigration of millions of Germans after the Second World War, it has few inhabitants. *Green Magazine*[9]

'It' is the Polish-German border area, and 'it' must not be said to be 'due' to anything. Here 'as a result of' would make the best correction. *As a result of the forced emigration of Germans after the Second World War, it has few inhabitants.*

> Due to his penetrating realism, compositional pyrotechnics and violent temper . . . Caravaggio was denounced in his own day as the Antichrist who had come to murder painting . . . *The World of Interiors*[10]

Because of his penetrating realism, compositional pyrotechnics and violent temper . . . Caravaggio was denounced in his own day . . .

> Due to the closed nature of the auditing firms, we know little about the standards of Britain's auditors. *Times*[11]

But owing to the open nature of the press, we know a good deal about the standards of British journalists (and, in this case, university teachers). *Owing to the closed nature of the auditing firms . . .*

> Due to increased cats and rats, the magpie robin is on only one island of the Seychelles where its numbers are declining. *Country-Side*[12]

It is not 'increased' (larger) cats and rats that must be blamed for the loss of the magpie robin, but the increase in cats and rats: *Owing to the*

*increase in cats and rats, the magpie robin can be found on only one
island of the Seychelles.*

> Usually due to damaged Fallopian tubes, a fertilised egg will
> become embedded in the tube itself . . . *Woman*[13]

A fertilised egg must not be said to be due to damaged Fallopian tubes.
As often, one could well substitute a causal clause for the misused 'due
to': *because the Fallopian tubes are damaged.*

3 'due to': where needed

In view of the widespread use of 'due to' where it is incorrect, it is ironic
that there are instances where it is badly needed and is not used.

> Faced by the virtual elimination of deep-mined dry steam coal as a
> result of South Wales pit closures, some of Britain's leading steam
> railways are running their locomotives on imported coal . . . *Steam
> Railway*[14]

Just as 'due to' cannot hang on a verb, so 'as a result of' cannot qualify a
noun. 'As a result of' introduces an adverbial phrase. We say 'The
vehicle deteriorated as a result of neglect' where the phrase hangs on
the verb 'deteriorated', but we cannot speak of 'the deterioration as a
result of neglect' where the phrase hangs on the noun 'deterioration'.
We have examined sentences already in which 'due to' could have been
replaced by 'as a result of' instead of 'owing to' or 'because of'. But here
the need is for an adjectival construction to depend on the noun
'elimination', and 'due to' would serve. *Faced by the virtual elimination
of deep-mined dry steam coal (which is) due to South Wales pit
closures, some of Britain's leading steam railways are running their
locomotives on imported coal.*

> The unspoilt aspect of the West Country owes some credit to its
> conspicuous lack of motorways. *In Britain*[15]

'Owes some credit' will not do. Credit is not an issue. Use either 'due to'
– *The unspoilt aspect of the West Country is partly due to its conspicuous
lack of motorways* – or the idiomatic 'owes something to': *owes
something to the conspicuous lack of motorways.*

> Empty weight 45 tons 3 cwt, working weight 48 tons 9 cwt. This
> discrepancy can only be accorded to the materials Swindon used in
> construction. *British Railways Illustrated*[16]

The verb 'to accord (with)', meaning to be in harmony with is wrong
here. Change it – *This discrepancy can only be attributed to the
materials Swindon used* – or use 'due to' instead: *This discrepancy
can only be due to the materials Swindon used in construction.*

But the proliferation of kinship connections because of the rise in the number of spouses a person may have, may turn out to be an unexpected source of support for those in need of it. *History Today*[17]

We have seen 'due to' used where 'because of' was required. Here the converse applies: *But the proliferation of kinship connections due to the rise in the number of spouses a person may have.*

4 'like/as if'

Much the most common use of 'like' is as an adjective. It is safest to avoid other uses, with certain well-known exceptions. There are some acceptable non-adjectival uses of 'like' ('I wouldn't do it like that' and 'She dresses like her mother'), but extensions of the few acceptable exceptional uses of 'like' are to be avoided. So too are attempts to make 'like' do the work of a conjunction. Perhaps the worst such misuses are those that occur when 'like' is regarded as the equivalent of 'as if' or 'as though'. There is a special temptation to lapse in this way after expressions such as 'it looks' or 'it seems'.

It looked like the great American portraitist was trying to hit us with the most banal of *double entendres* . . . *Independent*[18]

It looked as though the great American portraitist were trying . . .

When we first bought our house, it looked like the previous owners had moved in just after Charles Dickens had moved out. *Country Living*[19]

When we first bought our house, it looked as if the previous owners had moved in just after Charles Dickens had moved out.

At first it looked like the females were making the running, with one or more approaching the displaying male of their choice. *BBC Wildlife*[20]

For the misuse of 'with' see Chapter V, 4. *At first it looked as if the females were making the running, with one or more of them approaching the displaying male of their choice.*

The closet shopper in every Cancerian could be dipping into her purse like there is no tomorrow. *Options*[21]

This usage may be on the increase, but it remains incorrect: *could be dipping into her purse as if there were no tomorrow.*

5 'like/just as'

Equally slovenly is the misuse of 'like' where 'as' or 'just as' is intended.

If someone can get their nose in front of you they will take your line at a fence like in polo. *The Field*[22]

If someone can get their nose in front of you they will take your line at a fence just as in polo.

On the road for almost half the year, Wheeler updates his passport like the rest of us renew TV licences. *Gentlemen's Quarterly*[23]

On the road for almost half the year, Wheeler updates his passport just as the rest of us renew TV licences.

Like in the case of test-tube babies – it was questionable when it first started happening, but it's becoming more and more common. *New Woman*[24]

Just as in the case of test-tube babies – it was questionable when it first started happening . . .

I was very happy and I was respected like my father was respected. *Times*[25]

Rhodes Boyson is talking about his schooldays: *just as my father was respected.*

A London ironmonger, Thomas Deakin, had patented a portable range back in 1815 but, perhaps being entirely enclosed like many similar later ranges were, they did not at first prove popular with the British public who still preferred to see the glow of a fire. *Old-House Journal*[26]

Either change 'like' to 'as' or omit 'were'. Moreover, by 'perhaps being entirely enclosed' the writer really means 'perhaps *because* they were entirely enclosed'. 'Perhaps' applies to the theory that their being enclosed is the possible cause of the poor sales. And the sentence shifts from a singular 'portable range' to a plural 'they'. *A London ironmonger, Thomas Deakin, had patented a portable range back in 1815 but, perhaps because it was entirely enclosed as many similar later ranges were, it did not prove popular with the British public who still preferred to see the glow of a fire.*

6 'like/such as'

The third kind of misuse of the word 'like' occurs when it replaces 'such as'.

Gone are the days like [*such as*] Frank experienced in the 1970s, when his boat landed 40 stone of codling ashore and went back and took another 30 stone. *Sea Angler*[27]

I want a steady boy friend like [*such as*] all my friends have . . . *Catch*[28]

> It went on smoothly and had a brilliant finish, there were no ridges or brush marks like [*such as*] you tend to get with cheaper ones. *Catch*[29]

> Well, if we're talking about choice at Asda, then how about fresh potatoes which aren't packed in peat like you get in other supermarkets? *Green Magazine*[30]

Merely to change 'like' to 'such as' here ('potatoes which aren't packed in peat such as you get in other supermarkets') leaves a certain ambiguity. Is it 'potatoes which aren't packed in peat' that you get in other supermarkets? We guess that it isn't, but the grammar doesn't help. The meaning needs to be clarified. *Well, if we're talking about choice at Asda, then how about fresh potatoes which aren't packed in peat as they are in other supermarkets?*

7 'unlike' + preposition

In 'Unlike the town, the countryside has few amenities' the word 'unlike' has a two-way link with 'town' and 'countryside'. In 'Unlike the town, country people miss the amenities', one of the links (with 'the country-side') is lost. We explored that kind of error in Chapter I, 1. In 'Unlike in the town, country people have few amenities' both links have gone. 'Unlike' lacks a connection either way. Combined with 'in' it is masquerading as some kind of adverbial construction. The construction is barbaric.

> Moreover, unlike in the 1980s, there are few talented ministers of state ready to replace them. *Times*[31]

If 'unlike' is kept, it must be properly attached. *In the 1990s, unlike the 1980s, there are few talented ministers of state ready to replace them.*

> Fortunately, we don't have capital punishment in this country, unlike in the United States . . . *Spectator*[32]

Either simply omit 'in' – *in this country, unlike the United States* – or change the construction: *as they do in the United States.*

> All of which made for remarkably quick lock operation – unlike on the GU today. *Waterways World*[33]

If 'unlike' is to be kept, tie it in: *remarkably quick lock operation – unlike today's provisions on the GU.*

> What is clear is that, unlike with most epidemics, prevention is simple. *Times*[34]

. . . unlike most epidemics, it is simple to prevent.

8 Bogus adjectives

There is an increasing tendency to drag other parts of speech in to do the work of an adjective. We take a noun, 'methods', and we put another noun in front of it, 'business methods', and then we put a third noun after it, 'business methods conference'. And so we go on, referring perhaps to a 'business methods conference programme' or even a 'business methods conference programme coordinator'. The practice is to be deplored. There is a world of business jargon (*sic*) which we cannot hope to free of this grammatical slovenliness, but we ought certainly to guard against it in the ordinary practice of journalism. That does not of course mean that every use of a noun as an adjective is bad. When I am backing up a disk on my word-processor and see the instruction 'Insert source disk' or 'Insert destination disk', I may feel uncomfortable in view of the substance of this book, but I am bound to concede that the message is concise and exact and defies any attempt to improve upon it. Commonsense must be our guide in this respect.

ARD A and B together, the total Germany sell is going up 21 per cent. *Marketing Week*[35]

'Sell' is a verb used here as a noun. 'Germany' is a noun used here as an adjective. We are in a linguistic jungle.

Bergevin has a clear agenda, drawn up with industry consultation. *Marketing Week*[36]

'Industry' is a noun. *Bergevin has a clear agenda, drawn up in consultation with industry.*

Most of Richmonds books cost about £15, but Thorsons have been publishing American origin motivational books for years at much more modest prices. *Money-Maker*[37]

The adjective 'motivational' qualifies the noun 'books'. The adjective-noun combination 'American origin' operates as a further adjective. There need be no end to this kind of accumulation. ('They have been publishing high value quick sale American origin motivational books for years'.) Is not the word 'origin' redundant? *Thorsons have been publishing American motivational books for years.*

Like Grasmere it has close associations with William Wordsworth – though in a more business than poetic sense. *Cumbria Life*[38]

(The place referred to is Ambleside.) This sentence compounds the error of using the noun 'business' as an adjective by introducing the word 'more'. Can one thing be 'more business' than another? Can a thing be 'more business than poetic'? The mind boggles. *Like Grasmere it has close associations with William Wordsworth, though those associations have more to do with business than with poetry.*

> But *Panorama* is regarded with almost paranoia in some Tory circles after a series of programmes ministers believe to have been totally biased. *Times*[39]

'Almost' is an adverb. You can almost have an accident, but you cannot have an almost accident. Use the adjective 'near'. *But Panorama is regarded with near paranoia in some Tory circles.*

4 MISUSE OF 'WITH'

'With' is now the most overworked word in the language. It is a preposition. There are no problems about the most basic use of the word. 'He took a walk with his dog', we say. Unfortunately usage of the word has been extended quite outside the scope of this simple function. The result is that for the writer who wants to write well it is a dangerous word. An attempt is made here to illustrate what the dangers are.

1 'with' + present participle: causal/temporal
We say 'He strode down the road with his wife'. We also use the construction in which 'with' is followed by a phrase that includes a participle, 'He strode down the road with his coat flying open'. It must be noted that this is very different from saying 'He strode down the road with the town clock striking three' or 'With the town clock striking three he strode down the road'. The wife was indeed with him according to the first sentence, and his coat was with him according to the second, but the town clock did not accompany him. There are perfectly good expressions for indicating that two events happened at the same time. ('He strode down the road as the town clock struck three.')

The misuse of 'with' followed by a participle is not restricted to contexts in which time is a predominant concern. 'With the rain now falling heavily, he decided to take a bus.' In that sentence the heavy rainfall not only marks the point at which he decided to take a bus, it indicates the cause which prompted him to take a bus. 'With' is no more fitted to introduce causal connections than it is to indicate temporal connections. Nevertheless it is now widely used for both. More often than not causal and temporal aspects are blended in the use of this construction, though one or the other is likely to be predominant. Where the temporal aspect is predominant, 'now that' will often serve as a satisfactory construction.

With Labour leaders facing mounting pressure to reverse their public commitment to back the Lloyd's 'lifeboat' operation, that tactical ploy could now backfire. *Independent*[1]

This sentence exemplifies the connotative blend referred to. *Now that Labour leaders are facing mounting pressure to reverse their commitment to back the Lloyd's 'lifeboat' operation, that tactical ploy could backfire.*

With the economical use of space playing a more important part in our lives, a foldaway bed helps solve that problem. *House Beautiful*[2]

Use 'now that' again, and deal with the words 'that problem', for no problem has been directly posed. *Now that using space economically is more important, a foldaway bed is useful.*

With both of you being unemotional and cool-headed, this may be a good time for singular activity, as the common ground between you may be a little depressed. *New Woman*[3]

By 'singular' the writer means 'separate'. And it is not the 'common ground' that is depressed. *Now that both of you are unemotional and cool-headed, this may be a good time for separate activity, as your shared interests may not be stimulating.*

With the growth of special features, with writers being interviewed or, worse still, allowed to write about their own books, book reviews start to get squeezed out. *Times*[4]

The repetition of 'with' draws attention to the bad usage: *Now that there are more special features and writers are being interviewed.*
Where the causal element in the connotation is predominant, 'now that' is less likely to be a suitable correction of 'with'.

With a global shortage of quality sparkling wine looming, these wines have a great future. *Decanter*[5]

Here 'since' could be used: *Since a global shortage of wine is looming, these wines have a great future.*

The new GCSE Sport is proving popular at Lisa's school – and with it now involving a formal exam, it is a definite 'career' option. *19*[6]

Use 'since' again: *since it now involves a formal exam.*

With most hotels offering only a continental breakfast it was a real treat to indulge in a full English breakfast of sausages, bacon, egg and tomatoes, every morning! *Waterways World*[7]

'As' is the most obvious word here – *As most hotels offer(ed) only a continental breakfast* – but there would be stronger ways of making the point: *Knowing that most hotels offer(ed) only a continental breakfast, we found it a real treat . . .*

> With eight out of nine people in the UK living in towns and half the population having no easy access to a car, our belief was that care for wildlife on the doorstep held the key to political pressure for countryside conservation. *BBC Wildlife*[8]

Correcting 'with' – *Since eight out of ten people in the UK live in towns and half the population has no easy access to a car* – leaves us with the problem of the subsequent metaphorical confusion. Caring for wildlife 'on the doorstep' is an odd way of finding a key.

> With Folkestone being a tidal harbour, many of them would be returning before the water fell too far. *Sea Angler*[9]

'Since' or 'because' could be used here – *Because Folkestone is a tidal harbour* – but so could the now absurdly neglected absolute participle construction: *Folkestone being a tidal harbour, many of them would be returning.*

2 'with' + present participle: explanatory

'With' followed by a noun and participle frequently introduces an explanation or elaboration of what has already been said.

> Thatching is at present undergoing a considerable revival, with even owners of new houses wanting a thatched roof. *In Britain*[10]

The irony of this clumsy use of 'with' is that the word could be omitted altogether, leaving a satisfactory absolute participle construction. *Thatching is at present undergoing a considerable revival, even owners of new houses wanting thatched roofs.*

> Essex has literally thousands of very small woods, with even the ancient ones often growing inside town, and sometimes new-town boundaries. *BBC Wildlife*[11]

Again omit 'with': *Essex has literally thousands of very small woods, even the ancient ones often growing inside town.*

> These symptoms do vary, with some unfortunate people also suffering from nausea, vomiting and dizziness. *New Woman*[12]

Again omit 'with': *These symptoms do vary, some unfortunate people also suffering from nausea.*

The series was shot in Italy, New York and London, with O'Neill visiting places associated with the singer and talking to people about him. *Opera Now*[13]

(The subject is a documentary about Caruso.) Either simply omit 'with' – *The series was shot in . . . London, O'Neill visiting places associated with the singer* – or use 'and': *The series was shot in . . . London, and O'Neill visited places associated with the singer.*

In the sentence above 'with' was used to add information while avoiding use of the natural word 'and'. The practice is not rare.

Trusteeship of pension funds needs to be tightened, with the board of trustees striking a reasonable balance between the different interests in the pension fund. *Investors Chronicle*[14]

. . . and the board of trustees should strike a reasonable balance between the different interests . . .

A short term cycle seems to be at work here, with whatever is initiated in personal affairs at the beginning of the month coming to fruition by the 20th. *New Woman*[15]

Once more, in this horoscope, the natural construction requires 'and': *and whatever is initiated in personal affairs at the beginning of the month will come to fruition by the 20th.*

The misuse of 'with' now under scrutiny sometimes calls for a more radical change of construction.

For most people, August is traditionally a holiday month with the majority of the population departing for their sunshine break. *Annabel*[16]

Here is a case in point. *For most people, August is traditionally a holiday month when the majority of the population depart for their sunshine break.*

The judge said that last year he had advised Mr Seelig to seek medical help with the doctor reporting to the judge, but he had replied that his time was better spent on his defence. *Times*[17]

'With the doctor reporting' is a tortuous device for avoiding directness and simplicity. *The judge said that last year he had advised Mr Seelig to seek medical help and asked that the doctor should report to him.*

Consequently there is a shorter ripening period and often a battle to get the correct balance between sugar and acidity, with the resulting wines being rather too high in alcohol and somewhat flabby on the palate. *Decanter*[18]

It would be absurd to say 'He struck me violently, with the resulting pain being severe', but probably no more absurd than the above. The expression 'with the resulting' (instead of 'so that') is a dangerous one: *a battle to get the correct balance between sugar and acidity, so that the wines are rather too high in alcohol.*

> 'Werther' can count as the first international literary craze, with Chinese porcelain factories taking in orders for dinner plates with scenes from the novel, and with a rash of suicides-by-shooting in imitation of the hero . . . *Economist*[19]

Eliminate the two bad uses of 'with' here. *'Werther' can count as the first international literary craze: Chinese porcelain factories took in orders for dinner plates . . . and there was a rash of suicides.*

3 'with' + past participle

The combinatiion of 'with' and the past participle gives rise to the same errors and awkwardnesses.

> With tourism set to become the biggest industry in the world, Ark, the environmental charity, has launched a colour travel magazine called *Going For it* . . . *New Woman*[20]

Here we have the causal/temporal connotation involved in use of 'with' followed by the past participle ('With . . . set'). It requires the same treatment that we gave to the combination of 'with' and present participle: *Now that tourism is set to become the biggest industry in the world.*

> With the social problems bred by 20 per cent unemployment, high emigration and a narrow economic base, Mr Haughey's fall is a mercy. *Times*[21]

'With . . . problems bred' is no more graceful than 'with tourism set'. Mr Haughey's fall with a heavy suitcase might prove undignified. His fall with the load listed here is grammatically inelegant. *In view of the social problems bred by 20 per cent unemployment . . . Mr Haughey's fall is a mercy.*

> With a strong order book geared to the oil, gas and water industries, Weir's trading has been good despite recession. *Investors Chronicle*[22]

The connotation of 'with . . . geared' here is causal rather than temporal. *Since Weir's order book is geared to the oil, gas and water industries, the firm's trading has been good despite recession.*

With the fire safely enclosed behind heat-resistant doors, it can be left burning overnight . . . *Traditional Homes*[23]

The use of 'the fire' and 'it' in parallel is absurd. It is like saying 'With the baby safely tucked into its cot, it can be left to sleep', instead of 'Safely tucked into its cot, the baby can be left to sleep'. *Safely enclosed behind heat-resistant doors, the fire can be left burning overnight.*

The airport's spare capacity could also be used for an expansion of international services with passengers fed into Brussels instead of the heavily congested Heathrow. *Independent*[24]

The 'absolute' construction can serve here: *The airport's spare capacity could also be used for an expansion of international services, passengers being fed into Brussels.*

With the debate hampered by lack of direct, quantitative evidence, it is at least possible to draw some conclusions . . . *History Today*[25]

As an alternative to the use of 'since' – *Since the debate is hampered* – use the 'absolute' construction again: *The debate being hampered by lack of . . . evidence.*

With appetites flayed by the summer heat, nothing beats the simple cool of chilled fruit. *Elle*[26]

Why not the obvious preposition? *For appetites flayed by summer heat nothing beats the simple cool of chilled fruit.*

4 'with' + participle: award of wooden spoons

There is a remarkable ingenuity about the way 'with' is misused, especially when followed by a noun and participle. Exploration in this area of misusage shows journalists seemingly competing enthusiastically for the award of wooden spoons. A question arises. If there is to be a 'With it' award in this field, should it be given for sheer quantity, or for the single misuse displaying the maximum degree of contortion? Let us consider applicants in the first category.

The Confederation of British Industry estimates that wage rises in April averaged 6.8 per cent, with many firms offering much smaller increases . . . With one in five firms freezing pay, some economists regard the income statistics as evidence that the recession is deepening . . . This is the sharpest quarterly fall for more than ten years and it appears to have been a prelude to an even bigger drop, with the CBI estimating that settlements in April may have averaged 6.8 per cent. *Times*[27]

The first 'with' ('with many firms offering') can go without replacement: *wage rises averaged 6.8 per cent, many firms offering much smaller increases*. The second 'with' ('With one in five firms freezing pay') requires to be replaced by 'as': *As one in five firms freezes pay*. The third 'with' ('with the CBI estimating') could be replaced by 'for': *for the CBI estimates that settlements in April may have averaged 6.8 per cent*. The score of three misuses of 'with' and participle in one piece might seem to put the *Times* correspondents here well ahead. But the *Independent* can challenge the achievement.

> With deep Tory divisions on Europe still to be settled, Mr Major spent five hours yesterday in talks at Chequers with the German Chancellor . . . But with the Tories moving into their thirteenth year of office, Neil Kinnock called for a general election now . . . With Labour this week to promise new incentives to British and foreign firms for research and development investment, Conservative strategists are concerned that the electorate has lost sight of the difference between the two parties.
>
> With the Citizen's Charter seen as crucial to outlinining Mr Major's new approach, speeches strongly outlining 'Majorism' may have to wait until next month . . . *Independent*[28]

The first 'with' might reasonably be replaced by 'while': *While the deep Tory divisions on Europe are still to be settled*. The second ('with the Tories moving into their thirteenth year') calls for 'as': *But as the Tories moved into their thirteenth year of office*. The third ('With Labour this week to promise new incentives') might be replaced by 'now that': *Now that Labour is this week to promise new incentives to British and foreign firms*. The fourth ('With the Citizen's Charter') is purely causal: *Since the Citizen's Charter is seen as crucial to outlining Mr Major's new approach*. It will be observed that the first and third instances above combine 'with', not with a participle, but with an infinitive. This usage is equally regrettable.

It is to the *Times* City Diarist that we must turn for the single most excruciating misuse of 'with' and participle. The Diarist is light-heartedly concerned with signs of an end to the recession.

> The *City Diary* is keen to hear of other such bottom-of-the-cycle indicators, with the occasional bottle of Krug Grande Cuvée champagne being awarded for particularly amusing ones. *Times*[29]

If a teacher said 'I want you to submit your essays with a box of chocolates', you would know what was meant. But if it was 'I want you to submit your essays with a box of chocolates being awarded for the funny ones', you might rightly think that the teacher in question had chosen the wrong profession. In this case there is no escape from error except by scrapping 'with': *and bottles of champagne will be awarded for particularly amusing ones*.

5 'with' (no participle): causal/temporal

The thoughtless use of 'with' is most offensive when it is followed by a phrase containing a participle. But irrespective of the participle construction the word is often forced into doing work which would be more naturally and exactly done by other constructions. The reader will notice that 'with' is an especially dangerous word when used as the first word in a sentence.

> With scarcely enough money to eat, paying expensive medical bills is out of the question. *Guardian*[30]

Here there are causal and (to a lesser degree) temporal aspects to the connotation of 'with'. 'When' can supply both. *When there is scarcely enough money to eat, paying medical bills is out of the question.*

> With white collar job losses on the increase, the Employment Service is now offering unemployed managers and executives job review workshops. *New Woman*[31]

Again there are causal and temporal connotations which ought not to be forced on the word 'with': *Now that white collar job losses are on the increase.* Alternatively use the absolute participle construction: *White collar job losses being on the increase.*

> With the numerous horse insurance policies available today the choice is a difficult one, especially when they all vary in cover and price. *Horse & Hound*[32]

The alternative to adding a clause – *As there are numerous horse insurance policies available today* – is again to use the absolute construction: *Numerous horse insurance policies being available today.*

> With the return of some food to the shops, a breath of reconciliation between reformist communists and radical democrats has blown through Moscow. *Times*[33]

Here the word 'with' introduces an explanation part-causal, part-temporal: *Now that some food has returned to the shops.*

> With a toehold in Europe, with its higher health-care spending, Intercare's shares are still good value. *Investors Chronicle*[34]

Here the misuse of 'with' is duplicated. *Because Intercare has a toehold in Europe, where health-care spending is higher, its shares are still good value.*

> However, with any one of the company's creditors able to seek its winding up, celebration would be premature. *Times*[35]

However, since any one of the creditors can seek the winding up . . .

> With no advanced planning we were lucky to discover that a ship was due to leave later that day for Romblom, our island stepping-stone to Boracay. *Complete Traveller*[36]

The obvious construction here would be a participle: *Having made no advanced planning, we were lucky to discover.*

> With the experts not all in agreement as to the causes and treatment of IBS, where does that leave the unfortunate sufferer? *New Woman*[37]

In conversation we might allow 'With the cat out of the bag, what am I to do?' but surely not 'With the cat out of the bag, where does that leave me?' *Since the experts do not all agree about the causes of IBS, what is the unfortunate sufferer to do?*

6 'with' (no participle): additional

There is a habit of sticking on an extra bit of information by using 'with' where 'and' or a relative clause might be more natural.

> He was an outstanding Beethoven interpreter, and with a particular affinity for the works of Debussy . . . *Independent*[38]

. . . and had a particular affinity with the works of Debussy . . .

> If they'd stayed together she could have been more emotionally disturbed with a less positive view of future relationships. *19*[39]

. . . and had a less positive view of future relationships.

> As one of the world's leading consumer marketing companies, Kimberley-Clark, with high profile brands such as Kleenex tissues, has an enviable position in European consumer and industrial markets. *Times*[40]

The layman, who understands what soap marketing is, may be puzzled by the words 'consumer marketing'. But 'with' is what concerns us: *Kimberley-Clark, whose high profile brands include Kleenex tissues . . .*

7 'with' ('in the case of' etc.)

We find 'with' used to mean 'in the case of', or something very like that.

> With these companies there are generally more kitchen styles to choose from . . . *Traditional Homes*[41]

If the obvious correction seems too wordy – *In the case of these companies there are generally more kitchen styles to choose from –*

change the order of the sentence: *These companies generally have more kitchen styles to choose from.*

> As usual with this young Scottish director, MacKinnon bears down on the action like an enraged bull. *Times*[42]

Here 'with' adds nothing. Omit it: *As usual this young Scottish director, MacKinnon, bears down on the action like an enraged bull.* If that does not satisfy there is an alternative: *As is his wont, this young Scottish director bears down on the action.*

> The shed was completely reconstructed in the new style during 1938/1939; as with its predecessors a steel frame was employed . . . *British Railways Illustrated*[43]

The simplest correction here would be to replace 'with' by 'for': *as for its predecessors a steel frame was employed.*

> Apart from with the obvious victimised crimes like child pornography or victimisation of women, I think censorship is dangerous. *More!*[44]

There is of course no such thing as a 'victimised crime' and 'with' here does not mean 'with'. *Except in the case of giving publicity to victims of crimes of violence and pornography, I think censorship is dangerous.*

> Yet the cost of this permanent protection is very little higher than it would be with untreated wood. *Horse & Hound*[45]

There is a conditional aspect to the use of the word 'with' here and it would be better to clarify this by the use of 'if': *than it would be if untreated wood were used.*

The variety of other ways in which 'with' can be misused is exemplified below.

> Admission to the railway will only be with a special ticket . . . *Steam Classic*[46]

Here 'with' is the equivalent of 'by means of'. Changing 'with' to 'by' would still leave us with misuse of the verb 'to be'. Rewrite. *A special ticket will be required for admission to the railway.*

> There has been no compromise with the structural restoration of the house. *Period Living*[47]

The words 'compromise with' have a distinct meaning. You can reach a compromise with someone by meeting him half way over a dispute, but you cannot make a compromise with a structural restoration. *There has been no compromise over the structural restoration.*

With over 300 fully crewed yachts and 200 villas whether you are looking for a sailing yacht or a luxurious motor yacht, a farmhouse or a mansion, for the holiday of a lifetime or that memorable business venue call Carte Blanche. *Harpers & Queen* [48]

In 'With a mobile phone call Carte Blanche' or in 'With a fifty penny piece call the AA' the function of 'with' would be clear. But how you (and it is you, the subject of the sentence, who are addressed by the imperative 'call') can 'call' with 300 yachts and 200 villas is obscure.

You should not shoot. In practice, with the necessity to achieve high cull numbers, a short stormy season and for reasons particular to that stalk, you sometimes do. *The Field* [49]

You ought not to shoot. But in fact, because of the need to cull extensively, because the season is a short and stormy one, and for other reasons pertinent to the particular stalk, you sometimes do.

There are approximately 70 houses, with the intention of limiting development to 120. *Times* [50]

The houses surely have no such intention. *There are approximately 70 houses, and the intention is to limit development to 120.*

5 Prepositions

Prepositions help to establish connections. A preposition generally precedes a noun and indicates the relationship between it and some other element in the sentence. We have already studied misuse of the preposition 'with' at some length because of the current epidemic of misuse. We look now at some of the ways in which various other prepositions are used incorrectly or infelicitously.

1 'of' and 'for'

With the ambidextrous qualities necessary of someone in his position, Dennis has in recent weeks turned his attention to the bogie . . . *Steam Railway* [1]

We say 'necessary to', and 'ambidextrous' (meaning 'equally skilled with both hands') is not what is wanted here: *With the versatility necessary to someone in his position.*

One of those closely involved in the project was scathing of the refusal of companies to contribute. *Independent* [2]

You can be contemptuous 'of', but you are scathing 'about': *scathing about the refusal of companies to contribute*.

> When reading about Bali, I had got bored of the subject, and therefore always made an excuse. *Harpers & Queen*[3]

You can be 'tired of', but you get 'bored with': *I had got bored with the subject*.

> And they were anxious not only because of the physical intrusion of their bodies . . . *Nursing Standard*[4]

The subject is the taking of cervical smears. If you said 'I was disturbed by the intrusion of a visitor', you would mean that the visitor had entered, not that somehow he had been entered. But 'their bodies' did not intrude; someone intruded into them: *And they were anxious not only because of the physical intrusion into their bodies*.

> . . . the spoliation of the country side and the pollution of additional car use. *Times*[5]

This is a similar error. 'Car use' does not suffer pollution but produces it: *the pollution caused by additional car use*.

> While there is understandable caution among the Dublin chattering class of predicting Mr Haughey's immediate demise . . . *Times*[6]

There is fear 'of' undertaking something, but there is caution 'in' undertaking something: *there is caution among the Dublin chattering class in predicting Mr Haughey's immediate demise*.

> The earth has an amazing capacity of regeneration . . . *Green Magazine*[7]

The earth has an amazing capacity for regeneration . . .

> And that great act of faith that asks you to believe of their existence is not necessary any more. *Complete Traveller*[8]

You do not believe 'of' something, but 'in' it. Moreover an act of faith does not *ask* you to believe; rather believing is itself the act of faith. *And that great act of faith by which you believe in their existence is not necessary any more*.

> To begin with, there was a consensus in favour for this national park. *Green Magazine*[9]

We say 'in favour of', not 'in favour for': *there was a consensus in favour of this national park*.

> This fascination for automata was inspired by the discovery of one

of the odder examples, Vaucanson's defecating duck, a machine which consumed fodder one end and excreted it at the other. *Times*[10]

If a beautiful girl fascinates me, then I am fascinated 'with' her (or 'by' her). If steam railways become my obsession, then *they* have a fascination 'for' me: *This fascination with automata was inspired* . . . Moreover 'a machine which consumed fodder one end' is an illiterate expression: *a machine which consumed fodder at one end.*

ı don't keep them for companionship, but out of respect and interest for the natural world. *Wild about Animals*[11]

Where there are two nouns requiring to be followed by two different prepositions ('respect for' and 'interest in') the needs of both must be met. *I don't keep them for companionship, but out of respect for and interest in the natural world.*

Added to this is the fear that . . . agriculture will be forced to bear the brunt of concessions with further adverse effects for the prosperity of rural populations. *The Field*[12]

We speak of 'effects on' this or that, not 'effects for': *to bear the brunt of concessions and have further adverse effects on the prosperity of rural populations.* (See Chapter V, 4–6 for 'with'.)

We have to be sure that the vision we have as to where we are aiming for in two or three years' time is so well understood that people will accept the difficulties. *Meridian*[13]

We cannot allow 'where we are aiming for'. Change 'where' to 'what' and 'for' to 'at' – *what we are aiming at* – or supply a verb to go with 'where' – *where we are aiming to be* – and make sense of 'in two or three years' time'. *What* we are aiming at we are aiming at now; *where* we shall be is a matter for the future. *We have to make sure that the vision of where we shall be in two or three years' time is so well understood that people will accept the difficulties.*

2 'to'

. . . there are plenty of bronzing powders on the market to create shadow and definition to the face . . . *Hello!*[14]

You cannot 'create' something *to* the face. You may 'give' something to it: *to create shadow and give definition to the face.*

We approached the Farriers Registration Council at various times . . . to ask them to look at focusing the training to those areas of the country where there was genuine need. *Horse & Hound*[15]

149

We do not 'focus to'; we 'focus on'. But 'focus' is the wrong verb anyway for what is meant: *to ask them to look at concentrating the training in those areas of the country where there was genuine need.*

> It should be noted that the self-employed cannot participate to SERPS which is exclusively for Class 1 N.I. Contribution payers only. *Money-Maker*[16]

You participate 'in', not 'to'. And there is redundancy here. If something is 'exclusively' for me, then it is for me *only* and there is no need to say so twice: *the self-employed cannot participate in SERPS which is exclusively for Class 1 N.I. Contribution payers.*

> The fact that farmers will not be forced to set land aside . . . goes some way to accommodating the objections of the National Farmers Union . . . *Independent*[17]

Here we have 'to' where 'towards' would be right: *goes some way towards accommodating.*

> So far, there is little sign of an end to the current recession and the likelihood is that a modest upturn in activity will be delayed towards the end of the year. *Times*[18]

Here, by contrast, 'towards' is used where 'to' would be nearer the mark. The sentence says that towards the end of the year there is going to be a delay. The writer means something very different: *a modest upturn in activity will be delayed until near the end of the year.*

> But most of all it is disgusted at the complacency of a government which lurches from one mistake to another, oblivious to the pain its incompetence causes . . . *Sunday Times*[19]

It would be a pity if carelessness allowed the distinction between 'oblivious *of*' and 'indifferent *to*' to be blurred: *oblivious of the pain its incompetence causes.*

> The Real Meat Company . . . suggests you ask the following questions to suppliers . . . *Green Magazine*[20]

You ask questions 'of' people, not 'to' them: *suggests you ask the following questions of suppliers.*

> . . . the construction of the Kingston by-pass in the late 1920s set the scene for the rapid transformation of the surrounding pastureland, to the urbanized sprawl we know today. *British Railways Illustrated*[21]

You transform something *into* something else: *transformation of the surrounding pastureland into the urbanized sprawl we know today.*

> A spokesman said that Mrs McGinnes had made her children intentionally homeless by 'acquiescing' to her husband's behaviour. *Times*[22]

You do not acquiesce 'to', but 'in'. And the word order is not good. *Mrs McGinnes had intentionally made her children homeless by acquiescing in her husband's behaviour.*

3 Other prepositions

> Freshwater fish are better at teaching principles of ecology . . . *Wild about Animals*[23]

One schoolmaster may be better 'at teaching' than another, but one kind of fish? Do not attribute pedagogic skills to fish. *Freshwater fish are better for teaching principles of ecology.*

> . . . the rivers authority says its investigation is part of planning into the next century. *Times*[24]

You can't 'plan' *into* anything: *planning for the next century.*

> Power-assisted steering as standard, combined with a smooth gearbox, allowed our testers to feel completely in control of the outfit during the varying conditions of our test route. *Caravan Magazine*[25]

'During' can be used only with reference to time. You can say 'I felt tired during the afternoon', and you might even say 'I felt tired during the long country walk', but you cannot say 'I felt tired during the steep hills and the bad weather': *to feel completely in control of the outfit under the varying conditions of our test route.*

> Those of my colleagues still making an appearance at working during those damp August days . . . were pestered with queries . . . *Times Higher Educational Supplement*[26]

The expression 'making an appearance' has a definite meaning, and it is not this. 'At' is totally wrong: *Those of my colleagues still putting on an appearance of working during those damp August days.*

> This is a rare opportunity for an ambitious personnel professional to contribute to the commercial success of the business against an overall objective of continuous improvement. *Times*[27]

Why 'against'? If you are working towards a given objective, you are certainly not working *against* it. And if your aim is to do better every day, you need not smother this simple purpose under a weight of verbiage.

Finally, the swivels tied into the rigs can also be major contributor factors in a good or bad rig. *Sea Angler*[28]

The swivels are not factors 'in' a good rig, but factors 'in making' a good rig. *Finally, the swivels tied into the rigs can also be major factors contributing to the quality of the rig.*

Now that society has become 'moral', many individuals find recourse in immorality. *Times*[29]

You have recourse 'to', not 'in', and you do not 'find' it: *many individuals have recourse to immorality.*

. . . I was far more interested in following up on the tip I'd picked up about a roving shepherd. *Harpers & Queen*[30]

The 'on' is redundant and vulgar. *I was far more interested in following up the tip I'd picked up.*

The clues are nearly always subtle, and the number you pick up on depends largely on how perceptive you are. *New Woman*[31]

After 'following up on' we now have picking 'up on'. It's a funny way of saying 'understand': *and how many you understand depends largely on how perceptive you are.*

Already the weaker players are being driven out and Lime Street will soon be littered by underwriters looking for jobs. *Independent*[32]

To litter is to scatter objects around. If you say 'The shore has been littered with paper by the trippers', it is quite clear that the trippers did the littering. And that is why the preposition 'by' is employed. The journalist did not really mean to say that the underwriters are a pack of rubbish-scatterers: *and Lime Street will soon be littered with underwriters.*

. . . and the emphasis turns towards what is good for the team. *Times*[33]

You don't turn emphasis towards something, you lay or put emphasis 'on' things: *and the emphasis is laid on what is good for the team.*

The emphasis of the position is very much geared to European expansion . . . *Times*[34]

Nor do you 'gear' emphasis in any direction: *is very much placed on European expansion.*

Beyond 16, Mr Major's aim of raising the status of vocational qualifications is laudable. *Times*[35]

Mr Major's aim of raising the status of vocational qualifications for the over-16s is laudable.

> . . . many from throughout his life have paid tribute to his concern .for the individual . . . *Independent*[36]

You cannot turn the phrase 'throughout his life' ('He was respected throughout his life') into a composite noun. No one can come 'from' throughout-his-life: *many who have known him at different stages of his life have paid tribute.*

4 'from . . . to'

It is important to preserve parallelism in what follows 'from' and 'to' in the construction 'From the youngest to the oldest, the members were all enthusiastic'.

> There's plenty to do here, from museums and galleries to swimming and sailing. *Prima*[37]

Whereas 'swimming and sailing' are things that you *do*, 'museums and galleries' are places that you *visit. There's plenty to do here, from visiting museums and galleries to going swimming and sailing.*

> Getting people into wild and open country obviously demands a great deal of co-operation, from public transport to support groups. *Green Magazine*[38]

The subject is the needs of the disabled. Grammatical horses are changed in midstream. 'From' is first used to complete the construction 'co-operation from public transport', but before the ink is dry 'from' has introduced the 'from . . . to' construction. This must go. *Getting people into wild and open country obviously demands a great deal of co-operation from public transport and from support groups.*

> With the coming of sound cinema, she, Berry, and many others like Louis Jouvet, Gaby Morlay and Arletty, duplicated their careers from stage to screen. *Independent*[39]

You may 'move from' stage to screen, but you cannot 'duplicate from' one thing to another: *duplicated their stage careers on the screen.*

> It has changed radically over the past two decades from being dependent on farming, fishing and tourism to its role today as an offshore financial centre. *Times*[40]

This is about the Isle of Man. Grammatical parallelism should be established between 'being dependent' and 'its role'. Change either the first – *from its dependence on farming . . . to its role today* – or the second: *from being dependent on farming . . . to acting today as an offshore financial centre.*

> It is good to see how many women poets are here, from Anne Finch (d 1720), Countess of Winchilsea, to the no less aristocratic 'Walled Garden' by Dorothy, Duchess of Wellington (d 1956). *Oldie*[41]

You would not speak of 'poets from Shakespeare to "If" by Kipling'. Don't mix up poets and poems: *from Anne Finch . . . to Dorothy, Duchess of Westminster, author of 'Walled Garden'.*

> From eighteenth-century parks and houses, through Schinkel's homage to our northern factories, to the careful study of the Arts and Crafts Movement which pre-dated the thoroughly German Bauhaus, a lack of restrictive chauvinist pride at the right moments has resulted in ever greater creative fertility. *Tatler*[42]

'Parks and houses, homage to factories, study of a movement', each item belongs to a different category, and none belongs to the category represented by 'a lack of restrictive chauvinist pride'. The real subject ought to be German art. *In its design of eighteenth-century parks and houses, in Schinkel's homage to our northern factories, and in the careful study of the British Arts and Crafts Movement which pre-dated the thoroughly German Bauhaus, German art has, at the right moments, displayed a lack of restrictive chauvinistic pride which has resulted in ever greater creative fertility.*

5 Omission of preposition

> Apply the lipstick first, followed by lipliner – this way they both wear away at the same rate. *New Woman*[43]

The preposition 'in' is omitted ('in this way they both wear away at the same rate'). But we are still left with a problem of logic. It is not 'in this way' that they both wear away. For 'this way' is a mode of application not of wear. *Apply the lipstick first, then the lipliner – as a result they both wear away at the same rate.*

> The trouble is, we don't choose our boyfriends the same way as we choose friends. *Catch*[44]

. . . we don't choose our boyfriends in the same way as we choose friends.

> . . . you'll have difficulty persuading any employer that you genuinely want this job if you've just picked it out of thin air. *Catch*[45]

. . . you'll have difficulty in persuading any employer . . .

> You'll have to see them to believe them, but then you can. *Ideal Home*[46]

Magnet kitchens are being advertised. You cannot speak of 'believing' a kitchen. Even 'corrected' in this respect, the use of the cliché is not effective. *You'll have to see them to believe in them.*

All the entries will be exhibited at Swanage Station the day of judging . . . *Steam Classic*[47]

Do not omit the preposition when citing a time. *All the entries will be exhibited at Swanage Station on the day of judging.* We commend the writer for avoiding the ambiguity of 'the day of judgment'.

Your ideas a few weeks ago about travelling . . . are now a reality. *More!*[48]

Your ideas of a few weeks ago . . .

The conglomerate share index lagged the market in 1991 . . . *Investors Chronicle*[49]

You can 'lag' hot water pipes to prevent escape of heat. The market does not require insulation: *share index lagged behind the market.*

It's a good landmark to look back on several points along the route. *Country Walking*[50]

. . . to look back on from several points along the route.

Not every personal assistant has to organise her boss a Peter Pan fancy dress costume . . . *Best*[51]

There are verbs in English which can govern both a direct object and an indirect object. Thus you can say 'I bought him a book' or 'I told her a story'. You cannot treat the verb 'to organise' like that. What is done here is done *for* the boss (and 'organise' is not the best word). *Not every personal assistant has to prepare/arrange a Peter Pan fancy dress costume for her boss.*

. . . Li Ka-Shing . . . who was rumoured to be close making an offer for the two last Autumn. *Investors Chronicle*[52]

. . . who was rumoured to be close to making an offer . . .

6 Omission of repeated preposition

We saw in Chapter I, 3 how crucial the repetition of the preposition may be in using the construction 'rather than'. It is equally crucial in other contexts. If someone said 'The walker was hurt as much by the lightning as the dog', you would guess that walker and dog were suffering comparably. But if it was 'The walker was hurt as much by the lightning as by the dog' you would recognise a totally different comparison. So crucial is the repetition of 'by'.

Wildlife and plants are vanishing from British rivers and the problem is caused as much by water companies, businesses and individuals extracting water to sell to customers as the three-year drought, according to Lord Buxton, a leading conservationist. *Green Magazine*[53]

Here, too, a crucial 'by' is omitted before 'the three-year drought'. The gerciple (see Chapter III) 'extracting' also needs to be dealt with: *the problem is caused as much by water companies, businesses and individuals who extract water to sell to customers as by the three-year drought.*

Look, as always, at the views you will get from various angles and particularly the house. *Practical Gardening*[54]

The failure to repeat the preposition 'from' gives a touch of ambiguity here: . . . *the views you will get from various angles and particularly from the house.*

'It was nothing,' she said, which could equally have been a reference to the match as her adventures on the streets. *Times*[55]

. . . *which could equally well have been a reference to the match as to her adventures on the streets.*

We have been delighted at the sympathetic response you have given to us and the ever increasing financial difficulties we face with the present regime. *College Newsletter*[56]

It ought not to be suggested that delight is taken in financial difficulties. Even corrected – *given to us and to the ever increasing financial difficulties* – the sentence is not felicitous.

7 *Omission of final preposition*

We have a respectable English construction which allows us to say 'This is a nice house to live in' instead of the clumsier 'This is a nice house in which to live'. There were purists who used to insist that you should never end a sentence with a preposition, but that view is happily discredited. Unfortunately the freedom to place the preposition late sometimes leads to its being omitted.

In the centre of the room a simple curtain pole is suspended from the ceiling for hanging some decorative wicker baskets. *Ideal Home*[57]

. . . *for hanging some decorative wicker baskets on.*

Our land journey started with a 230-mile trip across country to a small town called Saeby, where we found a camp site to stay. *Caravan Magazine*[58]

. . . where we found a camp site to stay at

> It lists more than 3000 places to stay, eat and drink (everything from hostels to bunkhouses) . . . *Country-Side*[59]

You cannot stay a place, eat a place, or drink a place. *It lists more than 3000 places to stay, eat and drink at.*

> Maybe someone will buy up some of the main stations, and make them jollier (and warmer) places to wait. *Times*[60]

You cannot 'wait a station': *jollier and warmer places to wait in.*

> Some will be thinking of places to go, museums, steam parks, etc. to visit. *Old Glory*[61]

Some will be thinking of places to go to.

> On policy, Mr Smith and his allies have achieved more than they are usually given credit. *Times*[62]

. . . have achieved more than they are usually given credit for.

8 'from' after 'prevent'

> In the beginning you should write everything down so you don't forget – this will prevent you having two choices, thinking it's one. *Bella*[63]

There are two alternatives here for correcting the gerciple ('you having'). Either make it a proper gerund – *prevent your having two choices* – or, more naturally perhaps, use the preposition 'from': *prevent you from having two choices.*

> If the British Government had such a problem with the word because of an impending general election that it would prevent it signing the treaty, a compromise may be possible. *Independent*[64]

The same alternatives apply: use the (rather awkward) gerund – *that it would prevent its signing* – or 'from': *prevent it from signing.*

> Similarly, polarised lenses can be extremely effective in reducing glare by preventing reflected light to pass from horizontal surfaces, such as the sea or ground. *Outdoors Illustrated*[65]

The verb 'to prevent' cannot be followed by the infinitive: *reducing glare by preventing reflected light from passing.*

– VI –

PRESERVING DUE SEQUENCE

Accuracy in the use of language demands that writers keep their heads from the beginning of a sentence to the end. When you begin a sentence with a certain construction you must make sure that you complete that construction. Errors occur when a writer starts a sentence with a certain construction and then, as the words flow, forgets exactly what that construction was. He finishes a sentence which he did not begin and fails to finish the sentence which he did begin. This error is called *anacoluthon*, the failure to preserve proper grammatical sequence. In its crudest form it can produce extreme absurdities. Very often syntactical collapse caused by failure to preserve grammatical sequence occurs in the use of quite simple constructions.

1 GRAMMATICAL CONTINUITY

1 Sequence after 'and'

When items are listed in sequence, care must be taken to preserve grammatical continuity. 'Fetch me some bacon, some eggs and some tomatoes' is a satisfactory sentence. 'Fetch me some bacon, some eggs and be quick' is not. The listing process begun with 'some bacon, some eggs' must be completed with a third item after 'and'.

> The matching Overtrousers have back pocket, zipped leg openings and pack down very small. *Country Walking*[1]

Here the listing process begun with 'back pocket, zipped leg openings' must be completed with a third item after 'and'. The construction must not be changed. And 'small' is an adjective which cannot qualify the verb 'pack'. *The matching Overtrousers have back pocket and zipped leg openings, and they fold into a small package.*

> Long ago, the house would have been self-sufficient, producing its own butter and cheese, fruit from the orchard, vegetables, and even livestock would have been kept. *Period Living*[2]

The list of items introduced by 'producing' is broken after 'and': *the house would have been self-sufficient, producing its own butter and cheese, fruit from the orchard and vegetables, and even keeping livestock.*

His enthusiasm, kindliness and *eminence grise* will be sadly missed. *Horse & Hound*[3]

An '*eminence grise*' is a person exercising great influence behind the scenes. While 'enthusiasm' and 'kindliness' are human qualities, '*eminence grise*' is a human being. *His enthusiasm, kindliness and unobtrusive guidance will be sadly missed.*

Exhibitors will include conservation organisations, optical equipment, outdoor clothing and footwear, wildlife holidays, special events and more. *Outdoors Illustrated*[4]

The word 'include' promises a list of 'exhibitors' but only one is named ('conservation organisations'). Optical equipment, clothing and footwear, holidays and events are none of them 'exhibitors'. Scrap the word 'include', which must introduce a series of exact parallels in substance and in grammar. *There will be exhibitions dealing with conservation and wildlife holidays, displays of optical equipment, outdoor clothing and footwear, and other special events.*

On his retirement to Boxford he played a full part in village life including the church and as chairman of the Boxford Society. *Times*[5]

'He liked games, including cricket and football' is a satisfactory sentence because cricket and football can both be properly listed as 'games'. But 'He liked games, including cricket and as full back in football' is not because the sequence after 'including' is broken. A second game must be named. Likewise here the 'village life' in which the subject of the obituary 'played a full part' may be said to include 'the church' and the 'Boxford Society', but 'as chairman of the Boxford Society' completes a construction which has not been used ('He acted as chairman of the Boxford Society'). *On his retirement to Boxford he played a full part in village life including the church and the Boxford Society, of which he was chairman.*

Researchers also found other safety problems such as lack of guards and long blade-stopping times. *Times*[6]

(The piece is about a *Which* report on compost-shredders.) The clumsiness could be avoided by getting rid of the word 'problems': *Researchers also found other possible dangers in the lack of guards and in the time it took for the blades to stop.*

My reason for saying this is that some of the alternative 'controls' used by these people are snaring (and you know my views on that), gassing, poisoning (illegal and indiscriminate), foot-hold traps (barbaric), and the camouflage jacket brigade with their terriers and warped ideas of 'sport'. *Cumbria Life*[7]

This outburst about fox-hunting shows how a writer can be led astray by sheer fervour. The 'controls' listed are all methods of control ('snaring . . . gassing, poisoning, foot-hold traps') until we come to 'the camouflage jacket brigade' who are not 'controls' but people. This last item after 'and' must be brought into line: *snaring . . . gassing, poisoning . . . foot-hold traps, and hunting with terriers.*

There were the common birds and flowers, the naming of hills and streams, described with apparent simplicity but also so animated by Wordsworth that they represented a mood or understanding in him. *Viva*[8]

And here is Melvyn Bragg listing incompatibles. The birds and flowers may well be described with apparent simplicity and even animated by Wordsworth. But we are told too that the 'naming of hills and streams' is described and animated. One can but guess at what is meant: *the common birds and flowers, the named hills and streams.*

2 Sequence after 'and': more complex cases

So far we have been concerned with fairly simple itemised listing which has broken down syntactically after 'and'. When the sequence '*a*, *b*, and *c*' occurs, whether the pattern is simply 'bacon, sausage, and chips' or, more complicatedly, 'stopped at the garage, filled up with petrol, and drove off', there must be no change to a discrepant construction after 'and'. The more complex the sentence, the greater the care needed to avoid syntactical breakdown.

It is a tremendous achievement to have followed a dream, realised your goal, grown through it and then be ready to move on. *Cosmopolitan*[9]

'Followed a dream . . . realised a goal . . . and then be ready': that is syntactical collapse. The construction after 'and' must be brought into line with the construction that precedes it. Moreover, the 'it' of 'grown through it' must be identified. Grown through the goal? Surely not. Grown through the dream? Scarcely. *It is a tremendous achievement to have followed a dream, realised your goal, and grown through the experience, and then to be ready to move on.*

Fledgling Stock Exchanges launched in Moscow and Leningrad might be enlarged and started in other Russian cities. *Sun*[10]

'Enlarged and started' will not do. The verbs cannot apply to the same subject. The Stock Exchanges that have been launched in Moscow and Leningrad, and may be enlarged, can certainly not be started elsewhere. *Fledgling Stock Exchanges launched in Moscow and Leningrad might be enlarged, and Stock Exchanges established in other Russian cities.*

> My ideal man's intelligent, someone from whom I can learn and see the world with. *Woman*[11]

You might speak of 'someone from whom I can learn and borrow money' because you both learn *from* and borrow money *from*. But you cannot speak of 'someone from whom I can learn and live with' because you learn *from* and live *with*. Change the position of 'from' and all could be well: *My ideal man's intelligent, someone whom I can learn from and see the world with.*

> A lot of work has gone into producing this catalogue. It is the single most expensive cost we have, but this year we are very fortunate to have it partly sponsored, which has enabled us to make it larger, and, we hope easier to see the goods we are offering. *Samaritans Catalogue*[12]

Again two discrepant constructions are hinged on 'and'. You can make a catalogue larger and easier to read, but you cannot make it larger and easier to see the goods. It is only for the reader that the goods can be 'easier to see': . . . *which has enabled us to enlarge it and make the goods we are offering more easily seen.*

> John Major yesterday joined Norman Lamont, the Chancellor, in a delicate balancing act on economic and monetary union. While both assert an unchanged approach to EMU, they share private sympathy for the compromise which avoids the 'imposition' of a single currency and leaving the political decision to join to a future Parliament. *Independent*[13]

What items are joined together by 'and' here? Do Major and Lamont (1) share sympathy for the compromise . . . and leaving the political decision to join to a future Parliament? Or do they (2) share sympathy for the compromise which avoids the imposition and leaves the political decision to join? If (1) is correct, insert the word 'for': *they share private sympathy for the compromise which avoids the 'imposition' . . . and for leaving the political decision to join to a future Parliament.* If (2) is correct, change the word 'leaving': *the compromise which avoids the 'imposition' of a single currency and leaves the political decision to join to a future Parliament.*

With a Prestige pressure cooker you can significantly cut down on cooking time, save energy and, because the fruit is cooked at a high temperature, more of the nutrients and flavour of the fruit is retained. *Practical Gardening*[14]

What follows 'and' here has no grammatical connection with what precedes it. We have the first half of one sentence and the second half of a different one. *With a Prestige pressure cooker you can significantly cut down on cooking time and save energy. Moreover, because the fruit is cooked at a high temperature, more of the nutrients and flavour of the fruit is retained.*

3 Sequence after 'or' and 'but'

When 'or' is used in listing options we need to ensure that what follows the word is grammatically in tune with what precedes it. Do not make 'or' a hinge on which to hang a new construction.

Always stop if you feel pain, dizziness, or unusually tired. *Family Circle*[15]

The third item, 'unusually tired', must match the first two items. *Always stop if you feel pain, dizziness, or unusual tiredness.*

Whether you are an antique devotee, a collector wishing to expand your knowledge, or just simply enjoy the atmosphere of a fascinating weekend in comfortable surroundings, you're sure to find these tours both rewarding and exceptional value. *The World of Interiors*[16]

Here 'or' is used like 'and' in previous examples, not to introduce a third matching item, but as a hinge on which to swing a new construction. The item introduced by 'or' does not match the previous ones grammatically. (You may be an antique devotee or a collector, but you cannot be a 'just simply enjoy'.) There is also a similar broken sequence around 'and' ('both rewarding and exceptional value'). *Whether you are an antique devotee, a collector wishing to expand your knowledge, or just simply a person who enjoys the atmosphere of a fascinating weekend in comfortable surroundings, you're sure to find these tours both rewarding and exceptionally valuable.*

He called for an urgent review of mortgage lending in Britain to stem the losses, or he warned lenders that premiums on mortgage indemnities would have to rise by three or four times. *Times*[17]

This use of 'or' is indefensible. To be defensible it would have to introduce an alternative to 'he called . . .' ('He called . . . or he warned'). In fact he did both. The 'or' does not apply to either the calling or the warning. *He called for an urgent review of mortgage lending in*

162

Britain to stem the losses and he warned lenders that otherwise premiums on mortgage indemnities would have to rise by three or four times.

A decision can always be made at the end to continue or have follow-up meetings if that is wanted or practicable. *Nursing Standard*[18]

Plainly 'practicable' cannot here be an alternative to 'wanted'. It is no good wanting something if it is not practicable. Change 'or' to 'and': *if that is wanted and is practicable.*

But of all his extracurricular activities it was for his music that he will be best remembered: playing duos with his second wife, Charlotte, or the chamber musician who was rarely at a scientific meeting without his clarinet. *Independent*[19]

There are two possible intepretations here: that he was in the habit of playing duos with either Charlotte or the clarinet-carrying musician; that he was in the habit of playing either duos or the chamber musician. Neither interpretation is intended. But there is no possible grammatical match between 'playing duos . . . or the chamber musician': *it is (not 'was') as a musician that he will be best remembered, playing duos with his second wife, Charlotte, and usually carrying his clarinet with him when he went to scientific meetings.*

In the use of 'but' there is the same need to preserve parallelism between what precedes the word and what follows it. You can say 'His life is not active but studious', where the two adjectives 'active' and 'studious' balance each other. But you cannot say 'His life is not active but as a scholar' where there is no grammatical match between what precedes and what follows 'but'. Yet the sentence below commits this error.

Its most useful functions are not constitutional but as an unmatchable PR agency for good causes, and some not so good. *Independent*[20]

(The subject is the monarchy.) 'But' is a hinge on which discrepant constructions swing. Bring what follows 'but' into line grammatically: *Its most useful functions are not constitutional but promotional: it is an unmatchable PR agency for good causes, and some not so good.*

There are a few registered equine hospitals and their high standards are inspected but the others are not. *Horse & Hound*[21]

The word 'others' goes back to 'standards' in grammar, but to 'hospitals' in intention. It is not the 'standards' that are inspected but the hospitals. *The few registered equine hospitals have their standards guaranteed by inspection, but the others do not.*

The loss of another Fitzrovian, Albert Pierrepoint, will be sadly missed but never forgotten by many of that era. *Times*[22]

It is not the 'loss' of Pierrepoint that will be sadly missed, but Pierrepoint himself. *Another lost Fitzrovian, Albert Pierrepoint, will be sadly missed and never forgotten.*

4. 'either . . . or'

In the use of 'either . . . or' (as in the use of 'both . . . and') what goes wrong is generally a matter of word order. You can say 'I will have either tea or coffee', because 'either' and 'or' define the alternatives. But you cannot say 'I will either have tea or coffee', because 'either have' requires a follow up, as in 'I will either accept the post or turn it down'.

Depending on the type of PEP you choose, your investment goes into either a basket of shares or into a unit trust or investment trust. *Moneywise*[23]

Switch round 'into either' – *your investment goes either into a basket of shares or into a unit trust* – or scrap the second 'into': *your investment goes into either a basket of shares or a unit trust.* But it is better to change 'either . . . or', which ought not to be used when there are more than two variables (alternatives): *your investment goes into a basket of shares, a unit trust, or an investment trust.*

Either place your fruit in a colander or a seive, and wash under water. *Prima*[24]

Place your fruit in either a colander or a seive.

The Italian political system can either be considered damagingly unstable, since there have been no fewer than 50 governments since the end of the Second World War; or a miracle of stability, with the Christian Democrats forming the backbone of all of them and the same leading characters tending to reappear in each new production. *Independent*[25]

The leader-writer for the *Independent* falls down here. If 'either' is placed before 'be considered', then an alternative to 'be considered' must be provided when 'or' comes along. Replace it before 'damagingly unstable'. Moreover, 'with' is unnecessary (see Chapter V, 4). And so is 'same', because if characters 'reappear', they cannot be other than the 'same'. *The Italian political system can be considered either damagingly unstable . . . or a miracle of stability, the Christian Democrats forming the backbone of all of them and the leading characters tending to reappear in each new production.*

The four piano concertos immediately preceding No. 15, which

Mozart had written since moving to Vienna, had been meant principally either for publication or aimed at amateurs to play . . . *Programme Note*[26]

A second verb ('aimed at') could be introduced here only if 'either' had preceded 'meant' ('had been either principally meant for publication or aimed at amateurs'). But there could be no point in thus duplicating the verb. Moreover 'aimed at amateurs to play' makes nonsense. *The four concertos immediately preceding No. 15, which Mozart had written since moving to Vienna, had been meant primarily either for publication or for amateur performance.*

5 'both . . . and'

What applies to 'either . . . or' applies also to 'both . . . and'.

Divided into four sections, the book charts the development of both the individual painters and of the impressionist movement. *Artists & Illustrators Magazine*[27]

Either remove the second 'of' – *the book charts the development of both the individual painters and the impressionist movement* – or move the first 'of': *the book charts the development both of the individual painters and of the impressionist movement.*

Presence of RDB species on a site demonstrate both habitat quality and point to the type of management needed to maintain them since the data sheets give information on habitat requirements as well as the known threats. *Country-Side*[28]

'Presence' is a singular subject and is here given a plural verb ('demonstrate'). 'Both' is misplaced and there should be parallelism also before and after 'as well as'. *Presence of RDB species on a site both demonstrates habitat quality and points to the type of management needed to maintain them (it?), since the data sheets give information on habitat requirements as well as on the known threats.*

Positioning the solo cellist at the centre of a crescent-shaped orchestra was both a metaphor of the composer's main idea and had the practical benefit of facilitating the role of a soloist who is also a conductor. *Independent*[29]

You can say 'He was both cheerful and helpful', where the two adjectives 'cheerful' and 'helpful' balance each other. But you cannot say 'He was both cheerful and helped me a lot', leaving the construction introduced by 'both cheerful' incomplete. In the above sentence 'both' is unncessary anyway. *Positioning the solo cellist at the centre of a crescent-shaped orchestra was a metaphor of the composer's main idea and also had the practical benefit of facilitating the role of a soloist who is also a conductor.*

6 The placing of 'only'

'Only' is another word which constantly gets misplaced. The rule is to place 'only' next to the words it directly affects.

> Sometimes they'll only see each other for a few snatched days. *Woman*[30]

Sometimes they'll see each other for only a few snatched days.

> The Met has only been responsible to the Home Secretary. *Guardian*[31]

The Met has been responsible only to the Home Secretary.

> It is an offence for a restaurant only to have a menu or wine list which they merely hand to you, once you are inside. *Moneywise*[32]

'Merely' seems to have been inserted in order to avoid repeating 'only'. In fact no repetition is called for. *It is an offence for a restaurant to have a menu or a wine list which they hand to you only when you are inside.*

> I only began to worry when financial incentives were added. *Guardian*[33]

I began to worry only when financial incentives were added.

> Sir Nicholas Goodison, the chairman, said the loss, caused by a £440 million bad debt provision, was not only due to the recession. He also blamed poor management and poor judgment. *Independent*[34]

Replace 'not only' by 'not solely' and adjust word order: *the loss, caused by a £440 million bad debt provision, was not due solely to the recession.*

2 COHERENCE AND INCOHERENCE

Proper continuity is a matter of meaning as well as of grammar. There is nothing grammatically wrong with the sentence 'The desk sprouted theorems', but the words do not fit together. By virtue of their respective meanings the words 'desk', 'sprout', and 'theorems' can be used in combination with certain words and not with others. Commonsense and logic are our guides in this respect. Convention is also important, and establishes certain usages as acceptable and others as unacceptable. For instance, you 'make' an application, but 'offer' your resignation, and to speak of 'offering an application' or 'making a resignation' would sound unnatural. We must not give the impression that we are ignorant of accepted usage. Consistency in the structure of a sentence must be matched by the compatibility of word with word.

1 Incompatibility: noun and verb

> Although little progress has been reached, French cooperation on defence could have far-reaching consequences for procurement projects . . . *Independent*[1]

You do not 'reach' progress, you 'make' it: *Although little progress has been made.*

> A repertoire of cleverly cut black evening dresses, short or long, with beaded or lace panels or cunningly draped, ran through this collection of polished, wearable high style. *Times*[2]

You can 'run through' a repertoire, but a repertoire cannot 'run through' anything. *A range of cleverly cut black evening dresses . . . distinguished this collection of polished, wearable high style.*

> . . . the main stumbling-block had been resolved. *Radio 4*[3]

Stumbling blocks cannot be 'resolved': *had been removed.*

> So how does he see himself as bridging this disparity? *Times*[4]

You cannot 'bridge' a disparity: *reconciling these extremes.*

> Single item measures are least preferable because it is doubtful one question can effectively tap a given phenomenon . . . *Nursing Standard*[5]

This piece on the use of statistics in health care has three errors: (1) 'whether' should be inserted after 'doubtful'; (2) 'least preferable' appears to mean 'least desirable' (i.e. not 'preferable' at all); (3) you can 'tap' a barrel of beer, but not a 'phenomenon'. *Single item measures are least desirable because it is doubtful whether one question can effectively test opinion on a given issue.*

> With this in mind, a far-sighted, extensive and on-going plan was drawn up to completely modernise and expand the winery, a plan which is currently taking place. *Decanter*[6]

A plan does not 'take place': *which is currently being executed.*

> This is done by re-educating the way we perform simple actions, such as sitting down and standing up. *She*[7]

Here is advice about projecting one's body 'more positively'. You can educate people but you cannot educate a way of doing something: *reforming the way we perform simple actions.*

Topics that were sacred or taboo are openly reviled and aired. *Times*[8]

This piece is about the situation in Moscow after Boris Yeltsin took over. A 'topic' cannot be 'reviled'; it is a subject or theme of discussion. Only the views expressed, the principles enunciated, or the people holding them can be 'reviled', that is, subjected to abusive criticism. Moreover, 'and aired' is redundant since a view cannot be 'openly reviled' unless it is aired. *Topics that were taboo are aired and principles that were sacrosanct are reviled.*

He lists post-war landmarks, such as devaluations and entry into Europe, that would have happened which ever party was in power. *Times*[9]

Landmarks do not 'happen'. *He lists important post-war changes, such as devaluations and entry into Europe, that would have happened whichever party was in power.*

. . . small checks are not suitable because they show a sort of fuzzy effect on the screen. *My Weekly*[10]

The topic is what to wear when you are forecasting weather on the BBC. You cannot 'show' an effect, but you can 'produce' one: *because they produce a sort of fuzzy effect on the screen.*

Nadège, a Parisian prostitute, fulfils such sexual desires as this gross man can summon the energy to enjoy. *Independent*[11]

The gross man does not 'enjoy' desires, he indulges or satisfies them.

Staff who fulfil certain performance criteria have no opportunity to earn additional salary points. *Times*[12]

'Criteria' are not things that can be 'fulfilled': *Staff who match up to certain performance criteria.*

2 Personal for impersonal

There are expressions which properly apply only to human or other living beings. We ought not to use them out of context.

Yesterday's Budget expects to be judged not today but next month, and by the whole nation. *Times*[13]

A person can 'expect' something; a budget cannot. Either get rid of 'expects' – *Yesterday's Budget is designed to be judged* – or change the subject of the sentence: *The Chancellor expects yesterday's Budget to be judged not today but next month.*

168

So the payment of £40 million by Peat to Ferranti may have its own reasons . . . *Times*[14]

A heart may have its own reasons, but a payment cannot. *So the payment of £40 million by Peat to Ferranti may be explicable.*

Over the past nine days the Yorkshire and Humberside coast has kept up the momentum, with reports of at least four bee-eaters while an American spotted sandpiper has been found near Wakefield. *Daily Telegraph*[15]

To 'keep up momentum' is a process which living beings and perhaps mechanical contrivances can accomplish. It is beyond the powers of a coast: *Over the past nine days reports of at least four bee-eaters have come from the Yorkshire and Humberside coast.*

Such gestures will have little impact, however, if planning does not respond. *Times*[16]

'Planning' cannot 'respond' as though it were a living creature. *Such gestures will have little impact, however, if plans are not made accordingly.*

But the government had now started a job creation scheme to reduce unemployment, a scheme which would pay the first three months' wages of any worthy new job that an employer proposed. *Independent*[17]

The 'scheme' will not pay the wages: *a scheme to pay the first three months' wages for any worthy new job.*

How many other gardens offer six varieties of Brussels sprouts and how many others assiduously label every vegetable? *In Britain*[18]

Usage may allow the writer to ask the first question; how many gardens offer this or that produce? But the act of assiduously labelling the vegetables must not be attributed to the garden: *and in how many other gardens is every vegetable assiduously labelled?*

3 Dislocation of terms

One can speak of 'dislocation' in the terms used when the elements of a sentence fail to hang together, either because of incompatability in the meanings of related words or because of grammatical breakdown.

Kaufmann became the Gerald Priestland of Swiss Radio – except that he did it for much longer. *Independent*[19]

If the sentence began 'Kaufmann acted as the Gerald Priestland of Swiss Radio', the words 'he did it' (i.e. 'acted') would make sense. But 'he did

169

it' cannot refer back to 'became'. *Kaufmann became the Gerald Priestland of Swiss Radio – though he remained so for much longer.*

> CJD in humans is a similar disease to BSE in cattle. The nervous system degenerates and results in death. *Essentials*[20]

We are told here that the nervous system 'results in death'. It doesn't. It is the degeneration of the nervous system that results in death. *The nervous system degenerates and the result is death.*

> Business expanded rapidly and construction of a new factory in Great West Road commenced in November 1933 and was opened on 19/1/34. *Automobile*[21]

Here is another sentence in which two verbs linked by 'and' follow the subject, the one correctly, the other incorrectly. The construction of a new factory commenced in November 1933, but the construction was not opened in 1934. *Business expanded rapidly; a new factory began to be constructed in Great West Road in November 1933 and was opened on 19/1/34.*

> . . . Lord Mackay's zeal. He has pushed through an end to the conveyancing monopoly . . . *Times*[22]

You cannot push through an 'end'. *He has pushed through legislation to end the conveyancing monopoly.*

> The long-term future for wages, both nominal and real, is the principal doubt. *Financial Times*[23]

The future cannot be a 'doubt'. *The main uncertainty is about what the nominal and real levels of wages will be in the long-term future.*

> The unobtrusive yet deceptively spacious design . . . *Cumbria Life*[24]

A 'deceptively friendly' man would be a man concealing his hostility. A 'deceptively spacious' house would be a house concealing its smallness. *The unobtrusive yet deceptively compact design . . .*

> The islands are home to forty percent of the bird's British population, but a lack of their main food, sand eels has seen tern numbers fall by over a half in just ten years. *Wild about Animals*[25]

The expression 'I have seen their numbers fall' has been idiomatically extended so that it is permissible to say 'The last decade saw their numbers fall'. But 'a lack of their food has seen their numbers fall' is surely absurd. The lack of food is the cause, not the witness, of the falling numbers: *but a lack of their main food, sand eels, has caused their numbers to fall by half in just ten years.*

Boothby married twice, first a cousin of Dorothy, Diana Cavendish – it lasted little more than a year – and then in 1965 to Wanda, an Italian student he met ten years before when she was 23 and he was 56. *Daily Mail*[26]

'Boothby married . . . first a cousin . . . then to Wanda'. You cannot 'marry to' anyone, though you can 'be married to' someone. And the 'it' of 'it lasted more than a year' refers to a word 'marriage' which has not been used. *Boothby was married twice, first to a cousin of Dorothy, Diana Cavendish – the marriage lasted little more than a year – and then in 1965 to Wanda.*

Bats have been built a special roost at a church hall. *Sun*[27]

The roost has been built, not the bats. *A special roost has been built for bats at a church hall.*

Healthy-looking hair is determined by the state of its outer layer or cuticle. *New Woman*[28]

It is not the hair that is 'determined' but its apparent relative healthiness. *How healthy hair looks is determined by the state of its outer layer or cuticle.*

We will issue you with a Personal Number (PIN). *Midland Bank circular*[29]

If I said 'We shall issue a newspaper with coloured pictures', the message would be clear. What shall I look like when the Midland Bank issues me with a PIN? *We shall (sic) issue a PIN for you.*

4 Dislocation: more complex cases

Sometimes the verbal dislocation is such that it is less easy to disentangle the confused grammar or confused meaning.

There are mountains waiting to be conquered, valleys to be explored and roads to be mastered. With the new Mitsubishi, the challenge is even easier. *The Field*[30]

'Easier' than what? And why 'even'? Both words imply a previous reference which does not exist. *With the new Mitsubishi, the challenge is easily faced.*

For nurses, these patients provide considerable challenges as they do not present with a consistent problem, or one which steadily improves from day to day. *Nursing Standard*[31]

The reference is to patients with speech disorders. But surely a problem cannot 'improve'. As the situation improves the problem diminishes.

Moreover, either 'with' must go or 'them' must be added ('present them with'): *they do not present a consistent problem, or one which steadily diminishes from day to day.*

Most products are aimed at our faces . . . *Me*[32]

This comment on skin-care treatments is curiously ambiguous. *Most products are designed for our faces.*

. . . it is like so much of life, a much better idea than in reality. *Esquire*[33]

The subject is the English summer picnic. 'Idea' cannot be matched with 'in reality'. Better use 'in' twice: *much better in idea than in fact* or *in dream than in reality.*

One of the great glories of Japanese art, these hollow wooden sculptures almost seem to be alive, so skilled is the sense of movement – and so fierce the inlaid crystal eyes. *Viva*[34]

'Skilled' and 'fierce' do not match here. 'Fierce' applies to the artefact but 'skilled' applies to the creator. The 'sense of movemenet' must not be described as 'skilled'. It has no skill at all: *so skilfully is the sense of movement created.*

How many of the spiralling numbers of cancer sufferers can be attributed to the poisons that soak and infiltrate our food . . . no one can say. *Lancashire Life*[35]

You cannot 'attribute' either 'numbers' or 'sufferers' to poisons, only the disease. Moreover poisons 'soak *into*' food, and 'infiltrate' is redundant. *How many of the spiralling numbers of cancer sufferers can attribute their disease to the poisons that soak into our food.*

Nicholas Hawksmoor also utilised the bay, though to a lesser degree than by his contemporary baroque designers . . . *Old-House Journal*[36]

Two constructions are confused here. You cannot say 'Smith also drinks beer though less than by his mates'. *Nicholas Hawksmoor also utilised the bay, though to a lesser degree than did his contemporary baroque designers.*

The area may never rival the beauty of the Ribble Valley or the upmarket ambience of Lytham St Annes or Southport. *Lancashire Life*[37]

An 'area' cannot rival 'beauty'. It can only rival another area *in* beauty. *The area may never rival the Ribble Valley in beauty or Lytham St Annes or Southport in upmarket ambience.*

Success also reflects the role of Members of the European Parliament who pressed the commission and were responsible for improving the proposal in its passage through the Parliament, and to the government officials and ministers responsible for finalising the legislation in the Council of Ministers. *The Field*[38]

'Success also reflects the role of Members . . . and to the government officials.' The sentence begins with one construction and ends with another. Use the one – *the role of Members of the European Parliament who pressed the commission . . . and of the government officials* – or the other: *Success is due to Members of the European Parliament . . . and to the government officials.*

Both charges were this weekend being levied at the Bank; at once accused of shutting down the bank when the Sheikh stood ready to inject more money into it, and for ignoring a host of signs warning of its unsoundness over the years. *Times*[39]

You cannot say 'I was accused of breaking in and for stealing'. You must stick to the one construction: *at once accused of shutting down the bank, . . . and of ignoring a host of signs warning of its unsoundness over the years.*

5 Loss of coherence

We are investigating sentences whose parts do not fully 'cohere', that is, do not hang together properly. Failures of verbal compatibility and structural consistency destroy coherence.

If your mother was pear-shaped it's possible that your fat cells will be located in the same area. *Harpers & Queen*[40]

'Pear-shaped' is not an 'area'. No area is mentioned here or in the previous sentence. *If your mother was pear-shaped it's possible that your fat cells will be located where hers were.*

These new business barons gained extra respect from their escalating salaries, which attracted both criticism and awe. *Times*[41]

No one can gain respect from a salary, which is incapable of giving respect: *gained extra respect because of their escalating salaries.*

Blue Circle Cement at Beeding provided nearly 100 tonnes of clay free and when completed it will measure 25 metres in diameter. *Country-Side*[42]

Two sentences previously there was a reference to a project to build a new dew pond, so the reader can put two and two together. But as the

173

sentence stands 'it' can only refer to the firm or the clay. *When the dewpond is completed it will measure 25 metres in diameter.*

> From an early start as a portrayer of religious iconography, the ability to rapidly cover walls with symmetrical designs proved a popular device for enlivening the interiors of other great public halls, namely the theatre and the picture house. *Old-House Journal*[43]

The writer begins a sentence of which he intends to make a stencil artist the subject – 'From an early start as a portrayer'. But the artist is forgotten, 'ability' becomes the subject and is represented as having made an early start. *From an early start as a portrayer of religious iconographer, the artist found that his ability to cover walls with symmetrical designs proved a popular device.*

> The aria here, 'A te, fra tanti affani', in which the voice is required to compete with a superb woodwind obbligato, culminating in an *allegro* in which two components vie with exhilarating virtuosity for the listener's attention. *Opera Now*[44]

Here the writer forgets that a sentence needs an end as well as a beginning. After reading 37 words we are still waiting for the verb which must follow the subject 'The aria'.

> While smaller newsagents often carry a far wider range, more prominently displayed, it is precisely because W H Smith is such a large and supposedly respectable retailer which has made it the focus of recent moves to get porn banned from public sale. *Living*[45]

The sentence jams two constructions together incoherently. You cannot say 'It is because I am hungry which has made me eat'. The writer here must choose between the 'because' construction – *it is precisely because W H Smith is such a large and supposedly respectable retailer that it has become the focus of recent moves to get porn banned* – and the use of 'which' and a relative clause: *it is W H Smith's size and supposed respectability which have made it the focus of recent moves to get porn banned.*

> Certain artists who were involved in the origins of Pop Art from the beginning have moved away from it and some have never been anything else. *Viva*[46]

Anything else but what? *Certain people who were Pop Artists from the beginning have moved away from it and some have never been anything else.*

> Their chief problem is availability of serious well-financed candidates to take on vulnerable Democrats in the Senate. *Times*[47]

'Availability' could not be a problem for them. Unavailability could be. *Their chief problem lies in finding serious well-financed candidates.*

> The Trust believes that restoration by itself is not enough and that any building it saves must be combined with use and enjoyment as well. By letting the pigsty out for holidays, people will be able to enjoy it at their leisure at the same time as contributing in a positive way towards its upkeep. *Old-House Journal*[48]

The writer does not really mean that a building has to be 'combined with use and enjoyment', but that the building has to be both used and enjoyed. Nor will people enjoy the pigsty by letting it out for holidays, but by hiring or renting it. *The Trust believes that restoration by itself is not enough and that any building it saves must be used and enjoyed as well. By renting the pigsty for holidays, people will be able to enjoy it at their leisure.*

> The expulsion of a high commissioner can be borne lightly. More difficult is whether a cut in aid will bring greater suffering to the people who are abused by their leaders. *Times*[49]

More difficult than what? The writer appears to be making a comparison with what has gone before. The expulsion could be lightly borne, he tells us. We therefore expect 'more difficult' to mean 'more difficult to be borne'. But the question that follows, whether a cut in aid will bring greater suffering to the people, is not something that has to be 'borne', but answered. There is no escape from incoherence unless 'more difficult' is dropped. *The expulsion of a high commissioner can be borne lightly. The taxing question remains, whether a cut in aid will bring greater suffering to the people who are abused by their leaders.*

> Its attraction must be in treading carefully down the dividing line between the huge and empty expanse of ocean, while keeping in contact with the land, observing it from the periphery. *The Great Outdoors*[50]

The piece is about walking on a coastal path. A sentence is begun and not ended so that we ask 'Dividing line between the ocean and what?' It is like saying 'The pleasure lies in smoking between the meat course while keeping in contact with the dessert'. *The pleasure lies in walking on the boundary line between land and sea.*

> The mechanism of thinking, then, is this two-way play between what we gather through seeing, feeling and experiencing being constantly and instantly referred to the subconscious which is endlessly thumbing through the files recording, evaluating, com-

paring and giving us instant feed-back to guide and influence the next move. *Money-Maker*[51]

'The mechanism is this two-way play between . . .' The sentence sets out to define the play between what we gather . . . and something else. That something else never emerges, for construction is switched by the words 'being . . . referred'. What it amounts to is: 'Cricket is this two-way play between the batsman being constantly bowled at by the bowler.' Anyway, the jargon defies intelligent elucidation.

3 DISORDER AND DISTORTION

We have seen that a frequent cause of bad writing is the failure to preserve continuity from one part of a sentence to the next. The writer must always be on guard against writing something which would follow correctly only on something which has not been written. Faulty memory or faulty reasoning can cause lapses in this respect.

1 Crossover (parts of speech)
Here the term 'crossover' defines the shift by which a writer proceeds as though a certain part of speech has been used when in fact it has not.

> The design for the reserve has taken ideas from several Dutch schemes, a country recognised as the leading expert in the development of wetland nature reserve. *Times*[1]

The writer uses the adjective 'Dutch' and then continues as though he had used the noun 'Holland' ('a country'). Thus 'a country recognised' seems to stand in apposition to the word 'schemes', which is absurd. 'Dutch' must go if 'a country recognised' is kept. *The design for the reserve has taken ideas from several schemes in Holland, a country recognised as the leading expert.*

> Pierce, born in County Meath in Ireland, has not forgotten the career sacrifices Cassie made to forward his. *Hello*[2]

Although 'career' is a noun, it is used here as an adjective, qualifying the noun 'sacrifice'. The pronoun 'his' cannot refer back to the adjectival 'career', only to the noun 'sacrifices'. It would be clumsy to try to keep the present construction ('has not forgotten the sacrifices Cassie made in her career in order . . .'). Better rewrite. *Pierce, born in County Meath in Ireland, has not forgotten how his career was forwarded by sacrifices Cassie made in her own.*

But is the Gaulier effect touching the theatre establishment? He has
yet to reach a significant number of directors . . . *Times*[3]

Exactly the same error is made here. 'Gaulier' is used adjectivally to
qualify the noun 'effect'. 'He' will not do, because *he* has not been
mentioned, only his 'effect'. If a simpler construction were adopted
there would be no problem. *Is Gaulier having any effect on the theatre
establishment? He has yet . . .*

It would be the first time the factions have met in China, the main
backer of the Cambodian guerrillas . . . *Independent*[4]

Strictly speaking, 'China' first means the place (where the factions have
met) and then means the state or the government (the main backer of
the guerrillas). The purist might not like the transition.

To anyone visiting the great Mantegna exhibition at the Royal
Academy the superb display of his cartoons is as though seeing
them for the first time. *Times*[5]

The writer has not cited Mantegna by citing 'the Mantegna exhibition',
and 'his' has nothing to refer back to. And it is not the *display* that 'is as
though seeing it for the first time' but the viewer's experience of it.
*Anyone visiting the great Mantegna exhibition at the Royal Academy
will respond to the superb display of the artist's cartoons as though he
were seeing them for the first time.*

2 Faulty links
The sentence above illustrates that breaking sequence by transition
from one construction to another or one connotation to another
generally involves much more than merely forgetting what part of
speech has been used. It was the false link from 'display' to 'seeing
them' by means of 'is as though' which caused the trouble.

The great plantsman and gardening author William Robinson
regarded drifts of Michaelmas daisies as his favourite autumn
flowers. *Practical Gardening*[6]

He could not regard 'drifts' of anything as his favourite flowers. If the
rest of the sentence is to stand, 'drifts' must go: *regarded Michaelmas
daisies as his favourite autumn flowers.*

There is a genuine winegrower's house about 350 years old. The
open fire in the kitchen, the canopy bed and utensils used then give
an impression of life at the time. *Caravan Magazine*[7]

Here 'then' is the wrong word to link the two sentences together. The
house is 350 years old and the furniture used *then*, we are told . . . This

is like saying 'I am now 80 years old and the trains running *then* were wonderful'. If 'then' is to be kept, a period must be mentioned. *This is a genuine winegrower's house dating back to the sixteenth century. The open fire in the kitchen, the canopy and utensils used then give an impression of life at the time.*

The vocabulary is simple and boldly printed . . . *Parents*[8]

The thing that is 'simple' (the choice of words) is not exactly what is 'boldly printed'. *The vocabulary is simple and the print bold.*

Its dilemma is perhaps best summed up by a cab journey I once took. *Oldie*[9]

Harry Thompson is talking about Radio 5, but a cab journey is incapable of summing anything up. *Its dilemma is perhaps best summed up by what a cab driver once said to me.*

. . . but the whole story including the cars will hopefully feature in *The Automobile* one day. *Automobile*[10]

. . . the whole story and photographs of the cars, we hope, will feature . . .

The Department of Transport Art Competition is a new exhibition which is open to all artists in any medium to submit work on the theme of Transport. *The Artist*[11]

Two constructions are telescoped here. We know what 'a new exhibition which is open to all artists' means, and it cannot be followed by 'to submit work on the theme of Transport'. The idiom in mind is 'It is open to all artists to submit work on the theme of transport' where 'it' is impersonal and does not mean 'the exhibition'. Better rewrite. *The Department of Transport Art Competition is a new exhibition to which artists in any medium are free to submit work.*

That early study is one of the few books from any field which serves wonderfully well as a primer, yet can also enlighten the specialist. Davie's ability to address both audiences with equal persuasiveness makes his work all the more valuable . . . *Independent*[12]

We are in the world of highbrow reviewing, but the singular verb 'serves' should be plural. Moreover, having said 'This is a good primer and will please the specialist', the writer cannot then speak of 'both' audiences, because a primer is not an audience: only one audience has been mentioned: *one of the few books which serve wonderfully well for beginners, yet can also enlighten the specialist. Davie's ability to address both audiences.*

Even that approach, however, is not a guaranteed success. *Vivid*[13]

Even that approach, however, does not guarantee success.

A passionate guide and an authority on Cornwall's wildlife, mysterious history and hidden places, Martin takes small groups on journeys which are far from the superficial burblings usually offered to tourists. *Good Housekeeping*[14]

Journeys cannot be 'far from the superficial burblings usually offered'. Having referred to the guide's knowledgeableness, the writer appears to think that she has referred to his way of instructing tourists. *Martin takes small groups on journeys and his talk is far removed from the superficial burblings usually offered to tourists.*

. . . the product provides protection from ultraviolet light and any other particular requirements you may have. *Outdoor Illustrated*[15]

One does not 'provide' requirements; still less does one need protection from them: *and meets any other particular requirements.*

The Crewe-Chester-Shrewsbury-Hereford-Crewe 'Phoenix' was run in exhilarating style, and at a peak speed which dare not be quoted. *Steam Railway*[16]

. . . *at a peak speed which I hesitate to specify* . . .

The sound we heard here last year is looking increasingly like the sound of extinction. *Radio 4*[17]

Not knowing what 'extinction' sounds like, we cannot guess what the 'sound' of extinction 'looks' like.

Dragonfly specialists are especially in her debt for her definitive treatment of the Old-World genus *Orthetrum*, which is now less daunting as a result of her efforts to unravel its complexities. *Independent*[18]

What does the word 'which' refer to? It is neither the 'treatment' nor the 'genus' that is now less daunting, but study of the genus, which has not been mentioned: *the Old-World genus* Orthetrum, *whose study is now less daunting.*

He emphasised that the cost figures had to be treated with caution because they were a rough calculation spurred by the criticism which the research team has generated. *Times*[19]

It was not the calculation that was 'spurred', but the calculators: *they were a rough calculation made to meet the criticism* . . .

3 Misplaced phrases
Sometimes an ill-placed phrase can make for awkwardness or even for absurdity.

She was, at the time of writing, being sponsored to examine various aspects of GP fund-holding by management consultants Peat Marwick McLintock. *Options*[20]

It should be made clear that 'by management consultants' does not qualify 'fund-holding'. *At the time of writing she was being sponsored by management consultants Peat Marwick McLintock to examine various aspects of GP fund-holding.*

I have already slimmed down to six stone but wonder if you could advise me of how I could contract cholera in preparation for my departure. *Independent*[21]

The writer speaks as though he wishes to contract cholera in preparation for his departure. That last phrase must go where it belongs. *I have already slimmed down to six stone but, in preparation for my departure, I should be grateful if you could tell me in what circumstances cholera can be contracted.*

With the exception of Florida, we would pay on average about $10 to pitch our tent . . . *Complete Traveller*[22]

It sounds as though 'Florida' were one of the company who was allowed a cheaper rate. *Except in Florida, we would pay . . .*

In the smaller villages you can wake to find the hotelier's next door neighbour driving his pigs out of a stone shed thrown up against the side of his home towards the pastures. *Independent*[23]

Make clear that 'towards the pastures' has nothing to do with the side of the home, but a lot to do with driving the pigs: *to find the hotelier's next door neighbour driving his pigs towards the pastures out of a stone shed thrown up against the side of his home.*

It would give the two main agencies access to the $69 billion European market for the first time which is predicted to grow 9.2 per cent this year. *Marketing Week*[24]

Misplacing 'for the first time' creates a bad gap between 'European market' and 'which is predicted to grow'. *It would for the first time give the two main agencies access to the $69 billion European market which is predicted to grow 9.2 per cent this year.*

The worst performers are predictable, including textiles and footwear manufacture . . . *Times*[25]

It is not the performers that are predictable, but their worstness, and 'manufacture' is not a performer. *Predictably, the worst performers include textiles and footwear manufacturers.*

4 Connotational slippage

Slippage in meaning can occur between mention of a thing, be it a place, a fact, or an event on the one hand, and mention of the idea, the name, or the report of it on the other hand. The writer's safeguard is to focus with precision on every word written, carrying forward in the memory the exact connotation from each group of words to the next. We are again really concerned here with a kind of 'crossover' in which a writer loses track of his own words.

> The encouraging economic news is not yet established as a trend. *Times*[26]

It is not the *news* that may become a trend, but the matter reported in the news. The mind slides from the one to the other, and the 'slippage' occurs. *The economic improvement reported is not yet established as a trend.*

> The inflation rate has now fallen to 6.9%, taking it down towards the Chancellor's prediction of 4% by the end of the year. *Radio 4*[27]

The rate does not fall towards a prediction, but towards a predicted figure: *taking it down towards the 4% predicted by the Chancellor for the end of the year*.

> Conflict between mothers and daughters is a sure way of getting readers turning the pages. *Daily Mail*[28]

Conflict between mothers and daughters is not likely to lure people to read. Recording or imagining such conflicts may do so. And 'getting readers turning' is bad. *Recording conflict between mothers and daughters is a sure way of getting readers to turn the pages.*

> The events of the past week have reinforced the weakness of the court system as a means of establishing the truth . . . *Independent*[29]

It is not weakness that has been reinforced, but evidence of weakness. *The events of the past week have confirmed the weakness of the court system as a means of establishing the truth.*

> While the institute's final document disagrees markedly with the government over training . . . *Times*[30]

'Documents' do not enter into controversy. *While the institute's final proposals conflict markedly with the government's* . . .

> Mr Major hopes that the charter will enable the government to seize the initiative on public services. It will open a week in which the prime minister and his close advisers intend to dominate parliament and the media with a series of announcements including the

restructuring of the army and further trades union legislation. *Times*[31]

The charter is not going to 'open a week'. *Its publication will open a week* . . . The announcements are said to include a restructuring of the army, when what is meant is notification of such a restructuring: *a series of announcements including notice of the restructuring of the army and of further trades union legislation.*

In fact, at the risk of sounding conceited, I feel beautiful. *More!*[32]

The writer is rejoicing in what cosmetic surgery has done for her. But feeling is inaudible, and no one can *sound* conceited merely by having certain feelings. *In fact, at the risk of sounding conceited, I must tell you that I feel beautiful.*

With the risk of engaging in too much hyperbole – none of which is unwarranted – these stunning photographs, together with the measured yet informative text, are a true inspiration to all. *Outdoors Illustrated*[33]

As it was not *feeling* beautiful that might incur a risk of sounding conceited, but talking about it, so here no risk of hyperbole is incurred by the photographs in being a true inspiration, but only by the writer in saying so. *At the risk of engaging in too much hyperbole – justified though it might be – I must declare these stunning photographs . . . a true inspiration to all.*

As my train approached Euston the other day, the guard announced very clearly: 'For the benefit of all passengers, the buffet bar is now closed'. *Times*[34]

This burlesques the error we are exploring – mixing up talk about something and talk about the talk. The presumed 'benefit' lies in passengers' having the information, not in the buffet's being closed. *For the benefit of all passengers, I am announcing that the buffet bar is now closed.*

Brian Blessed was involved with the film and was so impressed he commissioned Clive to sculpt Mallory and Irving, an exquisite finely-detailed piece which involved painstaking research. *Cumbria*[35]

You cannot say 'He was asked to paint his mother, a beautifully executed piece of work' because his mother was not a piece of work and, presumably, was not executed. Nor did Mallory and Irving constitute a finely-detailed piece. Moreover, 'impressed' should be followed by 'that': *so impressed that he commissioned Clive to sculpt Mallory and Irving. The sculpture was a finely-detailed piece which involved painstaking research.*

His name was Bernard Davenport, already an accomplished railway photographer and leading member of the Railway Correspondence and Travel Society. *Steam Railway*[36]

The subject of this sentence is 'His name', not 'Bernard Davenport', and his name was not a railway photographer. Why bother with the word 'name'? *He was Bernard Davenport, already an accomplished railway photographer.*

However, this isolated survivor well-illustrates the paucity of specimens that have escaped the pillaging of the last century. *Country-Side*[37]

(The 'survivor' is a mummified cat.) In itself the survivor does not 'illustrate' what is suggested. It is the *fact* that there is only one survivor that 'illustrates' the point. *However, the fact that there is only this isolated survivor well-illustrates how few specimens have escaped the pillaging of last century.*

The East End of London is probably stretching the concept of East Anglia too far . . . *BBC Wildlife*[38]

Obviously the East End cannot stretch anything, not even a concept. *To refer to the East End of London under the heading 'East Anglia' is probably to stretch a point.*

5 Loss of control

We turn now to sentences in which there is loss of control in respect of vocabulary, meaning, or syntax, and sometimes of all three.

Without any weight penalty the Micro has ended the compromise between a comfortable night and a back-breaking experience. *The Great Outdoors*[39]

(The 'Micro' is a new light-weight tent.) It is difficult to conceive of a 'compromise' between comfort and backache, but it is not hard to see what the writer ought to have said: *the Micro has eliminated the need to choose between comfort at night and comfort when walking.*

Even looking into the sun, which I love to do, whilst ironing out much colour, nevertheless has its own subtlety and appeal alongside the contrast. *The Artist*[40]

This sentence says that looking into the sun, while ironing out much colour, has its own subtlety and appeal. But is it the *looking* that irons out the colour? And is it the *looking* that has subtlety and appeal? And what is 'the contrast'? *The effect of looking into the sun is to iron out much colour, but it confers subtlety and appeal.*

To many the Great Western was all that was right with the world. Others could hardly bare to mouth its name . . . The old chestnut 'God's Wonderful Railway' or one of its many counterpoints 'Got Wet and Rusted'; whatever our cherished affinities we can all take pleasure in every aspect of the limitless railway bounty bequeathed us. *British Railways Illustrated*[41]

'Bare' of course should be 'bear'. By 'counterpoints' the writer probably means 'counterparts', though a better word would be 'variations'. By 'affinities' he probably means 'allegiances'. The second sentence begins with a subject ('The old chestnut') and exemplifies it, but then seemingly forgets it, for it leads nowhere.

If an Englishman's home is his castle, it would figure that his tent or caravan – home from home – would be the next best thing: almost equivalent to uprooting his house by its foundations and replanting it at his favourite holiday destination. *Weekend Telegraph*[42]

What is the 'it' of 'it would figure'? Is 'figure' a mistake for 'follow'? A caravan cannot be 'the equivalent of uprooting' a home, though betaking oneself to a caravan could be. *If the Englishman's home is his castle, perhaps his tent or caravan is the next best thing, a home from home achieved by removing the house to his favourite holiday destination.*

The respondents, however, in spite of their doubts about the single currency, foresaw many benefits, including the elimination of the risks involved with currency exchange . . . and the psychological benefits attached because of a strengthening of the bonds between countries and it being evidence of a united European economic power. *Marketing Week*[43]

A breakdown in sense and syntax comes with the word 'because'. The writer does not really mean 'benefits attached *because of*' this or that, but 'benefits arising from' this or that. Moreover the gerciple ('it being evidence of') must become a gerund ('its being evidence of') or go: *and the psychological benefits arising from a strengthening of the bonds between countries and the evidence it provides of a united European economic power.*

In most towns and cities the local museum is a potted history of British ceramic design, and many of the names synonymous with the first splendid blaze of English china design – Wedgwood, Spode, Doulton, Derby and Minton – are still with us, albeit in diluted form. *Harpers & Queen*[44]

Surely the 'local museum *provides*' (not 'is') a potted history. For the misuse of 'synonymous with' see Chapter VIII, 1. How can 'names' such as Wedgwood be 'with us . . . in diluted form'? What is the diluted form of 'Wedgwood'? Obviously the writer means something that she has not said, something, presumably, pertaining to the quality of the china and its design, not to that of the names.

> You are flexible on what you charge people, remember do not be too greedy as repeat custom is the best custom and so are the people they refer you to. *Money-Maker*[45]

This is advice on starting a travel-agency. Something more than a comma is needed before 'remember', and the construction is 'remember not to', not 'remember do not'. The worst error is the use of 'they', which has nothing to relate back to. *Be flexible on what you charge people: remember not to be too greedy, for customers who come a second time are what you want, and so are the people they recruit for you.*

> Midsummer's day saw the departure of the Brixham trawler Lorne Leader (built in 1892) for a birdwatching week with. Carrying twelve visitors and four crew plus bird-watching leader, a route through the inner Hebrides gave plenty of choice to allow for wind and weather. *Country-Side*[46]

You might say 'He was a nice chap to get along with', but you would not speak of the departure of a boat 'for a holiday with'. Moreover, the above sentence tells us that a route through the inner Hebrides carried twelve visitors and four crew. *Midsummer's day saw the departure of the Brixham trawler Lorne Leader for a bird-watching trip. It carried twelve visitors and four crew with a bird-watching leader, and the route through the inner Hebrides was to be chosen according to the weather conditions.*

4 ILLOGICALITY

1 Non sequitur after 'although/despite/if'
'Although he was clever, he missed the point.' That represents typical usage of 'although'. A clever person is not expected to miss the point, and therefore the sentence makes sense. But 'Although he was clever, he took the point immediately' does not make sense because the contrast expected after 'although' has failed to appear.

> Mbabane itself, though small with only 40,000 people, is not particularly attractive. *Independent*[1]

Even so the expected contrast fails to appear here. 'Though' is misused for there is no necessary connection between being small and being attractive. *Mbabane itself, a small place with only 40,000 people, is not particularly attractive.*

> Although the guidelines, produced principally for consultants, fail to define extra capacity, that could include paying for closed beds or wards to reopen or by funding extra clinics over the week-ends. *Times*[2]

This is a criticism of the GPs guide on queue-jumping. 'Although' is again misplaced. There is no relationship of logical contrast between the failure of the guidelines to define extra capacity and what that extra capacity might amount to. Use 'but' and get rid of the ungrammatical 'by'. *The guidelines . . . fail to define extra capacity, but it could include paying for closed beds or wards to reopen, or funding extra clinics over the week-ends.*

> Although I only came to know her well towards the end of her life, she really was an extraordinary character . . . *Times*[3]

Once more there is no proper relationship of contrast between getting to know her only towards the end of her life and the fact that she was an extraordinary person. The word 'although' must go. *I only came to know her well towards the end of her life, but I found her an extraordinary character.*

> Despite his international reputation as a financier, Hurl was a man of great natural charm and modesty. *Times*[4]

'Despite' also should introduce a contrast. It is invidious to suggest an accepted antithesis between being an international financier and having charm and modesty. Cut out 'despite'. *Hurl, a financier of international repute, was a man of great natural charm.*

> If banking appeals to you or you are currently working in the financial sector, we are looking for bright young secretaries with at least a year's experience. *Times*[5]

This is a false conditional. The firm is presumably looking for bright young secretaries whether banking appeals to you or not. Get rid of 'if' : *Does banking appeal to you? Are you currently working in the financial sector? We are looking for bright young secretaries.*

> If you fail to find the name of the new company, there is now a pensions tracing service, the Pensions Registry, which may be able to help. *Good Housekeeping*[6]

Again the conditional is false. The pensions tracing service is there whether you fail or not to find the name of the new company. Either remove 'if'– *For anyone who fails to find the name of the new company there is now a pensions tracing service* – or complete the conditional sequence: *If you fail to find the name of the new company, you should consult the pensions tracing service.*

> If you were thinking about making some sort of long-term commitment, this is the best time to start thinking about it. *Me*[7]

'If you were thinking . . . this is the time to start thinking.' This astrologer seems to have been learning from the Delphic oracle.

> Opaque tights are still big business this year and can be worn with anything and they have a real slimming effect on the legs, if that's why Alison doesn't like to show them off! *Catch*[8]

One has to guess at the meaning here. 'If' won't do as it is, for plainly the slimming effect of the tights is not dependent upon Alison's reason for disliking something. Presumably 'show them' refers to the legs and not to the tights. I'm inclined to paraphrase thus: 'They have a slimming effect on the legs, which will be relevant to Alison, should she think her legs too fat to exhibit.'

> Time passes while they are found and brought, unless, of course, they are missing or the form has not been filled out right. *Times*[9]

Time passes anyway. It will not cease to pass even if the forms are missing or incorrectly filled in.

2 Inherent contradiction

Sometimes the logical sequence is disturbed to such an extent that an element of contradiction enters into what is said.

> A supranational authority, least of all one so ruthlessly centralised in its power structures as the Soviet Union, is not essential to the peace and prosperity of disparate peoples: indeed this thesis is one of the most awful fallacies of history. *Times*[10]

To what does 'this thesis' refer? If I said 'Two and two make four: this thesis is incontrovertible', you would know that the thesis in question was 'Two and two make four'. But the *Times* leader-writer says that a supranational authority is not essential and then contradicts himself by declaring 'this thesis' to be a terrible fallacy. *A supranational authority . . . is not essential to the peace and prosperity of disparate peoples: indeed, the thesis that it is so is one of the most awful fallacies of history.*

> Basically similar to the Johnson locomotives, the few differences were gradually eroded during overhauls and rebuildings and both

the Johnson and Pickersgill engines were put into the D41 class . . .
Steam Classic [11]

The 'few differences' of course are not 'similar'. *Basically similar to the Johnson locomotives, the Pickersgill models had a few differences which were gradually eliminated* (*sic*).

His formidable musical gifts allied to a monastic vocation never coexisted comfortably . . . *Times* [12]

If there was no comfortable coexistence then the musical gifts cannot be said to have been 'allied' to the monastic vocation. Omit the word. *His formidable musical gifts and his monastic vocation never coexisted comfortably.*

If you've followed your diet and lost the weight you wanted, you definitely deserve to have fun on holiday . . . *Prima* [13]

If I've lost the book I wanted, I regret the loss. If you've lost the weight you wanted, you are slimmer than you want to be. *If you've followed your diet and lost the weight you wanted to lose . . .*

Non-response to individual items on the questionnaire may also occur. *Nursing Standard* [14]

Non-events cannot 'occur'. *People may fail to respond to individual items on the questionnaire.*

It's true that my mother was left a large sum of money by one of her admirers, so there wasn't much talk of survival. *Artists & Illustrators Magazine* [15]

In fact what is meant here is that there was not much talk of possible *failure* to survive: *so there was no threat to our survival.*

According to Mr Nantke, it will take 10 years to bring the level of air and water pollution up to west German standards . . . *Independent* [16]

No one, we hope, is trying to raise the level of pollution. Either change 'pollution' – *it will take 10 years to bring the level of air and water purity up to west German standards* – or substitute 'down' for 'up': *It will take 10 years to bring the level of air and water pollution down to west German standards.*

He possesses a charisma which reaches a wide field, and his continuing high-profile involvement with the game is essential if variety of character and style of approach is not to reduce the appeal of cricket. *The Cricketer* [17]

This appears to say the opposite of what is intended . . . *is essential if cricket is going to keep the variety of character and style of approach which gives the game its appeal.*

. . . the machinery devised by the UN (for arranging the release of hostages) is working steadily, if erratically. *Radio 4*[18]

To use 'steadily' for 'slowly' might pass if you were speaking about, say, the approach of a car. But 'steadily' really means 'with steadiness' and you can't be steady and erratic at the same time. Rewrite: *working slowly, if erratically.*

Though it shouldn't present any significant risks if you buy through a franchised dealer, it's inconvenient and time consuming, and not a little worrying that everything will work out as planned. *Moneywise*[19]

One doesn't worry *that* everything will work well: *not a little worrying lest everything may not work out as planned.*

3 Irrationality

The delay is caused by the company's decision to enlarge the ship while it is still being built. *Caravan Magazine*[20]

Until the thing is actually 'built' there is no ship to enlarge. You can increase the planned size. *There is delay because the company has decided to increase the planned size of the ship under construction.*

Sprinkle the grated chocolate over the top then sprinkle the cinnamon. If your spice jar has sprinkle holes in the top be careful they are not large ones. *Lancashire Life*[21]

If your jar has sprinkle holes, no amount of care on your part can make them either smaller or larger. *Take care not to use a sprinkle jar with large sprinkle holes.*

The new wheels and con-rods are two big hurdles climbed . . . *Steam Railway*[22]

Wheels and con-rods are not hurdles to be climbed. *The acquisition of new wheels and con-rods is a great achievement.*

Like Tenterden before it the village of Rolvenden was some distance away . . . *British Railways Illustrated*[23]

The context is that a new railway has reached Rolvenden and a station has been built there. *As was the case at Tenterden, the village of Rolvenden was some distance away from the station.*

The nanny, then called Carol Prowling as she has since married, told the parents that Simon . . . had rolled on to toy keys left in his cot. *Times*[24]

It is not because she has since married that she was then called Carol Prowling. Indeed she would have been called Carol Prowling then even were she still single now. Better use brackets: *The nanny, then called Carol Prowling (she has since married), told the parents.*

I don't see any reason why you should ever deny yourself any visual reference. In the past the photograph would have been the engraving which every studio had in great numbers. *The Artist*[25]

Photographs are always photographs. *In the past the equivalent of today's photograph was the engraving.*

The reasons go back to the beginnings of modern European civilisation, when art was, as it is again now, a commodity. *Harpers & Queen*[26]

The question answered above is, why have wealthy tycoons always collected works of art? The 'reasons' do not 'go back'. The 'reasons' are the substance of the explanation for the phenomenon in question as now advanced. They stay with us in our own age as we formulate them. The fact that they direct our minds backwards does not set them in motion. *For an explanation we must look back to the beginnings of modern European civilisation.*

Several dew ponds in West Sussex are now being restored or even created like the one at Truleigh Hall, near Shoreham. *Country-Side*[27]

The word 'or' is used but no true alternatives are presented. If you have a dew pond, you cannot choose between restoring it and creating it. *Several dew ponds are now being restored in West Sussex and some new ones created like the one at Truleigh Hall.*

Do present-day Christians really believe, as many of our forbears undoubtedly did, that all unevangelised souls go straight to Hell? Or is it more true to say that goodness forced on people under threat of torture is not goodness at all? *Independent*[28]

The writer, the Archbishop of York, misuses 'or'. After the question 'Do presentday Christians really believe something?', his 'or' should introduce a genuine alternative, 'Or do they believe something else?' Instead of which he asks 'Is it more true to say? . . .' It is elementary to understand that there are no degrees of being 'true'. Nothing can be 'more true' than something else. And what is the force of 'to say'? Why include the words? The succeeding logic is equally faulty. If 'goodness forced on people' is 'not goodness at all', then why call it goodness in the first place? The argument lacks any precision. *Does belief in Hell hold water? Can fear of punishment ever have any place in fostering goodness?*

4 Degrees of absurdity

The danger of peanuts can be quite as severe as that found in those who suffer from allergy to penicillin, bee-stings, shellfish . . . *Times*[29]

The danger from peanuts must not to be compared with something 'found' in people who have allergies, but with the danger from penicillin, bee-stings, shellfish etc. *Peanuts can be as dangerous to those with a particular allergy as are penicillin, bee-stings, shellfish.*

Gifford is now preserved by the Boat Museum at Ellesmere Port. Unfortunately, being built of wood, time has taken its toll and she is the object of a restoration appeal. *Old Glory*[30]

It sounds as though time is built of wood. *Unfortunately, being made of wood, she has suffered from the passage of time . . .*

But a particularly narrow piece of road meant that anything bigger than a couple of cars couldn't pass at the same time. *Cumbria Life*[31]

Replace 'meant' by 'ensured' and 'anything bigger . . . couldn't' by 'nothing bigger . . . could'. Vehicles can pass each other only if they are present simultaneously. Therefore 'at the same time' is redundant. *The narrowness of a certain section of the road ensured that no vehicles larger than cars could pass each other there.*

Willy Forde met us with the comment that he was glad we had not been drinking the night before, a fact with which my head begged to differ. *The Field*[32]

The writer is implying that the 'fact' was not a fact. If it were, it would not be disputable: *a theory which my head begged to dispute.*

Do you wear rings? The fingers you wear them on are very revealing. *New Woman*[33]

The fingers are not revealing. It is the positioning of the rings, or the *choice* of finger which can be called 'revealing'. *Which fingers you choose to wear them on can be very revealing.*

The minimum investment is £2,000 up to a maximum of £6,000. *Moneywise.*[34]

Why 'up to', which implies that the 'minimum' rises? *The minimum investment is £2,000 and the maximum £6,000.*

> Stagnant economic growth in the West, mild weather in Europe and the US and high prices because of the Gulf crisis lessened the world's thirst for oil last year. *Independent*[35]

There can be no such thing as 'stagnant' growth. The two words cancel each other out. The phrase introduced by 'because' cannot qualify 'high prices' (see Chapter V, 2). *Lack of economic growth in the West, mild weather in Europe and the US and high prices caused by the Gulf crisis lessened the world's thirst for oil last year.*

> Never ostentatious, but with perfection in every respect, you could find yourself sitting next to Nancy Mitford, a prince, a prime minister, or a curate. *Times*[36]

The gracious description ('never ostentatious . . .') is meant for the subject of this obituary, who is not mentioned at all in the sentence. Instead the obituarist applies it to 'you'. *In entertaining guests she was never ostentatious . . . and you could find yourself sitting next to Nancy Mitford.*

> But good walking shoes are a far better way to see the sights . . . *Times*[37]

Shoes are not a way of seeing anything. *It is far better to see the sights in good walking shoes.*

> Rogue Male became a classic. Stephen Leather has written another on the theme . . . His Chinaman is actually Vietnamese, but that is deliberate. *Daily Mail*[38]

Since the writer is talking about the content of a book, how could any of it be other than 'deliberate'? *. . . but that is significant.*

5 'no exception'

The expressions 'is no exception' is frequently misused. Before defining something as not being exceptional, you must establish clearly what the generalisation is which the given instance exemplifies.

> Brookner couldn't write a bad story if she tried and *Brief Lives* is no exception. *New Woman*[39]

If the sentence had read 'Brookner generally writes good books and *Brief Lives* is no exception' we should recognise the generalisation to which the new book provides no exception. The new book would *exemplify* the general rule advanced. But it would be impossible to exemplify the generalisation that Brookner couldn't write a bad book if she tried. *Brookner always writes good stories and* Brief Lives *is one such.*

> Relations between chief executives and their finance directors
> become tense at times and bowling-to-discos combine First Lei-
> sure is no exception. *Daily Telegraph*[40]

In this case there is no *general* rule to which the facts given might
supply an exception, for relations between executives and finance
directors, it is said, become tense only *at times*. Thus neither a given
instance of tension nor a given instance of lack of tension could ever
provide an 'exception'. *Relations between chief executives and their
finance directors become tense at times, as has happened at bowling-to-
discos combine First Leisure.*

> Rarely do Court of Chivalry depositions provide a complete picture
> of a man's military career and Goushill's is no exception: a man of
> seventy years, he tells the court rather endearingly that his memory
> is not what it was. *History Today*[41]

The word 'rarely' here makes it illogical to speak of a given instance as
either an 'exception' or 'no exception'. The generalisation allows of
instances either way: . . . *and Goushill's is a case in point.*

> When Reader's Digest bring out the latest of their chunky books,
> you can bet it was produced with a cast of thousands. Their new
> gardening volume *A Garden for All Seasons*, £21.95, is no excep-
> tion. *Practical Gardening*[42]

Their new gardening volume . . . illustrates the point.

> I've driven a variety of cars and few fall into the memorable
> category, but the XM is an exception. *Good Housekeeping*[43]

Here we have the converse error. The XM clearly is *not* an exception,
for the operative word in the generalisation is 'few': *few fall into the
memorable category, but the XM is one of them.*

– VII –

VERBAL SENSITIVITY

Sensitivity in the use of words is a matter of good taste as well as of accuracy. Here we consider various forms of laxity and imprecision which mar contemporary writing.

1 ERRORS OF EXCESS

1 Duplication

You might say 'He gave me a bracelet' or 'His gift to me was a bracelet', but you would not say 'He gave me the gift of a bracelet'. That is one kind of duplication.

> A major source of such funding would have to come from Scottish owners and those who fish in Scotland . . . *Times*[1]

(The issue is the future of salmon fishing.) You might say 'A major source of such funding would be Scottish owners' or 'Such funding would have to come from Scottish owners', but not that the source would have to come from Scottish owners, because the Scottish owners are themselves the source. *A major source of such funding would have to be Scottish owners and those who fish in Scotland.*

> The Palestinians will obtain a homeland and Yasser Arafat, Saddam's ally, will watch with satisfaction as the genesis of a Palestinian state is created on the West Bank . . . *Independent*[2]

To talk of creating a genesis is similarly duplicative. Either cut out 'is created' – *Yasser Arafat will watch with satisfaction the genesis of a Palestinian state on the West Bank* – or change the word 'genesis': *Yasser Arafat will watch with satisfaction as the nucleus of a Palestinian state is created on the West Bank.*

> With its origins founded more than two centuries ago this company, now part of a major multi-million pound group, has established an enviable reputation . . . *Times*[3]

You can found a company, but you cannot found an origin. Cut out 'with its origins'. *Founded more than two centuries ago, this company . . . has established an enviable reputation.*

As well as requiring that the job was done to the highest standards, and conserving as much of the house as possible, the newspaper's requirements imposed a particular timetable on the renovation. *Old House Journal*[4]

We cannot have requirements requiring something. Moreover you require that a job 'be done' not 'was done'. And it is a mistake to make 'conserving' parallel to 'requiring' as though the newspaper was (1) 'requiring' and (2) 'conserving'. That the job be done to the highest standards and that as much of the house as possible be conserved are two parallel requirements. *As well as requiring that the job be done to the highest possible standards and as much as possible of the house be conserved, the newspaper imposed a particular timetable on the renovation.*

As the conical form of Stromboli looms large on the horizon there is no mistaking its volcanic ancestry – it epitomises the archetypal textbook volcano. *Complete Traveller*[5]

To 'epitomise' is to typify in perfection and an 'archetype' is a perfectly typical example. The use of the two words is duplicative. Moreover 'textbook', as here used, seems to turn duplication into triplication. Better economise: *it is the archetypal volcano.*

The depersonalisation of sex is not only confined to men. *New Woman*[6]

The word 'only' is out of place. If something is not confined to men then it does not concern or apply *only* to men. That is what 'confined' means. In any case, if you are going to say that something is 'not only' confined, you must go on to explain what else it is. *The depersonalisation of sex is not confined to men.*

The result of the poll tax fiasco has not merely wasted public funds, it has also meant that voters are effectively unable to make choices about the level of services they like locally. *Times*[7]

You might say 'Eating raw apples gives me indigestion' or you might say 'My indigestion is the result of eating raw apples', but you cannot say 'The result of eating raw apples gives me indigestion'. In the same way it is the poll tax fiasco, not the result, that has 'wasted public funds', for the result is itself the wastage of public funds. *The poll tax fiasco has not only resulted in the waste of public funds, it has also meant . . .*

What makes this book such a success, and a pleasure to read, owes much to the visual impact made by the delightfully drawn humorous characters depicting the action and illustrating the text. *Cumbria Life*[8]

Surely the choice should be between 'What makes this book such a success . . . is the visual impact', and 'The success of this book . . . owes much to the visual impact'. It is wasteful duplication to conjoin 'What makes . . . such a success' and 'success . . . owes much'.

2 Anticipatory duplication

It must ·be seen with deep regret the way in which the financial institutions have dealt with George Walker. *Times*[9]

This is 'anticipatory duplication'. The word 'it' anticipates 'the way'. The substance of the sentence is 'The way in which the financial institutions have dealt with George Walker must be seen with great regret'. The natural construction after 'It must be seen with deep regret' would be 'that the financial institutions have dealt harshly with George Walker'. Better scrap 'it'. *We see with deep regret how the financial institutions have dealt with George Walker.*

In a recent article by Richard Stapley he said 'I have never subscribed to the rather hair-shirt view that gathering bait is in some way superior to buying it.' *Sea Angler*[10]

Here the duplication 'Richard Stapley' and 'he' is absurd: *In a recent article Richard Stapley said 'I have never subscribed to the view.'*

For example, by not going out or talking to anyone, it ensures that however much you want to meet someone you won't – it's a physical impossibility. *19*[11]

Once more the trouble arises through starting a clause with a preposition. In the previous example it was 'in'. Here it is 'by'. Omit 'by' and omit 'it' along with the comma that precedes it. *For example, not going out or talking to anyone ensures that however much you want to meet someone, you won't.*

For the last four days I have been motoring in Holland with a friend, it being my idea to show her the finer points of north Holland . . . *The Oldie*[12]

The writer is Germaine Greer and the construction is barbaric . . . *motoring in Holland with a friend, my idea being to show her . . .*

Sheep dog trials are also included in the programme, although it must be pointed out that to anyone brought up on the series of 'One Man and his Dog', they may not quite appreciate the lack of cooperation on the part of the sheep . . . *Cumbria*[13]

'To anyone brought up . . . they may not appreciate'. Again it is the fatal introductory preposition ('to') that ensnares: . . . *although it must be pointed out that anyone brought up on the series 'One Man and his Dog' may not quite appreciate the lack of cooperation.*

> So for those who don't yet own their own yacht, or don't want the costs of running their own holiday home, they can 'borrow' Necker and make it theirs for a few days or a few weeks. *Lancashire Life*[14]

Apply the same treatment here. Get rid of 'for' and 'they'. *So those who don't yet own their own yacht, or don't want the costs of running their own holiday home can 'borrow' Necker.*

3 Duplication of construction

Errors of this kind seem to spring as much from carelessness as from ignorance of grammar.

> Starting with picture or 'baby' books that have one picture on each page, lovely bright colours to attract a child's eye, you can start to connect pictures with words. *Annabel*[15]

This is surely a case in point. *Using picture or 'baby' books . . . you can start to connect pictures with words.*

> If the Middle East peace process breaks down in mutual recrimination, the West should not be surprised if hostage-taking is resumed. *Daily Telegraph*[16]

This is not a gross example, but it occurs in a leading article. English does have alternative usages which save a writer from having to repeat 'if' in this way. *Were the Middle East peace process to break down in mutual recrimination, the West should not be suprised if hostage-taking is resumed.*

> It is often forgotten that the clergy stipend is stretched to breaking point when two or three children are at school when, even in the maintained sector, music lessons, school travel and uniform must be paid for. *Times*[17]

The first 'when' (meaning 'at the time when') is a thoroughgoing 'when' which can stand, but the second 'when' (meaning 'in circumstances where') is not irreplaceable. *It is often forgotten that the clergy stipend is stretched to breaking point when two or three children are at school for, even in the maintained sector, music lessons, school travel and uniform must be paid for.*

> To allow us to build on that success and achieve the necessary change in perception to allow us to remain at the heart of the weight control business we had to focus our attention on far more than just a range of new products. *Money-Maker*[18]

The repeated 'to allow us' will not do. Change the first – *In order to build on that success* – or better still, change both: *In order to build on that success and achieve the necessary change in perception to enable us to remain at the heart of the weight control business.*

> Paint can be used wet over dry paint, dry paper or using a rather dry brush. *Artists & Illustrators Magazine*[19]

.You cannot say 'Paint can be used using a dry brush', for the paint does not use a brush. Moreover, the grammatical sequence which should follow 'or' is broken. It would be correct to say 'You can walk over his footpaths, his lawns, or his flower beds', but incorrect to say 'You can walk over his footpaths, his lawns or using a spade'. I am not sure what the sentence means.

> . . . friendly staff members are vitally important to the venture's success, and thus the volunteer's ability to be able to share their hobby with the public. *Old Glory*[20]

Repeat the preposition 'to' and cut out 'to be able': *and thus to the volunteers' ability to share their hobby.*

4 Redundancy

> Its main weakness is that it lacks wardrobe space, which means the space provided for hanging clothes is limited. *Caravan Magazine*[21]

One is tempted to say 'It does indeed mean that'. What else could 'wardrobe space' mean? This is straight repetition disguised as explanation. *Its main weakness is that it lacks wardrobe space.*

> There are two different uses that a compass can be put to. Both are linked, in as much as they help you to get from A to B, but they involve using the compass in different ways. *Country Walking*[22]

If there are two and they are linked, then the word 'both' adds nothing. You cannot have one 'linked' on its own. Moreover 'in as much as' is here a lengthy way of saying 'in that'. Either disconnect 'both' from 'linked' and attach it to 'help' – *They are linked, in that they both help you to get from A to B* – or, better still, get rid of all the waste words: *Both help you to get from A to B.*

> Still, the GWS could never quite escape the recurring suggestion that the Didcot locomotive collection would always be incomplete without a 'King' and thus there is a certain degree of inevitability that the works overhaul now being conducted on 'KEII' at Didcot, would always happen one day. *Steam Railway*[23]

There cannot be degrees of inevitability. If a thing is inevitable it is inevitable, and if it isn't it isn't. In any case to say that something 'would always happen one day' is merely to repeat that it was inevitable: *and thus the works overhaul now being conducted on 'KEII' at Didcot was bound to happen one day.*

> The Shawl is a limestone ridge extending almost to Preston under Scar, in the process providing glorious views up the length of Wensleydale. *Dalesman*[24]

The phrase 'in the process' is wordily inappropriate. *The Shawl is a limestone ridge extending almost to Preston under Scar and providing glorious views up the length of Wensleydale.*

> Although other studies have been published during the same time period, comparisons cannot be made . . . *Nursing Standard*[25]

Omit the redundant word 'time': *during the same period.*

> It will not happen overnight, of course, and nor should it. *The Cricketer*[26]

The word 'nor' combines the two meanings, 'and' and 'not'. It is redundant therefore to add another 'and'. *It will not happen overnight, of course, nor should it.*

5 Adjectival overkill

There are some adjectives which by their very meaning cannot have comparative and superlative forms. For instance, if a thing is 'unique', it is the only instance of its kind, it is without equal or parallel. It is therefore illogical to call anything 'more unique' or 'less unique'.

> I can think of no more ideal gift than a season ticket to the Royal Shakespeare Company, allowing one to see all their current productions in a period of six weeks. *Meridian*[27]

This, alas, is Jeffrey Archer. He ought to know that 'ideal' is used of something that cannot be bettered or improved upon. It is therefore illogical to proclaim anything 'more ideal'. *I can think of no more desirable gift than a season ticket to the Royal Shakespeare Company.*

> I find it hard to imagine a more perfect paragon of undomestic bliss. *Times*[28]

Most of us find it impossible to imagine a '*more* perfect' anything. If a thing is perfect there can be nothing 'more perfect'. The concept is nonsensical. The error is compounded here. A 'paragon' is a pattern of excellence. It is not something that admits of degrees of quality. It is perfection. The writer is not only speaking of a 'perfect perfection' but of a 'more perfect perfection'. *I find it hard to imagine a better instance of undomestic bliss.*

> The Cabernet really comes through most strongly in the deep thick colour and the leafy nose, with the Nero d'Avola most present in the lighter fruit notes over young strong tannin. *Decanter*[29]

If a thing is 'present' it is present and nothing else can be 'more present' than it. Nor can there be a third thing, which would be 'most present' of all. *The Cabernet really comes through most strongly in the deep thick colour and the leafy nose, with the Nero d'Avola most evident in the lighter fruit notes.*

> Most areas will have further showers with more normal temperatures. *Radio 4*[30]

Can there be degrees of 'normality'? A temperature might be nearer to the average than another, and thus 'nearer to the normal'. But 'more average' and 'more normal' are not tenable concepts.

2 ERRORS OF OMISSION

1 Missing a step
In written English we have to avoid the kind of careless thinking which often governs our conversation so that we jump a step and, under strict scrutiny, the meaning is impaired.

> On Saturday we'll print the voucher you need to go with the tokens, as well as the stadiums across the country that will be taking part. *Sun*[1]

The paper will not print the stadiums, but their names. *On Saturday we'll print the vouchers you need to go with the tokens as well as the names of the stadiums across the country.*

> His most dangerous operation was a mine which had brought Chatham Dockyard to a standstill . . . *Times*[2]

His most dangerous operation was disposal of a mine . . .

> One obstacle to reform is simple, and should be easy to remove. It is Kenneth Baker. *Times*[3]

It is incorrect to describe the obstacle as simple when you mean that its removal would be simple: *one obstacle to reform could be simply removed.* (The joke is bought too dearly.)

Loyal readers will remember that some weeks ago I announced my intention of putting my goose eggs in an incubator in order to avoid last year's exploding egg disasters. *Oldie*[4]

Germaine Greer (for it is she) should know that it is far too late to avoid (or more correctly 'prevent') anything that happened last year: *in order to prevent a repetition of last year's exploding egg disasters.*

Proper police accountability should have been addressed long ago. *Guardian*[5]

You cannot 'address' accountability. *The need for proper police accountability should have been addressed long ago.*

The National Union of Public Employees has formally lodged a dispute with management. *Nursing Standard*[6]

You cannot 'lodge' a dispute. *The National Union of Public Employees has formally lodged notice of a dispute.*

Barry Jones, the shadow Welsh secretary, described the plans as 'unbalanced' by the lack of an assembly which, he said, was vital to the reform of local government. *Times*[7]

You would not say 'The architect's drawing lacked a WC' but 'provision for a WC'. *Barry Jones, the shadow Welsh secretary, described the plans as 'unbalanced' by lack of any provision for an assembly.*

There are no easy solutions to teaching deaf children . . . *BDA Newsletter*[8]

There are no easy solutions to the problems of teaching deaf children . . .

The ideas a choreographer has only come into existence through other people's bodies. *Viva*[9]

This suggests a peculiar relationship between mind and matter in the genesis of choreography. *The ideas a choreographer has only come into existence through observing other people's bodies.*

Specific recommendations, like the separation of chairman and chief executive, and a full quota of independent non-executive directors, make sense. *Independent*[10]

Neither 'the separation of chairman and chief executive' nor 'a full quote of independent non-executive directors' constitutes a 'recommendation'. Moreover, 'the separation of chairman and chief executive' makes it sound as though they are man and wife at loggerheads. It is their posts that are to be separated. *Specific recommendations, like the proposals to separate the posts of chairman and chief executive and to have a full quota of non-executive directors, make sense.*

> The memo to the Health Select Committee contained recommendations to improve the handling of child abuse, including an improvement in internal communications to identify and deal urgently with high risk cases. *Independent*[11]

Presumably the participle 'including' depends on 'recommendations'. But recommendations cannot *include* 'an improvement'; they can only recommend it: *recommendations for improving the handling of child abuse cases, in particular the internal communications by which high risk cases are identified and urgently dealt with.*

> Services over the whole line began almost a year to the day after the original section, on 28th May 1939. *British Railways Illustrated*[12]

The writer means to tell us that the services over the whole line began a year after they began over the first section of the line. *Services over the whole line began almost a year after the opening of the original section on 28th May 1939.*

> Would you like to spend a weekend away, staying in the luxury of a Hilton Hotel but at half the cost? *Woman's Journal*[13]

Half the cost of what? That is the natural question. 'Half the cost usually involved' is what is meant. We can abbreviate further: *staying in the luxury of a Hilton Hotel but at half the usual cost.*

> The alarm was summarised by Richard Solomon ... *Sunday Times*[14]

The cause of the alarm was summarised ...

> He has instructed his solicitor to explore an action for damages. *Independent*[15]

Either insert a word – *to explore the possibilities of an action for damages* – or change the verb: *to prepare an action for damages.*

2 Missing a word or words

The sentences under the heading 'Missing a step' showed how the mind makes a jump which in fact registers a loss of meaning. We now turn to sentences in which the omission causes a grammatical lapse.

> Our main concern is that because this bank was so in the news a report should have been given to councillors ... *Guardian*[16]

Correct 'so in the news': *because this bank was so much in the news a report should have been given to councillors.*

202

Instead, working with Julian Harrap, Foster has brought ultra-Modern Palladian and Italianate design together in a way that, while each is allowed to show off its particular qualities, none is allowed to stifle the others. *Independent*[17]

The phrase 'in a way that' requires grammatical completion in a relative clause – 'in a way that I like'. You cannot say 'I designed the rooms in a way that none is bigger than another'. Add the word 'such': *has brought ultra-Modern Palladian and Italianate design together in such a way that . . . none is allowed to stifle the other.*

The Field Studies Council has nine residential and one day centre across England and Wales . . . *Artists & Illustrators Magazine*[18]

It is incorrect to say 'The Council has nine . . . centre', whatever words may intervene between 'nine' and 'centre'. There is no escape from repetition. *The Field Studies Council has nine residential centres and one day centre across England and Wales.*

This gave me some breathing space away from Mike to think through my problems . . . *Family Circle*[19]

. . . breathing space away from Mike in which to think through my problems.

'O Tingis! Tingis! O dementa Tingis . . .' St Augustine lamented a city that allures in the same sudden, furtive manner it repels. *Harpers & Queen*[20]

The omission of 'as' is the colloquialism of the prole, scarcely to be expected here: *a city that allures in the same sudden, furtive manner as it repels.*

The inevitable of course happened, no sooner had the wagon stopped its forward momentum it started back towards Chessington . . . *British Railways Illustrated*[21]

Omitting 'than' is a comparable vulgarism: *no sooner had the wagon stopped its forward movement than it started back.*

To move from a saxophone-playing, motor-cycling dentist to become a world-renowned and world-respected surgeon might have turned the heads of lesser men. *Independent*[22]

To move from being a saxophone-playing, motor-cycling dentist to become a world-renowned and world-respected surgeon . . .

In the interests of spectator safety, the parade ring has been moved to between the tents and the lane so as to give horses direct access to the course. *Horse & Hound*[23]

You cannot move to 'between' things but only to the space between them: *has been moved to the space between the tents and the lane.*

> Not all the taverns in *Pickwick Papers* are as delightful as this one. English inns are still as variable as they were in Dickens' time, and probably since the day Chaucer's pilgrims met at the Tabard in Southwark to start their journey. *Times*[24]

In 'They are still as variable as they were in Dickens's time' the verb 'they were' is satisfactory, but add 'and probably since the day Chaucer's pilgrims met at the Tabard', and the verb 'were' will no longer serve ('they are what they have been since Chaucer's pilgrims met'). *English inns are still as variable as they were in Dickens's time, and probably have been since the day Chaucer's pilgrims met at the Tabard in Southwark to start their journey.*

> The comment made by a respondent from Toyota that 'centralisation is becoming more important to companies wanting or already dealing in Europe' typifies the attitudes of companies that have centralised their marketing operations. *Marketing Week*[25]

There is no escape for the logical mind from supplying 'wanting' with an infinitive: *centralisation is becoming more important to companies wanting to deal or already dealing in Europe.*

> Kaufmann's last book, in collaboration with his successor Nikolaus Klein, was an extended exegesis of that speech. *Independent*[26]

Kaufmann's last book, written in collaboration with his successor . . .

> The collection is spattered with childlike descriptive touches such as the house in 'Esmerelda'. *Times*[27]

A house cannot be a 'descriptive touch': *such as the picture of the house in 'Esmerelda'.*

3 More confusing omissions

Most of the examples given so far were able to be corrected by insertion of a word or two over which the writer had mentally skipped. Cutting corners sometimes leads to more complex mix-ups. To acquire command of English involves being wary of the damage to syntax and meaning which omissions can cause.

> These firms will spend a lot of time listening to what sort of kitchen design you're after . . . *Traditional Homes*[28]

The colloquialism here surely goes beyond what written usage should allow. *These firms will spend a lot of time listening to you as you explain what sort of kitchen design you're after.*

I would be grateful if I could record straight concerning the issue of farrier training. *Horse & Hound*[29]

We know what a man means when he says 'I would be grateful if I could think straight'. Neither grammar nor idiomatic usage allows of recording 'straight'. Direct correction would not do ('I would be grateful if I could correct the record') because the writer obviously *can* correct the record, and is going to. If 'grateful' is to stay, then the object of gratitude must be mentioned – *I should be grateful to be allowed to set the record straight* – but there are briefer ways of saying the same thing: *I should like to correct the record.*

You notice the plastic on the dash, console and doors, but the latter close with the firmness of any well-made car. *Tatler*[30].

Strictly speaking 'the latter' should be used only when two and not more things or persons have been mentioned. To say the doors close 'with the firmness of any well-made car' is an awkward short-hand for 'close as firmly as they generally do on a well-made car'. It is the firmness of door-fittings, not of the car as a whole, that is the issue. *You notice the plastic on the dash, console and doors, which close as firmly as those of any well-made car.*

Estate workers come and go, not in the casual sense, more long term, sons succeeding fathers. *Decanter*[31]

This passage tells us that workers come and go, and then proceeds to explain that in fact they do not 'come and go'. That is what the message really amounts to. *Estate workers come and go, not in the sense that they are casual workers, for sons follow fathers.*

As highly regarded marks of authenticity, blue plaques are attached only to the most historically correct of door posts. *History Today*[32]

The subject is the marking of houses in London where the great have lived. But door posts can never be correct, not even historically correct. It is the positioning of the plaques that is either correct or incorrect: *blue plaques are placed on door posts only when it is strictly justifiable on historical grounds.*

One place it was necessary to spend a good deal of money was on the extra large, German Duker bath to accommodate her client's 6ft 3in, 16-stone frame in comfort. *Times*[33]

One's first impulse in trying to correct this is to write 'One place *where* it was necessary to spend money', but this clarification only serves to highlight the fact that 'place' is the wrong word anyway. A bath is not a place. *One object on which it was necessary to spend a good deal of money was the extra large, German Duker bath.*

> Few industries attract more criticism and more myths, or touch so intimately the lives of those who use it, than the railway. A railway is perceived as a 'people' industry, so we blame management, staff, unions; yet stuck in a traffic-jam we blame *circumstances*. The double-standards between road and rail epitomise the dilemma. *Oldie* [34]

The subject of the first sentence, 'Few industries', is plural, so 'it' must become 'them' in back-reference. 'Few things attract more criticism' is rightly followed by 'than the railway'. But 'Few things . . . touch so intimately the lives of those who use them' cannot be followed by 'than the railway': 'as the railway' is required. Finally, the double-standards do not exist 'between road and rail'. They are applied in judgment upon road and rail. *Few industries attract more criticism and more myths than the railway, and few touch so intimately the lives of those who use them . . . The double-standards adopted in judging road and rail highlight the discrepancy.*

> I usually arrived just after five, parking my motor cycle in the goods yard, then up a flight of steps up to platform 3. *British Railways Illustrated* [35]

The second 'up' is redundant. The sentence suggests that the motor cycle is parked first in the goods yard and then up a flight of steps. *I usually arrived just after five, parked my motor cycle in the goods yard, and then went up a flight of steps to platform 3.*

> Drain the pasta well then turn into a flameproof dish. *My Weekly* [36]

The instruction to 'turn into a flameproof dish' sounds like an excerpt from a manual of necromancy. Since the verb 'turn' can be intransitive it is safest to give it an object when using it transitively: *turn it into a flameproof dish.*

> The responsibility of individuals who take action on behalf of charitable trusts is possibly even higher than for other voluntary organisations. *Old Glory* [37]

It would be awkward to correct this directly ('The responsibility of individuals who take action on behalf of charitable trusts is possibly even higher than that of those who act for other voluntary organisations'). Better rewrite. *A higher responsibility is perhaps imposed by charitable trusts than by other voluntary organisations on those who take action on their behalf.*

4 Omission of 'that'

There is an increasing tendency to omit 'that' after verbs of saying, thinking, ordering and so on.

He announced Italy would double the £45 million food aid . . . *Daily Mail*[38]

He announced that Italy would double the £45 million food aid . . .

China has announced dozens of executions of traffickers, signalling. the battle against a growing social menace will be fought with bullets. *Independent*[39]

. . . signalling that the battle against a growing social menace will be fought with bullets.

Studies show your metabolic rate is raised for longer than the duration of your exercise session. *Me*[40]

Studies show that your metabolic rate is raised for longer . . .

Peter Warburton agrees [*that*] the government now has to make people feel happier. *Investors Chronicle*[41]

Mazur discovered [*that*] the cell was using BCCI. *Gentlemen's Quarterly*[42]

But it did mean [*that*] they would have to set about job-hunting in a more professional and committed way . . . *Times*[43]

. . . yet I bet many of you don't know [*that*] the Cardiff-based company also make pierced bullet and trolling moulds. *Sea Angler*[44]

Go back to basics and check [*that*] your foundation matches your skin tone exactly. *New Women*[45]

. . . revelations in the last *Eye* that IEA bosses are worried its close relationship with the Tory party might endanger its 'charity' status . . . *Private Eye*[46]

To avoid the repetition of 'that' ('that IEA bosses are worried that') use 'lest': *that IEA bosses are worried lest its close relationship with the Tory party might endanger.*

What happens now the high court has ruled BCCI must give the Bank the documents it wants . . . *Private Eye*[47]

It may be acceptable to omit 'that' after 'now', but not after 'ruled': *now the high court has ruled that BCCI must give the Bank . . .*

'That' is now also sometimes omitted before 'result' clauses, that is to say after 'so' in statements such as 'She was so tired (that) she fainted'.

> . . . her attacks finally became so bad she was afraid that she couldn't sit through an exam in a large room full of people. *Annabel*[48]

The writer here was no doubt anxious not to use 'that' twice within half a dozen words ('so bad that she was afraid that she couldn't'), but the awkwardness could have been avoided otherwise: *became so bad that she began to doubt whether she could sit through an exam.*

> Many of those who phone are so disturbed [*that*] they ring off without saying anything. *Woman*[49]

> . . . a proprietor so enthusiastic you feel he might go in to orbit. *The World of Interiors*[50]

If 'so enthusiastic that you feel that he might' seems over-precise, sacrifice the the second 'that': *a proprietor so enthusiastic that you feel he might go into orbit.*

5 Omission of 'to'

The practice has crept in of omitting 'to' after the verb 'help'. It is now very widespread.

> The computerised pollen counts will be sent regularly to thousands of GPs and should help them [*to*] warn hay fever sufferers . . . *Times*[51]

> . . . and Cadbury helped [*to*] lay the foundations for British Telecom . . . *Independent*[52]

> The session helped me [*to*] realise that I was capable of overcoming depression . . . *New Woman*[53]

> . . . in effect, Peel helped [*to*] educate the Irish in the effectiveness of popular pressure . . . *History Today*[54]

3 OTHER ABERRATIONS

We turn to a variety of faults caused by laxity in the choice of words or in grammatical control.

1 Use of negatives

To use a double negative is supposed to be a mark of illiteracy. Yet people who would be incapable of saying 'I don't want no more tea' sometimes seem to be capable of errors which match that one.

A tourist war erupts between the cities of Durham and York, with the former unable to contain its jealousy no longer. *Independent*[1]

The double negative is illogical, for the second negative cancels the first out. There are two options: 'I am unable to contain my jealousy any longer' and 'I am no longer able to contain my jealousy'. To be 'no longer unable' is obviously the same thing as to be able. (For the infelicitous use of 'with' see Chapter V, 4.) *A tourist war erupts between the cities of Durham and York, the former being unable to contain its jealousy any longer.*

The reliability of the Duke of Hamilton's own account, especially his repeated denials never to have met or recognised Hess, is contradicted by contemporary reports in *The Times . . . Times*[2]

The Duke did not deny that he had never met Hess (thereby admitting that he *had* met him). He denied that he had *ever* met him: *especially his repeated denials ever to have met or recognised Hess.*
Other misuses of the negative are easier to find.

I have read several articles on the benefits of seaweed in skin-care ranges, but all the chemists I have tried have never heard of it! *Chat*[3]

There is nothing illogical about saying that all chemists have never heard of something, but we don't do it. The English usage is 'No one has come', not 'Everyone has not come': *but none of the chemists I have tried has ever heard of it.*

All No7 products are not tested on animals. *Woman's Journal*[4]

The same rule applies here: *No No7 products are tested on animals.*

But one thing you can be sure every mother won't want to do on 29 March is cook lunch! *Homes & Gardens*[5]

Correct in the same way and add 'that' after 'sure' and 'to' before 'cook'. *But one thing you can be sure that no mother will want to do on 29 March is to cook lunch.*

Any individual has a right to bring a private prosecution if he chooses to do so, and would not have proceeded without the sound advice of an experienced and informed lawyer. *Daily Telegraph*[6]

'Any individual' cannot be followed by 'would not have proceeded', nor is 'would not have proceeded' the appropriate tense: *and no one would proceed without the sound advice of an experienced and informed lawyer.*

This would give you no access to the cash, but then you can only make withdrawals from the CapitalBond in the second year anyway. *Moneywise*[7]

The obvious correction here ('This would not give you any access') could be improved upon: *This would deny you access to the cash.*

Properly fitted child car seats reduce accidents by nearly three-quarters – yet more than 50% of seats in the UK aren't put in properly. *Parents*[8]

There are two alternatives here, both of which replace 'aren't' by 'are'. Either change 'more' to 'less' – *less than 50% of seats are put in properly* – or change 'properly' to 'improperly': *more than 50% of seats in the UK are improperly fitted.*

With an explosion of hind numbers in parts of the eastern Highlands the availability of discriminating stalkers able to conduct heavier than usual culls has been found wanting. *The Field*[9]

'The availability of stalkers has been found wanting' is a most awkwardly pretentious way of saying 'Stalkers are hard to find'. And need we talk of numbers 'exploding'? *At a time when hind numbers in parts of the eastern Highlands are rapidly increasing, discriminating stalkers able to conduct heavier than usual culls are hard to find.*

. . . and I must say I was a little disappointed to see a lack of photographs. *Sea Angler*[10]

'Seeing a lack' of something suggests remarkable powers. *I was a little disappointed that there were no photographs.*

2 Some common expressions

Certain much-used phrases spring all too readily to the lips of speakers or the pens of writers. Sometimes a fashion sets in – as has recently happened with the phrase 'at the end of the day'. Here we are not concerned so much with overuse as with evident misuse. Nevertheless, it is overuse which produces misuse.

At the other end of the summer, the bonus of autumn foliage needs no introduction. *Outdoors Illustrated*[11]

The article is recommending a trip to New England in the fall. To treat the hackneyed expression 'needs no introduction' as a suitable equivalent of 'well-known' in a context like this is insensitive. 'Bonus' is also inappropriately used. *At the other end of the summer, the beauty of the autumn foliage is renowned.*

Lighting up a loco can take a number of forms, the most common being to soak old rags in diesel or paraffin, ignite them, and put them inside the firebox on a bed of coal. *Steam Railway*[12]

Soaking old rags in paraffin is not a 'form' of lighting up a loco but a 'way' of doing it: *Lighting up a loco can be effected in many ways.*

The cover you slip your duvet into is where you can really go to town. *Family Circle*[13]

Misuse of a colourful colloquialism such as 'where you can really go to town' can easily become absurd. The more vivid the idiom, the sillier it sounds when it is out of place. *Choosing a cover for your duvet gives you a chance to use your imagination.*

Sauvignon Blanc is being made unwooded – which is where the future lies . . . *Decanter*[14]

The same applies here: *Sauvignon Blanc is being made unwooded – and this will be the accepted practice in the future.*

Finally, chewing fresh parsley is an old wives' tale that really works. *New Woman*[15]

We are receiving medical advice on the care of teeth and gums. A tale cannot 'work'. The writer could have adapted the idiom: *Finally, chewing fresh parsley is an old wives' remedy that really works.*

The United States and Australia have cleaned up their old bases, but so far Britain hasn't done a bean. *Green Magazine*[16]

Idiomatically, 'I haven't got a bean' means 'I'm penniless'. There is no usage which would allow one to 'do a bean'. *Britain hasn't done a thing.*

Sometimes, pleading a three-line whip, they will be discreetly chauffeured out again after the dinner interval, thus missing half the point of why they are there. *Times*[17]

The piece tells us how Cabinet ministers have to curtail their evenings at Glyndebourne. The idiom 'to miss the point' is used of failure mentally to grasp the essence of some matter. It cannot be used of behaviour which seems to make nonsense: *thus negating half the purpose of their visit.*

A bit obvious to point out that Pierre Frey, run today by the founder's son Patrick, is a French company, but the success of these simple teacups does beg the question of why more notice is not taken of the splendour of their heritage by our own potteries. *Harpers & Queen*[18]

The idiom 'to beg the question' means 'unwarrantably to take something for granted'. Here the writer appears to think that it means the opposite – 'raises the question'. Moreover you do not need 'of' after 'the question': *raises the question why more notice is not taken.*

> Not content with this, and other, misleading information in the article, including calling the canal society 'Developers', it was then issued as a press release. *Waterways World*[19]

You can say 'Not content with this, he then added insult to injury' because it is 'he' who is 'not content'. You cannot say 'Not content with this, it was also raining' because 'not content' is left hanging in the air. The word needed is 'notwithstanding'. 'Including calling' is ugly. *Notwithstanding this and other misleading information in the article, including a reference to the canal society as 'Developers', it was then issued as a press release.*

> Similarly the wardrobe would be well pushed to satisfy the needs of two people's clothes let alone a family. *Caravan Magazine*[20]

The colloquial idiom 'I should be pushed' to do this or that, meaning 'It would strain my resources', cannot be used of objects such as wardrobes. And clothes do not have 'needs' which wardrobes 'satisfy'. *Similarly the wardrobe is scarcely adequate to accommodate two people's clothes, let alone a family's.*

> The prospect of a hung parliament is not a result of the electorate wishing to see neither of the two main parties in power. In that case, the Liberal Democrats would win a majority of popular votes and doubtless form a government. *Times*[21]

Here is an illogical misuse of 'in that case'. The writer has said that a certain prospect is *not* the result of a certain situation, and now he wants to observe what would happen if that consequence *did* in fact obtain. If kept, the gerciple ('not a result of the electorate wishing') could be corrected by an apostrophe ('of the electorate's wishing'). *If we are to have a hung parliament, it will not be because the electorate wants to see neither of the two main parties in power. Were that its view, the Liberal Democrats would win a majority.*

> It seems that almost every week there's a new 'miracle' product. Basic moisturisers remain the bottom line. *Me*[22]

The article is about skin care. Careless use of the latest jargon suggests that moisturisers are normally applied to the buttocks.

> Many observers believe that Mr Buchanan-Smith's seat could be lost to the Liberal Democrats because of the big number of new settlers,

many from England, who hold no candle to the traditional Tory values of the farming communities of Kincardine and Deeside. *Times*[23]

'He could not hold a candle to his father' means that he is too inferior to be compared on equal terms with his father. The writer has got the wrong idiom. . . . *because of the big number of new settlers, many from England, who hold no brief for the traditional Tory values.*

Tears at bedtime can wreak havoc with artfully constructed make-up . . . water-proof mascara (now so advanced that it very rarely runs) should be a foregone conclusion. *Harpers & Queen*[24]

A 'foregone conclusion' is an *inevitable consequence*. But the writer regards water-proof mascara as a *necessary means*, for which the right expression is *sine qua non: should be a* sine qua non.

. . . and school grounds in particular have proved to be a hotbed of habitat recreation. *BBC Wildlife*[25]

This cheapens the potentially vivid word 'hotbed': *and school grounds have proved to be popular locations for habitat recreation.*

Each would-be diver is assigned a wet-suit . . . (Diving gear comes *ad hoc* with each dive.) *Outdoors Illustrated*[26]

We use the expression 'ad hoc' of a plan adopted or a committee formed on an impulse to serve one purpose only. It is not rightly used here. *Diving gear is supplied for each dive.*

Any indication from elsewhere in Britain that the popularity of contemporary dance is on the wane gets short shrift in the East Midlands. *Vivid*[27]

A 'short shrift' is a brief and unsympathetic response. The writer means that signs from elsewhere are at loggerheads with experience in the East Midlands: *that the popularity of contemporary dance is on the wane is at odds with what is happening in the East Midlands.*

3 'as it is known'

If the author has a bee in his bonnet, this is it. You can say 'He is called Slyboots' and in the passive form you can say 'Slyboots, as he is called'. You can say 'He is known as Slyboots', but if you want to use a corresponding passive form, you would have to say, 'Slyboots, as he is known *as*'. That is the only logical, grammatical thing to say. You would not say it, of course. Why bother, when you can say 'Slyboots, as he is called'? Let us have an end to the slovenliness of 'as he is known'.

These are practitioners of 'in-line skating' as America's fastest-growing new sport is officially known. *Times*[28]

. . . in line skating, or 'blading' as it's known [*called*] in the States. *Me*[29]

The Petrov affair, as it came to be known [*called*], caused a sensation in 1950s Australia . . . *Independent*[30]

The British Museum (Natural History), as it used to be known [*called*] before Dr Chalmers updated its title, has always been famous for its dinosaurs. *Viva*[31]

'Joppers', as he is universally known [*called*], drove the party through the lobbies 10 years ago . . . *Times*[32]

Death from overwork or *karoshi*, as the phenomenon is known [*called*] . . . *Times*[33]

This bad habit is now breeding others in its own mould. For instance, you can 'describe someone as "the monster of Chiswick"' but it is neither logically nor grammatically acceptable to say '"the monster of Chiswick", as he is described'. To satisfy the demand of logic and grammar, it would have to be '"the monster of Chiswick", as he is described *as*', which is not tolerable.

But while his wife of a year, former nightclub hostess Emily Bendit – as she is invariably described [*called*] by the tabloids – positively radiates New Age karma and tranquillity . . . *Esquire*[34]

The 'good doctor', as he tells our correspondent in Florence he is sick of being described [*called*], makes plain that his own land will be seeing little of his work in the future . . . *Daily Telegraph*[35]

What applies to 'describe as' applies also to 'refer to as'. In neither case can 'as' be jettisoned and since 'Slyboots, as he is referred to as' is not tolerable, change the verb.

May I suggest that this issue is well worth inclusion in the citizen's charter – or rather, consumer's charter, as Lord Gladwyn (July 25) refers to it. *Times*[36]

or rather, consumer's charter, as Lord Gladwyn calls it.

Twice this century there have been parades through the town in honour of Cap'n Dick, as he had been locally referred to [*called*]. *Old Glory*[37]

4 'this'

There is a growing tendency to use 'this' where 'so' or 'as' is needed. The practice of good writers does not yet sanction the development.

In fact, if you've read this far, there's no doubt of your capability to take the course. *She*[38]

Use either 'so' – *if you've read so far* – or 'as far as this': *if you've read as far as this, there's no doubt of your ability to take the course.*

To model perhaps? To become a film star? Could anyone this long-limbed and this fine-featured, with such impeccably histrionic credentials, want to do anything else? *Tatler*[39]

Repetition seems to make misuse of 'this' especially ugly. *Could anyone as long-limbed and fine-featured as she is, and having such impeccable credentials, want to do anything else?*

You might think something this special would be especially difficult to prepare. *Woman's Journal*[40]

You might think something as special as this would be especially difficult to prepare.

Even this early in the campaign, *The Times* would be dissembling to its readers if it did not admit a predisposition towards a new Conservative mandate. *Times*[41]

You do not 'dissemble' *to* people, though you might dissemble *before* or *with* them. *Even as early in the campaign as this,* The Times *would be dissembling with its readers if it did not admit a predisposition . . .*

5 Metaphorical anarchy

Great writers have been known to mix their metaphors. Shakespeare's Hamlet speaks of taking 'arms against a sea of troubles'. But the attentive reader will generally be uncomfortable with such discrepancies. The danger of lapsing into the absurd is increased by the ever-growing number of 'dead' metaphors in common use. We speak of a 'sphere of activity' or a 'field of activity' without actually picturing either a sphere or a field. A problem arises when such expressions are juxtaposed with other expressions which bring incongruous imagery to mind. Thus a writer might speak of 'launching out' into a new venture without bringing a ship to mind; but to speak of 'launching out into a new field of activity' would run the risk of bringing a smile to the mind of the person who is aware that vessels cannot launch out into fields.

Many of those who undergo this cultural chasm, particularly women, frequently refer to it as having a split personality. *Cosmopolitan*[42]

The topic is the collision between the attitudes of one's parents and those of one's peers – the 'Culture Gap'. If it is regarded as a 'chasm' then it not something you must *undergo*, but something you might have to cross. And what about the 'it', which is said to have a split personality? *Many who experience this collision of cultures feel as though they have acquired a split personality.*

> That is why we favour a Europe in which separate pillars of co-operation are maintained, each reporting to the heads of government sitting as the European Council. *Independent*[43]

Mrs Thatcher's metaphor pictures 'pillars' that report to heads of government. Get rid of the architecture: *a Europe in which separate participants co-operate, each reporting to the heads of government.*

> . . . the cellars hold some staggering bottles of wine. *Country Living*[44]

This recommendation of a hostelry in the French Alps suggests that the area is subject either to earthquakes or to spooky manifestations of the paranormal: *some magnificent bottles of wine.*

> Powergen's organisation is founded on business units, including power stations and sales marketing, which operate with considerable independence within rigorous financial targets. *Powergen: Annual Review*[45]

'Targets' are things you aim at. They cannot be 'rigorous', though they may be difficult to hit. They are not constraints. You cannot do anything 'within' them: *within rigorous financial disciplines.*

> In this situation the negative partner can help to keep the positive partner on the ground when new ideas are flowing, but they should try to avoid coming across as a wet blanket. *New Woman*[46]

Keeping someone 'on the ground' because new ideas 'are flowing' is not happily imaged as the possible function of a 'wet blanket': *they should try to avoid sounding like a killjoy.*

> And in London, city wildlife has been recognised as a politically powerful foot in the door of a wide range of environmental issues. *BBC Wildlife*[47]

The sensitive imagination is uneasy with this kind of thing. We picture 'city wildlife' and straightaway we are asked to conceive it, with all its vitality and variety, as a 'foot in the door'. *In London, the campaign for city wildlife has been seen as one by which a host of environmental issues can be given political leverage.*

216

As generation gaps go, this one is pretty tame. *Times*[48]

Gaps are not normally categorised as either 'tame' or 'wild'. They may be 'wide' or 'narrow': *this one is pretty narrow.*

If Quinn is right, and the ITC continues to 'relax' the quality threshold to force media which may never be profitable on to the market . . . *Marketing Week*[49]

Perhaps the quotation marks indicate the writer's discomfort with her imagery. You cannot 'relax' a threshold. You either raise it or lower it: *and the ITC continues to lower the quality threshold.*

. . . and you really do feel that the weather has an almost physical presence. *The Artist*[50]

What other kind of 'presence' can weather possibly have?

Other fields beginning to emerge or expand include environmental law, architecture, local authority planning, education, and the particularly healthy employment sector of environmental auditing . . . *Green Magazine*[51]

The writer is giving guidance on careers. As a conservationist he ought to be aware that *fields* do not 'emerge or expand': *Other occupations offering new or increasing openings include environmental law, architecture.*

If this scenario is compounded by the burden of care implicit in meeting the needs of a child who is hyperactive . . . *Nursing Standard*[52]

The writer is concerned with the crisis in caring for children in Romania. You cannot *compound* a scenario. You might 'complicate' it. Better get rid of it: *If this problem is made more intractable by the burden of care implicit in meeting the needs of a child.*

The day had been an unqualified success and has become an annual event, growing in stature all the while . . . *Old Glory*[53]

Days do not grow in stature: *growing in significance all the while.*

. . . then mergers as an issue will retreat to the back of the political agenda . . . *Independent*[54]

An agenda does not have a back and a front. Is the writer thinking of the much-cited cooking stove with front and back burners? *. . . will be pushed to the bottom of the political agenda . . .*

Despite the great progress of the past decade, the agenda for change stretches ever further ahead . . . *BBC Wildlife*[55]

The agenda has now acquired elasticity. *Despite the the great progress of the last decade, plans for change are ever more far-reaching.*

They fight life's well of loneliness . . . *Spare Rib*[56]

It is a pity to devalue a powerful metaphor ('well of loneliness') thus. You cannot 'fight' a well.

– VIII –

VOCABULARY

In this section we look at some individual words which are being notably and, in some cases, frequently misused. Sometimes the misuse arises from failure to understand the exact meaning of the word. Sometimes it arises because writers distort accepted usage in contexts where the word in question is out of place.

1 SOME OVERUSED AND ILL-USED WORDS

When words are popularly overused they tend to spring readily to our minds. They can supply a convenient substitute for thought. We use them without reflecting on their precise meaning. Mental laziness leads us to use them inexactly.

amount: The amount you bend the vanes governs how the spinner works. *Sea Angler*[1]

You cannot bend an amount of anything. *How far you bend the vanes determines how the spinner works.*

With new-wave salon perms you can control the amount of curl you get . . . *Company*[2]

It isn't a matter of controlling an 'amount': *you can control how much curl you get.*

The amount of water not only controls the strength of colour, but also the size of the area of colour . . . *Artists & Illustrators Magazine*[3]

How much water you use not only determines the strength of colour . . .

apply: 'Punctuality . . . is the politeness of kings.' But that particular virtue seldom seems to apply to game-shooting these days. *The Field*[4]

The writer does not mean 'apply'. *But that particular virtue seldom seems to be cultivated in game-shooting these days.*

approach: Most of the production is sold on the market either as easy drinking or blending wine. Cooks Hawkes Bay Chenin Blanc and

219

Gisborne Riesling Chenin Blanc are good examples of this approach. *Decanter*[5]

'Approach' has a very definite meaning, but increasingly it is devalued by this sort of thing. Brands of wine cannot be examples of an approach. No approach has been mentioned, only two methods of marketing wine: *... are good examples of this practice.*

Operating a Catering Trailer is simple, and falls into two distinct approaches. The operator must decide whether or not he or she wants a roadside or a market pitch ... *Money-Maker*[6]

Operating a trailer cannot 'fall' into 'two approaches'. There is no need for either expression. *There are two ways of running a Catering Trailer.*

area: ... a hybrid administration responsible for infrastructure and areas such as social services, building control, street cleaning and education. *Private Eye*[7]

These are not 'areas', but activities. 'Area' is now one of the most overworked words in the language. Hesitate to use it: *responsible for infrastructure and activities such as social services.*

We have tried to be even-handed in developing all areas of the club ... You have to treat all of them, players, members, spectators, sponsors as equal priorities. *Times*[8]

The players, members, and others would surely object to being categorised as 'areas'. *We have tried to be even-handed in catering for all the people involved with the club.*

After a short introduction to the book, each section has a short explanatory piece to set the scene for the photographs, each being a favoured area of the father and son team. *Steam Classic*[9]

To explain exactly what 'area' means here would test anyone: *a short explanatory piece to set the scene for the photographs, each focusing on a particular aspect of the work done by the father and son.*

... he will address three main areas; the role of advertising, ... the need for advertising, ... and the degree to which advertising revenue supports Europe's media. *Marketing Week*[10]

These are not 'areas' but topics.

aspect: ... I quickly noted that every aspect of food was constantly sharpened by the use of citrus fruits, spices or African influences, such as combining the very hot with the sweet or bland. *Independent*[11]

You cannot sharpen an aspect: *every flavour of food was regularly sharpened by the use of citrus fruits, spices or such African practices as combining the very hot with the sweet or bland.*

dimension: ORIENTEERING This gives an added dimension to cross-country running as you need to read a map to follow your course, giving you a mental and physical challenge. *Cosmopolitan*[12]

If cross-country running really did acquire an added dimension, then presumably the runners would fly part of the way. The word 'dimension' is now absurdly overused where it is quite out of place. *This gives an added interest to cross-country running.*

For women there's also the added dimension of children. *Me*[13]

The article is concerned with the risks of infecting others with HIV. *Women also have to reckon with childbirth.*

The bath is raised to a higher level, which gives an extra dimension and character . . . *Ideal Home*[14]

Where the concern is with measurement ('higher level') the misuse of 'dimension' is particularly absurd. *The bath is raised to a higher level, which adds character.*

example: From then on the original chimneys were discarded in favour of a taller example. *British Railways Illustrated*[15]

The word 'example' is quite inappropriate here. Perhaps the writer meant 'a taller model' but it is better to be straightforward: *the original chimneys were discarded in favour of taller ones.*

The response to the *Sunday Times* revelation has provided an example of one of my beliefs, which is that when nice people try to be nasty, the result is nastier than when nasty men act nasty out of their own nature. *New Statesman & Society*[16]

The revelation does not provide an 'example' of one of the writer's beliefs, but a corroboration or justification.

factor: Miniatures vary in price according to factors including the artist, the sitter and the condition of the piece. *Moneywise*[17]

Can the artist or the sitter be said to be a 'factor': *according to the identity of the artist and sitter*? As so often, 'including' is unnecessary.

feature: If you are buying a hand-held mixer or blender, size and weight will also feature in your decision. *Moneywise*[18]

Overuse of the verb 'to feature', meaning 'to play a part in', is insensitive: *size and weight will help to determine your choice.*

fulfil: One object to fulfil with a bargain break like this is to revisit old haunts. *Times*[19]

You don't 'fulfil' an object, you 'attain' it. Change either the noun – *One desire to fulfil* – or the verb: *One object to attain*.

> In vintage and PVT times plating was only rarely used on cars for protection alone, this role generally being fulfilled by paint. *Automobile*[20]

You do not 'fulfil' a role, you 'fill' it, but to talk of paint 'filling a role' instead of 'serving a purpose' is absurd: *this purpose generally being served by paint*.

function: How quickly ERM membership induces convergent price and cost structures is largely a function of conditions in the country that is joining. *Times*[21]

'Function' is the wrong word here. You would not write 'How quickly I run is largely a function of my legs'. You might write 'How quickly I run is largely determined by my legs'. *How quickly ERM membership induces convergent price and cost structures is largely determined by conditions in the country that is joining.*

> The most rapid growth in unit labour costs is to be found in Greece and Portugal, a function of the low level of labour costs there. *Times*[22]

This second erroneous use of 'function' treats it as though it could operate in place of a causal conjunction. Use 'because'. *The most rapid growth in unit labour costs is to be found in Greece and Portugal because of the low level of labour costs there.*

hopefully: With the 25th Anniversary coming up in 1993, hopefully this will prove to be the largest assembly of showman's engines gathered together on one occasion . . . *Old Glory*[23]

It is a pity that this word has been adopted as a quick way of interjecting 'I hope' into a sentence, because it has its own useful connotation. (For the misuse of 'with' see Chapter V, 4.) *As the 25th Anniversary comes up in 1993, we hope it will prove to be the largest assembly . . .*

idea: However, few anglers bother with the tank idea to induce peelers because it is so involved and requires a large tank . . . *Sea Angler*[24]

The word 'idea', as used here, appears to signify a process or a way of doing something. It should be omitted and the infinitive 'to induce' should be moved. *However, few anglers bother with a tank when they wish to induce peelers.*

importance: This reinforces the importance of Britain now making more of a reality of Hong Kong's 'high level of autonomy', formally guaranteed under the 1984 Sino-British declaration. *Times*[25]

The 'importance of Britain now making' includes a gerciple (see Chapter III, 5), but merely to correct that ('the importance of Britain's now making') would be inadequate. 'The importance . . . of making' is an awkward way of saying 'the need to make'. *This confirms the need for Britain to make more of a reality of Hong Kong's 'high level of autonomy'.*

incredible: . . . to see the synchronised aerobatics of Pinero's guacamayos, as they call them, is incredible. *Green Magazine*[26]

This illustrates the careless overuse of 'incredible', meaning 'unbelievable', where words such as 'remarkable' or 'astonishing' would be more appropriate.

I told Mick about the breakthrough Sarah had made and though he thought it incredible, he couldn't see how it had been possible. *Annabel*[27]

For this writer the word 'incredible' (unbelievable) is equated with 'wonderful'. Thus she produces a self-contradictory sequence. If Mick finds the thing incredible, then it follows that he won't be able to see how it has happened. This is like saying 'Although I find it impossible, I don't know how I can do it'. Remove 'incredible': *and though he thought it wonderful, he couldn't see how it had been done.*

incredibly: My family was incredibly conventional . . . *New Woman*[28]

My family was remarkably conventional . . .

integrate: Conservation priorities are integrated with the physical economic constraints of each project, in order to provide an approach that is both appropriate and viable. *Traditional Homes*[29]

You would not say 'My household spending is integrated with the financial constraints of my weekly income'. To 'integrate' something is to incorporate it into a whole with something else. The issue here is not integration but adjustment. *Conservation priorities are adjusted to fit the economic constraints of each project.* Consider too what is said about 'approach' above.

literally: Events have once again reminded the world not to take the appearance of peace literally. *Times*[30]

The only thing that can be taken 'literally' is a statement of some kind. You cannot take an 'appearance' literally. *Events have once again reminded the world not to take the appearance of peace at face value.*

The book starts with a met man's look at the seasons, showing how they move quite literally by degrees through Britain. *Practical Gardening*[31]

Seasons cannot 'move literally', not even 'by degrees': *showing how the seasons gradually change through Britain.*

mean: This is now perhaps the most abused verb in the language. It is used to express relationships which have little or nothing to do with what the verb properly connotes.

Having a European presence means a firm has to be flexible. *Marketing Week*[32]

Here we see a very popular usage of 'mean', conveying relationships of cause and effect or of fact and result. When 'mean' is used thus, there is always a verb that can be substituted and will be more precise: *Having a European presence requires a firm to be flexible.*

For children, however, brown bread's bulk can mean that it fills up before they have eaten enough calories. *Times*[33]

We must deal here with both the vague verb 'mean' and the objectless verb 'fills up'. *As for children, however, brown bread's bulk can make them feel full before they have eaten enough calories.*

Fewer school leavers mean that more women are needed to make up the shortfall. *New Woman*[34]

Because there are fewer school leavers, more women are needed to make up the shortfall.

Subsequent advances mean that today treatment can be completed in six to nine weeks. *Gentlemen's Quarterly*[35]

As a result of subsequent advances, today treatment can be completed in six to nine weeks.

A 'Passport' ticket, valid indefinitely until you have visited all the sites at Ironbridge, means that you can take your time to enjoy the whole experience of exploring what is now recognised as a world heritage centre. *Traditional Homes*[36]

This is a slightly different way of misusing 'mean'. The relationship established by the verb is a 'permissive' or 'enabling' one and calls for an appropriate verb. *A 'Passport' ticket . . . enables you to take your time to enjoy the whole experience.*

The 2m flex should mean you can find a socket within easy reach of a mirror. *Good Housekeeping*[37]

The 'enabling' relationship exists here too ('The 2m flex should enable you to find a socket') but there is an illogicality, for the flex will not enable you to *find* a socket. Should there happen to be a socket, the flex will enable you to make use of it. Flex serves only the one purpose – to link your hairdryer to the power supply. Its length determines its usefulness in this respect. So omit what is obvious: *The 2m flex should prove useful.*

> And the AM/FM radio means you can wake up to your favourite music when you set the radio alarm. *Chat*[38]

You do not want to wake up to music *when* you set the radio alarm, but rather next morning. *And the AM/FM radio will enable you to wake up to your favourite music if you set the radio alarm.*

> Numbers of salmon are also reported to have increased. This probably means an improvement in water quality. *Sea Angler*[39]

This is the 'evidential' use of 'mean'; perhaps it it is closer to the strict connotation of the verb than misuses already illustrated. *This probably is evidence of an improvement in water quality.*

myth: Some infant teachers will tell you that you shouldn't teach your child the three 'Rs' because it will only cause confusion when she is taught 'properly' at school, but this is a myth. *Annabel*[40]

The word 'myth' has its distinctive connotation, that of an ancient heroic or superhuman story of symbolic significance. It is a pity to vulgarise it as a mere synonym for what is false: *but this is an old wives' tale.*

optimistic: The future looks optimistic with the general opening up of the East . . . *Marketing Week*[41]

If you are optimistic about what is going to happen tomorrow, you are optimistic today, not tomorrow. The writer means that he feels optimistic about the future. If the future actually 'looked optimistic', that would be a different matter, a matter of prospects for the future's future. 'Hopeful' is similarly misused. So is the word 'forecast'. Weather men speak of 'tomorrow's forecast' when they mean today's forecast of what tomorrow will bring. Tomorrow's forecast would predict the weather on the day after tomorrow. *There is optimism about the future.*

> Dealing 2000–2 is due to start client testing around now and could be launched later in the month (although given past experience this might be a little optimistic). *Investors Chronicle*[42]

To the layman it is not clear what is to be 'launched later in the month'. The grammar implies that it is 'Dealing 20000–2', but 'client testing' seems a safer bet. If 'this' refers to the timing of the launching (as it appears to do) then 'optimistic' is clearly wrong. *Dealing 2000–2 is due to start client-testing around now and the project could be launched later in the month (although this may be too much to hope for).*

part: He was part of a great renaissance of talent, which turned a massive defeat into a springboard for a new golden age . . . *Tatler*[43]

'Part' means a portion of a whole, an amount less than the whole, or a constituent of something. It is not happily applied thus to a human being. Use 'took part in' or some such construction. *He contributed to the great renaissance of talent.*

There is a natural level of fitness which is part of a child's growing up. *Parents*[44]

There is a natural level of fitness which is appropriate to a growing child.

Part of the Trip includes visits to local women's projects . . . *Good Housekeeping*[45]

Here 'part of' is simply redundant. *The trip includes visits to local women's projects . . .*

He attributes this in part to the scramble for new franchises, without informing us what he attributes the other part or parts to. *Daily Telgraph*[46]

You can refer to 'the other part or parts' only if you have already mentioned 'a part'. But using the adverbial expression 'in part' does not constitute a fit use of the noun 'part' for this purpose. *He attributes this partly to the scramble for new franchises, without informing us what other causes are involved.*

plank: Two major planks of the Council for National Parks' charter are for the government to double its contribution to national park authorities and for all NPAs to be independent planning authorities . . . *The Great Outdoors*[47]

Can a 'charter' be said to have 'planks'? And if the word *were* allowed, could those planks be 'for the government' to do this or that? *Two major demands of the Council for National Parks charter.*

problem: If you are careful and think ahead, you can prevent most problems before they happen. *Horse & Hound*[48]

Problems do not 'happen', they arise. The context makes it clear that the right word would be 'accidents'.

Problems such as crooked, stained, chipped and generally unattractive teeth can be beautifully corrected using such techniques as veneers, bleaching, crowns and white fillings. *Lancashire Life*[49]

It is not the problems that are 'corrected' but the defects. 'Using' is an unanchored participle (see Chapter III, 2). Veneers are not 'techniques', nor are crowns and fillings. *Defects such as crooked, stained, chipped and generally unattractive teeth can be beautifully corrected by the use of such devices as veneers, bleaching, crowns and white fillings.*

result: Care services profits rose 86 per cent to £3.8m, but this was largely a result of six new nursing homes filling up. *Investors Chronicle*[50]

It is clumsy to use the abstract noun 'result' where a causal clause would be more natural. Here, as so often, it produces a gerciple (see Chapter III, 5) which would be awkward to correct ('a result of the filling up of six new nursing homes'). Better re-phrase: *but this was largely because six new nursing homes filled up.*

In the past few weeks, the society, which is the result of the merger last year of the Eastbourne Mutual and Sussex County . . . *Guardian*[51]

Why not say what you mean: *the society, which was formed last year by the merger of the Eastbourne Mutual and Sussex County?*

scene: Roy Heath believes the discounting scene in Germany has depressed margins . . . *Marketing Week*[52]

This appears to mean that the practice of giving discounts and the size of the discounts has depressed profit margins. Such a practice does not constitute a 'scene'. Why not simplify? *Roy Heath believes that discounting in Germany has depressed margins.*

solution: This combination of rock and electronics is now the solution to many films. *Vivid*[53]

You can have a solution to a problem, but a film does not require one. This is an instance of the 'any word will do' style.

solve: Not all the perils of the earlier medieval period had been completely solved, however. Servants and hosts were both equally likely to be in league with bands of highwaymen . . . *Heritage*[54]

You cannot *solve* a 'peril'. *Not all the perils of the earlier medieval period had been completely eliminated, however.*

The report . . . must further focus attention on solving two distinct, though often interlocking, parts of medical care provision in

London – the care of the district populations and the maintenance of excellence in specialist services and research. *Times*[55]

You cannot *solve* 'parts' of medical care provision. If 'solve' is kept, supply a 'problem': *must further focus attention on solving the problems associated with two distinct, though often interlocking, functions of medical care provision in London.*

substitute: A creamier, if less orthodox sorbet can be made by substituting the egg whites with a pint of cream. *Independent*[56]

If I substitute a full-stop for a comma, it is the full-stop that replaces the comma. What you substitute is what comes in, not what goes out. You substitute 'for', not 'with': *less orthodox sorbet can be made by substituting a pint of cream for the egg white.*

> The World Cup rules stipulate that the replacement of any named squad member, once the competition begins, is at the discretion of the Cup committee. The inference is that a player entering the tournament with an injury cannot be substituted. *Times*[57]

The conclusion here is absurd. No one would want to 'substitute' an injured player for a healthy one. *The implication is that a player entering the tournament with an injury cannot be replaced.*

substitution: When substitution of a hazardous material or process is impractical, protective clothing and mechanical safety devices are the next best way to reduce risks. *Artists & Illustrators Magazine*[58]

'Substitution' is misused just as 'substitute' is. 'Substitution' *of* a full-stop for a comma would replace the comma by the full-stop: *When replacement of a hazardous material or process is impractical.*

synonymous: Roses are synonymous with Chelsea. *The Lady*[59]

> Bogs are synonymous with Ireland . . . *The Field*[60]

> For Jerry 'lingeray' is synonymous with sexy. *Woman's Journal*[61]

> Lalique's designs have become synonymous with elegant and imaginative presentation. *Period Living*[62]

> To most people the names William Wordsworth and the Lake District are all but synonymous. *Cumbria Life*[63]

> Tomorrow, the latest in a range of bicycles bearing the name that has become synonymous with the small wheel is launched: the Alex Moulton Stainless Steel GT. *Times*[64]

Abuse of the word 'synonoymous' has reached a point of absurdity.

One word is 'synonymous' with another if the two are identical in meaning. In none of the above usages is the word appropriate.

> Schloss Freudenberg became synonymous as a home from home to royalty, prime ministers and international leaders of finance and business . . . *Times*[65]

This is like saying 'Your house is synonymous as a pig-sty' when you want to deplore its untidiness. Nothing can be synonymous *as* something else. *Schloss Freudenberg became known as a home from home.*

traditional: The traditional people getting help from benevolent funds – the elderly, retired and sick – are now heavily outnumbered by 30, 40 and 50-year-olds. *Times*[66]

In no sense are the elderly, retired and sick 'traditional people': *The people traditionally getting help from benevolent funds – the elderly, retired and sick.*

way: Creches and 'career-break packages' were just two of the ways in which employers hoped to woo female staff and keep them sweet. *New Woman*[67]

This illustrates the tendency to use the word 'way' where more exact words are available. *Creches and 'career-break packages' were just two of the devices by which employers hoped to woo female staff.*

> You need to think about your child's exercise in two ways – fitness and activity . . . *Parents*[68]

Neither 'fitness' nor 'activity' is a *way. You need to think about your child's exercise in relation to two matters – fitness and activity.*

> The government has got to grasp the nettle and introduce competition in the electricity industry the way it didn't do the first time. *Times*[69]

The last eight words would surely be red-inked in a lower form at school: *introduce competition into the electricity industry as it failed to do the first time.*

2 WORDS CONFUSED WITH OTHERS

We are here concerned with words which tend to be confused with other words. Sometimes the confusion arises because two words resemble each other closely in form, and sometimes because two (or more) words are closely related in meaning.

adverse (averse): ... the locals ... weren't adverse [*averse*] to shovelling their way out. *Cumbria Life*[1]

'Adverse' means unfavourable or antagonistic; 'averse' means disinclined.

affect (effect): Officials ... said that drinking water without boiling it could cause stomach upsets and that affects [*effects*] on the young and elderly could be serious. *Times*[2]

The verb 'to affect' means to influence or act upon.

... Rembrandt Painting Paste which has the same consistency as tube oil paint but does have a slight affect [*effect*] on its drying time. *The Artist*[3]

Laski thus effected [*affected*] her life profoundly. *Times*[4]

This is the converse error. The verb 'to effect' means 'to bring about' ('He effected a transformation in their attitudes').

appraise (apprise): ... today's immigrants are immediately embraced by a modern welfare state and ... vigorously supported by bodies only too eager to appraise [*apprise*] them of the rights they could scarcely dream of in their own land. *Daily Express*[5]

To 'appraise' is to assess the value of something. It is now often confused with 'apprise' which means to inform.

Now go down the list and tick those who, appraised [*apprised*] of the plastic sheet business and the explanation offered in support of it, you think would believe the Yard. *Times*[6]

This, alas, is Bernard Levin.

ascribe to (credit with): Take a cure at Evian les Baines ... and you'll find there's a lot more to Evian water than drinking it. Here, in addition to being ascribed many curative properties ... the water is used ... for a wide range of external hydrotherapy treatments. *Gentlemen's Quarterly*[7]

When you ascribe something to a person, you register that something to his credit. You do not ascribe *him*, you ascribe something *to* him. Likewise you do not ascribe Evian water, you ascribe curative properties to it. In the passive version you cannot speak of the water 'being ascribed curative properties'. Either rephrase the sentence – *in addition to having many curative properties ascribed to it ... the water is used* – or change the verb: *Here, in addition to being credited with many curative properties ... the water is used.*

attributable (applicable): . . . one word used to describe a kiln that dried malt or hops was 'oste'. By the nineteenth century this had metamorphosed into 'oast', and was attributable to a kiln that was specifically made for drying hops. *Traditional Homes*[8]

An attribute is basically some quality that belongs to a person. The authorship of *Hamlet* and *Macbeth* is attributed to Shakespeare, but you cannot say that the word 'tragedy' is attributable to *Hamlet.* The word needed is 'applicable': . . . *and was applicable to a kiln.*

avoid (prevent/forestall): Lower pay settlements should mean a quicker drop in the underlying rate of inflation, allowing the Chancellor to take measures to stimulate the economy and avoid [*prevent*] the rise in unemployment [*from*] worsening the slump. *Times*[9]

(Note the gerciple, 'rise . . . worsening'.) You turn your steering wheel and 'avoid' the cyclist, but you do not thereby 'avoid' an accident; you 'prevent' it. The same applies here.

A similar improvement in BR service would avoid [*forestall*] the need for any compensation payment. *Times*[10]

You might avoid a hurricane by leaving the threatened area yet you would not thus affect the course of events. But the whole point about the improvement recommended to BR is that it would decisively affect the course of events, removing the need for compensation payment. The word needed is 'forestall'.

Babylon (Babel): There can hardly be a greater need for the CLA's voice to be heard clearly amid the general Babylon [*Babel*] of organisations lobbying Government . . . *The Field*[11]

Because of its Biblical associations 'Babylon' has been used of corrupt societies. On the same basis 'Babel' is used of a confusion of voices or noises. Clearly the wrong word has been used here.

baited (bated): As the contracts of senior United Nations officials finish at the end of February, all have been waiting with baited [*bated*] breath to see how Boutros Ghali, the new secretary-general, fares. *Private Eye*[12]

'Baited' breath would be breath supplied with a 'bait' to attract as the angler's bait attracts fish. 'Bated breath' is breath suspended by apprehension.

chart (trace): Recent developments in the visual arts can be charted back to these striking paintings. *Artists & Illustrators Magazine*[13]

To chart a course is to plot it in advance. Here the attitude is retrospective: *can be traced back to these striking paintings.*

clause (phrase): 'We live in stirring times – tea-stirring times,' Christopher Isherwood, the novelist, once wrote. The image is apt for racing's predominantly mundane daily rounds, but in this sevenday period, with the Eclipse Stakes at Sandown this Saturday following Sunday's Irish Derby, we can safely drop the author's mordant second clause. *Independent*[14]

But 'tea-stirring times' is not a clause, which must contain a finite verb: *we can safely drop the author's final phrase.*

---

compliment (complement): She also built an extraordinary swimming pool, and would regularly invite the entire compliment [*complement*] of a passing cruise liner, passengers and crew, to lavish garden parties . . . *Decanter*[15]

A 'compliment' is a remark expressing admiration. A 'complement' completes something. A crew as a whole would be a 'full complement'.

comply (conform): My only complaint is that men will probably not read it and they are the ones who make us women feel inferior or frigid if we don't comply to the image they are so used to witnessing. *Company*[16]

You comply *with* some regulation or code, not *to* it. Acts of compliance are acts of the will. Substitute 'conform with' or 'match up to' for 'comply with'.

comprise (consist of): Colonel Gaddafi . . . has increased the power of the revolutionary committee comprising of young men raised on his slogans. *Times*[17]

To 'comprise' is to contain, embrace, or consist of. The writer's choice is to say either 'the committee comprised young men' or 'the committee consisted of young men'.

> They had experienced a 'support' group led by a psychologist some years before, which comprised of everyone sitting silently until someone 'cracked'. *Nursing Standard*[18]

'Of' follows 'consist', not 'comprise', and neither verb would be right here: *'support' group . . . in which everyone sat silently.*

convince (persuade/induce): But it is time you all had the opportunity to stop this guilt and blame that he has convinced you to carry. *Essentials*[19]

You *convince* a person of a fact, but you *lead* or *induce* a person to do something, and 'stop' is the wrong verb to govern 'guilt': *the opportunity to free yourselves of this guilt and blame that he has induced you to carry.*

We should, if we were to follow Fukuyama, convince [*persuade*] ourselves to be optimistic while we cultivate our tea ceremony. *Times*[20]

derisory (derisible): Full-year profits are forecast at only £150m – a derisory [*derisible*] return for a manufacturing company with sales of more than £10 billion . . . *Daily Telegraph*[21]

A 'derisory' attitude, like a 'derisive' attitude, is one which is scornful, not one which ought to be scorned. Increasingly 'derisory' is being misused where the correct word would be 'derisible', worthy to be scorned.

disabuse (refute): The myth that the affairs of voluntary organisations can be conducted as casually as we may conduct our own personal affairs should be disabused. *Old Glory*[22]

Only people can be disabused, for to 'disabuse' someone is to rid them of a false idea: *The notion . . . should be refuted/exploded.*

disinterested (uninterested): 'Disinterested' is not connected with the word 'interest' used in its most familiar way. It is connected with the word 'interest' as used in 'He has a financial interest in the business'. To be disinterested in something is to be impartial towards it, because there can be no personal advantage in a positive or a negative attitude towards it.

. . . they can't believe that British business is so disinterested. *Times*[23]

The issue is the British attitude to a Soviet Trade Exhibition in London: *they can't believe that British business is so uninterested.*

. . . and a Prime Minister who has shown himself to be disinterested [*uninterested*] in promoting women to his cabinet. *Options*[24]

educational (educative/informative): The main pictorial section of the book is prefaced by a brief, but educational [*informative*] history of the lines on the Island, including opening and closing dates. *Steam Classic*[25]

An 'educational' matter is a matter bound up with education. The adjective (unlike 'educative') is not normally used to mean 'instructive'.

entrance (entry): During August it will be on display at the Bethnal Green Museum of Childhood in London, where the entrance is absolutely free! *Prima*[26]

The 'entrance' is the doorway and vestibule, and no one is giving it away: *where entry/admission is absolutely free.*

erode (eliminate): Between 1911 and 1922, these eighteen were rebuilt along with the other Holmes 6ft 6in 4–4–0s and enough of the minor differences between the different batches were eroded that, at the grouping, the LNER placed the entire forty-eight together as class SD31. *Steam Classic* [27]

Erosion is a matter of wearing down. To speak of 'eroding' difficulties instead of just 'eliminating' them is absurd. The construction 'enough were eroded that' is inexact: *enough of the minor differences . . . were eliminated for the LNER to place the entire forty-eight together, at the grouping, as class SD31.*

expand (expatiate/enlarge): Oswyn Murray expands on banquets in Greece and Rome. *Oxford Today* [28]

The misuse of 'expand' is rapidly increasing, probably by confusion with the verbs 'expatiate' and 'enlarge'. You can expatiate on a theme or enlarge on it, but if you expand, whatever you are *on*, you will eventually explode. Of course you can 'expand' a tale, by lengthening it, but that is not expanding *on* it. *Oswyn Murray expatiates on banquets.*

> When you're in the interview, don't spout one-word answers; if possible expand on [*enlarge on*] your answers by giving examples. *More!* [29]

flaunt (flout): In the event Tchaikovsky did sanction 3 small cuts – but unfortunately these were flaunted in the first edition for more wholesale cuts to the first and second movements . . . *Programme Note* [30]

The word 'flaunt' means to display ostentatiously. It is now often confused with the verb 'flout' which means to disregard or defy. That is what happens here. And what is 'flouted' is Tchaikovsky's recommendation. *Tchaikovsky did sanction three small cuts – but unfortunately this recommendation was flouted in the first edition.*

forget (forgo): If you're buying a replacement, forget [*forgo*] testing it on the back of your hand – you wear foundation on your face, so test it there. *New Woman* [31]

'Forget testing it' is an unnecessarily awkward colloquialism. There is no need to misuse 'forget' when there is the exact word needed to hand.

grist (gist): Now an article in *Commercial Motor* August 1920 has come to light headed 'Char-a-bancs and Hooliganism'. The grist [*gist*] is that it is better to sell seats individually to strangers, rather than let a rabble who know each other hire your coach and fill it with crates of beer. *Automobile*[32]

'Grist' is grain that is going to be ground. Thus the phrase 'grist to the mill' is used of material which can be turned to advantage. The word is confused here with the word 'gist', which means the point or substance of an argument. For the ungrammatical duplication of 'better . . . rather than' see Chapter I, 3.

hearken (hark): Napoleon brought stability to France, preserving many of the achievements of the revolution . . . while hearkening [*harking*] back to certain values and systems of the Enlightenment era. *Programme Note*[33]

To 'hearken' is an archaic form of to 'hark' (listen). What is intended here is the verb 'to hark back', used of reverting to something in the past.

hoard (horde): Ironically the popularity of the Lakeland poets and Wordsworth in particular has brought hoards [*hordes*] of visitors invading the very privacy so revered by the poets. *Cumbria Life*[34]

A 'hoard' is an accumulated store of things, often treasure. A throng of people is a 'horde'.

incredulous (incredible): People looking at these photographs for the first time find it incredulous that there could be so many accidents when so few vehicles were on the road. *Cumbria Life*[35]

Presumably the writer meant 'incredible' (unbelievable) and not 'incredulous' (unbelieving) which can only apply to people. Even so the word would be too strong: *find it difficult to believe that there could be so many accidents.*

indoctrination (initiation): Frank Scaife, now living in retirement at Kendal, recalls his indoctrination to driving down Shap. *Cumbria Life*[36]

'Indoctrination' refers to the purely mental process of forcefully instructing people to accept systems of thought. Here the word wanted is 'initiation', used of introducing people into the practices of an organisation: *recalls his initiation into driving down Shap.*

instigation (initiation/installation): The revival was mooted when it was realised that it would have been the 100th anniversary of its instigation this year. *Horse & Hound*[37]

To 'instigate' is to be the driving force behind some (often drastic) action. To act at someone's 'instigation' is to act in reponse to their goading or prompting. What the writer means here is probably 'initiation', but there are better words to describe the setting up of a show: *when it was realised that it would have been the 100th anniversary of its foundation this year.*

> With the instigation of a smoke-free workplace, a black cloud has lifted from *Marketing Week's* editorial office . . . *Marketing Week*[38]

The causal/temporal 'with' is bad (see Chapter V, 4, 5) and should be replaced by 'since'. The word 'instigation' is wrong. Is the writer thinking of 'installation'? It would not be a very appropriate word anyway. 'Establishment' or 'inception' would do – *Since the establishment of a smoke-free workplace* – but it would be better to rephrase: *Since smoking has been banned in the workplace* . . .

introduction (innovation): A more recent introduction [*innovation*] is a specially formed division of the company to advise and encourage hotels and corporate organisations on the buying and placing of art works . . . *The Artist*[39]

If a new practice is brought into use in an organisation, that does not constitute an 'introduction' but an 'innovation'.

less (fewer): They are given eight hours of darkness to sleep, like us, and the rest of the time it has to be light or they produce less [*fewer*] eggs. *Cumbria Life*[40]

'Less' is the comparative form of 'little'. It refers to bulk, not to number.

> If Mr Ford Coppola is to be believed . . . the Mafia consists mainly of heavily-jowled psychotics with less scruples than clothes sense. *Decanter*[41]

If 'less scruples' is corrected to 'fewer scruples' then what follows will be ungrammatical ('fewer scruples than clothes sense'). Replace 'scruples' by a singular noun: *heavily-jowled psychotics with less conscience than clothes sense.*

loathe (loath/loth): Due to her strong sense of loyalty to her family, the Princess is loathe to come to any decision as yet. *Hello!*[42]

For misuse of 'due to' see Chapter V, 3, 2. The verb to 'loathe', meaning to detest, must be distinguished from the adjective 'loath' (or 'loth'), meaning reluctant. *Because of her strong sense of loyalty to her family, the Princess is loth to come to any decision as yet.*

> Most of us would be loathe [*loth*] to see the great country houses fall into disuse as homes. *Times*[43]

mantle (mantel): . . . As fashions changed the bracket clock lost its
   wall mounting and started to appear on tables and mantle pieces.
   Old-House Journal[44]

A 'mantle' is a cloak. The ornamental structure around a fireplace is
the 'mantelpiece' and the shelf on top the 'mantelshelf'.

miss (lack): Alex is still missing a front-axle . . . *Automobile*[45]

The verb 'to miss', when not used of failing to hit a target, conveys a
sense of emotional loss ('I miss my deceased husband'). It is a pity
therefore to misuse it in place of 'lack', which does not have the same
emotive overtones. *Alex still lacks a front-axle.*

mitigate (militate): It is hoped that this will mitigate [*militate*]
   against the tidy but sterile approach often adopted. *Country-Side*[46].

You cannot 'mitigate' *against* anything, for to 'mitigate' is to soften,
palliate or tone down. The word is now frequently confused with
'militate' which, followed by 'against', means to oppose.

   The emergence of a pay review body, which in other sectors has
   tended to mitigate [*militate*] against industrial action . . . *Times
   Educational Supplement*[47]

mutual (common): While our mutual [*common*] friend Daniel
   disappeared into a haze of drugs and unlikely jobs, Gaby became
   the role model for female tycoons . . . *Independent*[48]

This error was perpetrated by Dickens, but it remains an error. A
'common' friend, a friend of yours and mine, is not our 'mutual friend'.
'Mutual' means reciprocal. If you trust me and I trust you then we share
a 'mutual trust'.

nauseous (nauseated): I feel nauseous reading about 'perfect
   couple' Julie and David Field. *Today*[49]

It is what *causes* nausea that is 'nauseous'. In other words 'nauseous'
means obnoxious. To be repelled by something is to be 'nauseated': *I
feel nauseated when reading about 'perfect couple'.*

passim (pace): There is no argument, *passim* Professor Skidelsky,
   about the federal implications of the proposed revisions to the Treaty,
   nor to the federal intentions of many of the players. *Independent*[50]

'Passim' is a Latin word meaning 'far and wide' or 'scattered about'. Its
special usefulness is that it is a quick way of indicating that references to
a given topic may occur at many points in a book. The writer has
confused the word with another Latin word 'pace' from the noun 'pax'
meaning 'peace' or 'pardon'. The expression '*pace* Professor Skidelsky'

would mean 'with due deference to Professor Skidelsky' and would represent a respectful way of contradicting the Professor's view. That is what the writer intended.

pour (pore): There was the lone figure of Sir Charles, in his shirt sleeves, pouring [*poring*] over plans, analysing cash flows . . . *Times*[51]

What was being poured over the plans? The verb meaning to make a close study of something is 'pore over'.

principal (principle): There isn't even a principal [*principle*] at stake here . . . Sir Bryan said he still accepted the compensation principal [*principle*] but, as far as the BT is concerned, accepting the principal [*principle*] is unlikely ever to translate into actual contributions . . . *Guardian*[52]

The writer, Deborah Wise, has achieved a hat-trick here. 'Principal' is an adjective, meaning first or chief. It is used as a noun with reference to the chief of an institution (the 'Principal' of the college) or with reference to capital or property as opposed to interest or income. The word required here is 'principle' meaning a standard or rule of conduct.

Principle [*Principal*] events include the One Thousand and Two Thousand Guineas at the start of the season . . . *Lancashire Life*[53]

Here the boot is on the other leg.

promise (assure): Theresa has left her room in a complete mess. She promised [*assured*] you it had been tidied up when you gave her permission to go out. *Family Circle*[54]

The verb to 'promise' is to give a pledge for the *future*. You cannot 'promise' that you have done something.

purgatory (purdah): Mrs Thatcher has not – so far – been consigned to political purgatory. *Independent*[55]

'Purgatory' is a place of suffering for guilt. The context suggests that what the writer means here is that Mrs Thatcher has not yet been silenced, like Muslim women kept in seclusion. *Mrs Thatcher has not – so far – been consigned to political purdah.*

reason (cause): There is a problem and it stems from no other reason [*cause*] than understaffing. *Independent*[56]

The word 'reason' is used of purposes that are in the mind. You might say 'The reason why I came here is that I wished to please you', but not 'The reason why I fell was that there was ice on the road', where it is a *cause* and not a *reason* that is cited.

This unrivalled service is a further fulfilment of Brooks' commitments made to the auction market at the time of the company's launch and the reason behind their emergence as market leaders in 1991. *Automobile*[57]

Once more no 'reason' is being cited: *cause of their emergence*.

3 Words Misunderstood and Misused

We are concerned here with two categories of misuse. There are words which are being used in such a way as to reveal or suggest misunderstanding of their precise meaning. There are also words whose basic meaning seems to be understood by the writer, but which are ill-used in the context.

abort: The destruction of the earth in *Dinosaurs and all that rubbish* forces humans to abort earth for a new life in the stars. *Green Magazine*[1]

To 'abort', used idiomatically, is to 'forestall'. You cannot abort one place for another: *forces humans to abandon earth*.

accompany: . . . his wife Jeanie serves Devon cream teas accompanied by her own home-made jam. *In Britain*[2]

You might say 'Jeanie serves teas accompanied by her little daughter' but not 'by jam'. 'To accompany' is most often used of living beings: *serves her own home-made jam with her Devon cream teas*.

activity: The first fundraising activity is a book containing a compilation of the silliest answers given by students . . . *Times*[3]

A book is not an 'activity': *The first fundraising device is a book*.

affinity: The French have an affinity for cyclists unknown on the British side of the Channel. *Independent*[4]

Affinity is basically kinship and the natural sympathy which family relationship implies. You have an affinity *with*, not *for*, someone. It is unfortunate that the distinctive word is being increasingly used for 'liking'. *The French have a fellow-feeling for cyclists*.

alternative: Therefore English resorts are pooling resources on a promotional campaign . . . aimed at 'mid-market families with young children'. The aim is to present the seaside as an affordable and attractive alternative. *Lancashire Life*[5]

Alternative to what? You cannot speak of an alternative, the second possible choice of two items, unless you have mentioned the first. Nothing can be an 'alternative' except in relation to something else. *The aim is to present the seaside as an affordable and attractive option.*

appreciate: The magnitude of such assertions may be better appreciated by the fact that in this country alone the British Museum and the Ashmolean Museum in Oxford each claims to hold around this number . . . *Daily Telegraph*[6]

The magnitude of the assertion (that there are only about 80 genuine drawings by Michelangelo) cannot be appreciated by a 'fact', only by people. *We shall better appreciate the magnitude of the assertion if we recall that in this country alone the British Museum and the Ashmolean Museum in Oxford each claims . . .*

ask: I asked him the extent to which the plague is now spreading from its original source. *Radio 4*[7]

You can ask someone a question or a favour, but not an 'extent': *I asked him how far* (or *to what extent*) *the plague is now spreading.*

breathable: Their cagoules were purchased on the local market for about £6; they aren't breathable, but are certainly waterproof. *Country Walking*[8]

The only thing that is 'breathable' is air; that is to say, it can be breathed into the lungs. A material cannot be called 'breathable' because it is porous: *they aren't porous to air.*

cause: . . . it looked for a while as if planning regulations would cause this plan to be changed. *Old-House Journal*[9]

Regulations establish requirements, not causes: *it looked for a while as if planning regulations would require this plan to be changed.*

choice: As soon as you've left your suitcase at one of the pleasant choice of hotels . . . make for the harbour. *Homes & Gardens*[10]

You cannot stay at a choice or leave your suitcase at a choice. The writer means 'at one of the pleasant hotels among which you can make your choice' but introducing the word 'choice' does not help: *at one of the various pleasant hotels available.*

compile: Michael Mansfield Q.C. said it 'compiles hearsay upon hearsay'. *Times*[11]

To 'compile' is to gather together, most often used of assembling material for a book or a list. Here the speaker uses the verb as though it were a variant of 'pile': *piles hearsay upon hearsay.*

compound: Soaring unemployment merely compounds a gloomy economic picture. *Financial Times*[12]

Can you 'compound' a picture? . . . *intensifies the economic gloom.*

conceive: He actually conceived a lot of children as a young man. *Times*[13]

Here Valerie Grove is interviewing and quoting Lady Antonia Fraser on the subject of Henry VIII, so we cannot be sure whether we have one or two ladies who are unaware that women 'conceive' babies, while men 'beget' them. *He actually fathered a lot of children as a young man.*

congratulate: The Home Secretary, Mr Baker, has congratulated the vigilance of the prison staff. *Radio 4*[14]

The circumstances were that an escape had been foiled. Only living beings can be the recipients of congratulations: *congratulated the prison staff on their vigilance.*

co-ordinate: Literally thousands of fabrics are available to choose from for covering chairs allowing you to co-ordinate your room. *Lancashire Life*[15]

A comma is needed after 'chairs'. To 'co-ordinate' is to relate things together in an orderly fashion. It takes *two* things at least to be co-ordinated: *allowing you to co-ordinate the furnishings of your room.*

credit: She credits his campaign for [*with*] saving the Council . . . *Waterways World*[16]

You credit *with*, not *for*.

deliver: Yes, Alice the Large Black Sow has delivered us of a fine litter of nine healthy piglets. *Times*[17]

A sow may deliver a litter or be delivered of a litter. Though we might deliver a sow of a litter, the sow cannot deliver *us* of a litter: *the Large Black Sow has delivered a fine litter for us.*

demonstrate: You should also be able to demonstrate around five years' practical experience of computer systems . . . *Guardian*[18]

Why abuse the distinctive word 'demonstrate'? *should also be able to give evidence of around five years . . . experience . . .*

demonstrative: Demonstrative administrative ability is essential . . . *Times*[19]

This, like the previous sentence, comes from an advertisement for a post. The adjective 'demonstrative' is applied to persons who express their thoughts or feelings with eagerness. It cannot precede the adjective 'administrative' here, but 'demonstrable' or 'evident' could.

diminish: The fact that Gorbachev's heroism was not relayed by the world's television cameras should not diminish from our plaudits. *Times*[20]

To 'diminish' means to reduce, make smaller, and is transitive. Something might diminish our plaudits, but it could not diminish *from* them. The letter writer has used the wrong verb: *should not detract from our plaudits.*

discard: At first it was discarded by some academics as too commercial. *Viva*[21]

The topic is the attitude to a kind of artistic innovation. To 'discard' something is to cast it aside. You can only discard something which you already have. *At first it was ignored / rejected by some academics as too commercial.*

divest: Such is the power of the green vote that politicians anxiously divest themselves of criticism by green players and green distortions lest they be labelled as insufficiently enthusiastic for the environmental cause. *The Field*[22]

To divest oneself of clothes is to remove them, to strip. The verb cannot be used of deflecting criticism: *that politicians anxiously protect themselves against criticism . . .*

due: She claimed Sarah Farrell broke up her own best friend's marriage and boasted she was due the Queen's telegram for one night stands. *Sun*[23]

You might say 'She was due at the meeting at 7 o'clock' but no one can be 'due' any reward or gift. The reward or gift is 'due' to them: . . . *boasted that she merited the Queen's telegram for one night stands.*

You are due a repayment of income tax for the year shown above. *Inland Revenue*[24]

Welcome as the message is, it is wrong to declare me 'due'. *A repayment of income tax is due to you for the year shown above.*

embodiment . . . we all know that a kitchen hung with dried herbs and floral garlands from last summer's blooms is the very embodiment of the English country cottage. *Money-Maker*[25]

The kitchen is part of the cottage. You cannot 'embody' a building because it already has a body: *is characteristic of the ideal country cottage.*

enhance: Word of the phantom rustler soon spread, and the legend of an unearthly sheep thief was enhanced as animals continued to disappear over a period of two years. *Wild about Animals*[26]

To 'enhance' something is to increase its value; the writer needs some such word as 'amplify': *the legend of the unearthly sheep thief was elaborated as animals continued to disappear.*

establish: He began to establish a huge clinical experience . . . *Independent*[27]

You cannot 'establish' experience. Change either the verb – *He began to acquire a huge clinical experience* – or the noun: *He began to establish a huge clinical practice.*

event: . . . and some lovely events in northern Ireland, including a collection of hand-crafted Japanese dolls. *In Britian*[28]

A collection of dolls is not an 'event': *including an exhibition of hand-crafted Japanese dolls.*

exhibit: The only exhibits of contemporary volcanic activity here are thermal springs . . . *Complete Traveller*[29]

Volcanic activity does not manifest itself in 'exhibits': *The only examples of contemporary volcanic activity.*

force: Punishment and crowd control are forced to become horrifying when the offenders are outraged by the alien idea that they should be restrained in any way. *Times*[30]

A man can be 'forced' or compelled to do something, but 'punishment' cannot be 'forced' to do or become anything. Rephrase this. *Punishment and crowd control must necessarily become horrifying.*

fragile: Their future remains fragile, but at least they are back in a natural habitat after years of extinction in the wild. *My Weekly*[31]

'Fragile' is an inappropriate word to apply to the future. And if a breed is extinct, it no longer exists, and cannot go 'back' anywhere. *Their future remains uncertain, but at least they are back in a natural habitat after years of threatened extinction in the wild.*

give: To the outsider they give a bleak, inhospitable landscape . . . *Heritage*[32]

The subject is the Fens. The sentence illustrates a recent tendency to overuse the verb 'give', forcing it to serve purposes it is not fitted to serve: *they present a bleak, inhospitable landscape.*

happen: There is no evidence that a strategic reappraisal has happened . . . *Independent*[33]

Reappraisals do not 'happen': they are arranged by human beings. *There is no evidence that a strategic reappraisal has been made.*

hopeless: We'd been customers for 26 years, but they'd just changed their system from being really friendly to hopeless. *Moneywise*[34]

'Hopeless' too has its own useful connotation and it is not this. The system did not lose hope. It lost its friendliness: *they'd just changed their system from being really friendly to utterly unhelpful.*

include: His own health was precarious and included a heart attack . . . *Times*[35]

Health could never 'include' illness. This is logical topsy-turvydom. *His own health was precarious and he suffered a heart attack.*

inevitable: It seems to make inevitable sense that she should move to a more comfortable platform in the Lords . . . *Daily Mail*[36]

Kenneth Clarke is speaking about Mrs Thatcher's resignation. The word 'inevitable' is used of inescapable events, not of inescapable deductions. *It seems logical that she should move to a more comfortable platform in the Lords.*

ingredient: To the uninitiated, togs are the clothes you put on children's backs, but to duvet converts, they're an essential ingredient to the perfect bed-time partner. *Family Circle*[37]

An ingredient is an essential component of some kind of mixture. There cannot be an ingredient 'to', only 'of': *an essential complement to the perfect bed-time partner.*

jargon: We try to offer a reasonably friendly ambience; the jargon is quality. *The Field*[38]

Thus the managing director praises Sandown race course. 'Jargon' is the specialised vocabulary that belongs to a particular sphere of activity: *the key-word is quality.*

legion: Muscovites love a good conspiracy theory and such speculation was legion the moment Mr Gorbachev returned to the capital. *Times*[39]

'Legion' means a vast host of people or things. Stretching a point, you might say 'theories were legion', but you cannot declare 'speculation' (a singular noun) to be 'legion': *and such speculation was rife the moment Mr Gorbachev returned to the capital.*

limbo: The magazine is the solution to Mr Ingrams's mid-life crisis. It fills the limbo between being too old to edit *Private Eye*, and too young to die . . . *Times*[40]

'Limbo' means a place for lost, forgotten things. It does not mean a gap or vacancy which could be filled. *The magazine is the solution to*

Mr Ingrams's mid-life crisis. It fills the void between being too old to edit Private Eye, *and too young to die.*

logical: Laying a place setting is very logical. *Ideal Home*[41]

Logic is concerned with due reason and sequence in argument. It does not prescribe procedures for preparing to eat. *Laying a place setting should be done systematically.*

majority: Drove roads, green lanes, old Roman roads and well graded footpaths form the majority of the route . . . *The Great Outdoors*[42]

The word 'majority' can be used only where numbers of individual items or people are involved. You can refer to the 'majority' of an audience because an audience is a collection of individuals, but a 'route' is not a collection of items. *Drove roads, green lanes, old Roman roads and well graded footpaths make up most of the route.*

need: Win the ultimate Greenhouse plus all your growing needs. *House Beautiful*[43]

A 'need' is a requirement. You may have need of help or need of a doctor, but neither the help nor the doctor is a 'need', it is an answer to your need. In short 'needs' are things you want to shed, not to acquire.

numerate: With a degree in a numerate subject, you should have experience in accountancy or a related field . . . *Times*[44]

The adjective 'numerate' is a fairly recent innovation: it usefully complements 'literate' (able to use words) and means able to use figures. But there is no such thing as a 'numerate subject' for academic subjects cannot use figures: only people can. One probably could not improve on 'a degree in a subject that requires numeracy'.

percentage: Not only does it look fresher and brighter but it has a higher percentage of colour than at any time in the magazine's history. *Steam Railway*[45]

It is not good form to use 'percentage' in contexts where numerical proportion is not at issue: *it has a higher proportion of colour.*

perform: Today, the two prime ministers will perform the ostensible main object of the visit when they sign the Hong Kong airport agreement. *Times*[46]

You cannot 'perform an object'. *Today, the two prime ministers will fulfil the ostensible main purpose of the visit.*

proverbial: . . . a few words on a local radio or TV station can work proverbial wonders. *The Artist*[47]

You might say 'He seems to have nine lives like the proverbial cat' because there is a well-known proverbial saying that a cat has nine lives. But the cliché 'works wonders' does not constitute a proverbial saying. The word 'proverbial' is out of place. Omit it.

> As a professional traveller he is without the constraints of the proverbial package holiday or commercial demand. *Outdoors Illustrated*[48]

There is no traditional saying about a package holiday: *he is free from the constraints of the typical package holiday.*

regress: For a bowler to take 100 wickets at a better rate than Younis in 1991 we need to regress 60 years to Harold Larwood in 1931. *The Cricketer*[49]

To 'regress' is to go backwards and has a pejorative connotation: *we need to go back 60 years to Harold Larwood.*

see: A great album comes from Eddi Reader . . . and it sees her in more contemplative mood. *New Woman*[50]

Albums cannot 'see': *it reveals her in more contemplative mood.*

> No 80136, based on the North Staffordshire Railway at Cheddleton, should see progress made on its restoration now . . . *Steam Classic*[51]

It isn't the locomotive that will 'see' progress made, but we, the witnesses. *We should see progress made on the restoration of No 80136, based on the North Staffordshire Railway at Cheddleton.*

show: The home batsmen showed few difficulties in keeping their wickets intact . . . *The Cricketer*[52]

You don't 'show' difficulties. Either change the verb – *appeared to have few difficulties in keeping* – or change what follows the verb: *showed themselves at ease in keeping their wickets intact.*

stop: The NENE Valley Railway's ex-Polish State Railway Class Ty2 'Kriegslok' 2–10–0 No.7173 has been stopped following the discovery of a split left side crosshead . . . *Steam Railway*[53]

To 'stop' a locomotive is one thing; to withdraw it from service another thing. *No.7173 has been withdrawn.*

> The house stopped on the first floor when they bought it. But Harry decided to open up the dusty, forgotten attic. *House Beautiful*[54]

They used only two storeys of the house when they first bought it.

suit: I tied my hair up into a French plait so it wouldn't go frizzy in the damp. I glanced in the hall mirror and decided I suited it. *Catch*[55]

The question that arises is 'Does it suit me?' not 'Do I suit it?'. What is on trial is not 'me' but the hairstyle. It is the hairstyle that must go if it does not suit. I cannot decide that I am unsuitable and remove myself from the hairstyle like the Cheshire Cat from its grin. *I glanced in the mirror and decided that it suited me.*

time: . . . contracts should be reviewed or invalidated at crucial times such as the birth of a child or permanent disability of a partner. *Options*[56]

Neither the 'birth of a child' nor the 'permanent disability of a partner' can be called a *time: at crucial times such as when a child is born or a partner becomes permanently disabled.*

unwittingly: . . . she ultimately obtained acceptance by the British government of financial responsibility for the pensions of the Colonial Service. For that thousands are unwittingly grateful. *Times*[57]

'Unwittingly' means 'unknowingly' or 'unintentionally'. You cannot be grateful and not know that you are grateful, because gratitude is something of which you are conscious. You can, of course, be unaware *to whom* you owe gratitude, and this is the state of mind the obituarist is thinking of. *For that thousands are unwittingly indebted to her.*

upfront: An upfront deposit of between 25 and 40 per cent of the final cost of the kitchen is normally required . . . *Traditional Homes*[58]

This seemingly barbaric evasion of the word 'advance' ('advance deposit') is all the more regrettable in that the word 'deposit' *means* an advance payment anyway. *A deposit of between 25 and 40 per cent of the cost of the kitchen is normally required.*

urge: . . . we're encouraging our network of groups to go to their local authorities to urge for improvements. *Green Magazine*[59]

You press *for* improvements, but you 'urge' people to make them: *to go to their local authorities to press for improvements.*

use: Other clues, such as habitat, can be used to make a more exact identification. *Waterways World*[60]

The article is about animal tracks and traces. You do not *use* a clue; you study or follow it. *Other clues, such as habitat, can be studied.*

Wagner's influence is apparent in his own orchestral writing, but used with a lighter texture and a lighter touch. *Opera Now*[61]

247

The article is about Debussy's *Pelléas et Mélisande*. You do not *use* an influence, not even 'with a texture'. *Wagner's influence is apparent in his own orchestral writing, but Debussy's has a lighter texture and a lighter touch.*

versatile: Salmon and trout are extremely versatile fish, providing the cook with a wide variety of dishes. *The Field*[62]

A 'versatile' person is one who is skilled in many different directions. It requires no skill on the part of the fish to be able to be cooked in various ways. The versatility is the cook's. *Salmon and trout are extremely useful fish for the versatile cook, providing him with a wide variety of dishes.*

vulnerable: 'The period after the birth of a baby is an especially vulnerable one for men embarking on affairs,' she continues. 'The new father feels that he must restore his ego somehow.' *Cosmopolitan*[63]

It is not the *period* that is vulnerable ('capable of being hurt' or 'exposed to temptation') but the men. *The period after the birth of a child is an especially tricky one for men who are tempted to embark on affairs.*

whatever: Whatever, this gave the pantomime two distinct sections . . . *Vivid*[64]

Since there is an appropriate word available, why twist the usage of 'whatever' like this? *However, this gave the pantomime two distinct sections . . .*

wise: Manufacturers have wised up quickly to our enthusiasm for low calorie foods . . . *Company*[65]

To 'wise up' is American slang and better avoided. *Manufacturers have quickly cottoned on to our enthusiasm for low calorie foods.*

APPENDIX

I COMPARING AND CONTRASTING

1 'LIKE/UNLIKE'

1   Aug 91
2   29 Jun 91, David McKittrick
3   23 Apr 93, Peter Riddell
4   29 Jun 91, Richard Kay & Chris Jenkins
5   2 Nov 91, Maria Aitken
6   Feb 92, Euan Corrie
7   Aug 91, Carol Fewster
8   27 Feb 92, advert
9   23 Nov 91
10 29 Jun 91, advert
11 Sep 91, advert
12 11 Jun 91, advert
13 Jul/Aug 91, Christa D'Souza
14 Feb 92, Liz Shaw
15 11 Apr 92, Susan Crosland
16 Dec/Jan 92, Mark Appleton
17 Apr 92, Victoria Mather
18 29 Aug 91, 2nd leader
19 Mar 92, John McGurk
20 Feb 92, Charles Ward
21 25 Apr 92, Alastair Robertson
22 14 Feb 92, Sue Elms
23 Jan 92, Sir Derek Barber
24 16 Sep 91, 3rd leader
25 13 Dec 91, Peter Riddell
26 Aug 91

2 'MORE/LESS THAN'

1   Mar 92, Steve Bradford
2   26 Aug 91, Bernard Levin
3   Sunmed Holidays, Summer 91
4   12 Jun 91
5   Mar 92, Steve Bradford
6   Jan 92, James Shergood
7   Mar 92, Mark Azaredo
8   Feb 92
9   13 Aug 91, Rodney Hobson
10 Mar 92
11 May 91
12 19 Jul 91, Liz Smith
13 11 Dec 91, Anatole Kaletsky
14 20 Aug 91
15 Dec/Jan 92, Sandy Foster
16 Sep 91, Patrick Kingston
17 21 Feb 92, Lin Jenkins
18 11 Jun 91, obit
19 Mar 92, quoted
20 Aug 91, Eva Gizowska
21 13 Jun 91, Martin Fletcher
22 Issue 7, Summer 91, John Andrew
23 12 Jul 91, Jeffrey Sachs
24 27 Feb 92, advert
25 Jan 92, Jason Smalley
26 27 Feb 92, John Etheridge

3 'RATHER THAN'

1   Jan 92, Wilfrid Ward
2   4 Jul 91, Liz Heron
3   12 Sep 91, Sheila Gunn
4   8 Jun 91, Eric Christiansen
5   8 Jun 91
6   Sep 91
7   11 Jan 92, Mary Griffiths
8   Feb 92, Jonathan Plant
9   Aug 91, Jo Cooper
10 Feb 92
11 Aug 91, Jill Blake
12 Feb 92
13 Mar 92
14 29 Jun 91, Keith Botsford
15 Feb 92, Peter Gotzl
16 Dec/Jan 92, Richard Simpson
17 12 Jun 91, Jonathan Glancey
18 27 Jul 91, Elisabeth Mortimer
19 Feb 92

4 OTHER CONSTRUCTIONS

1   Feb 92, Editor
2   Feb 92, quoted

15 27 Jul 91, Ursula Buchan
16 25 Aug 91, Barbara Amiel
17 Aug 91
18 Aug 91, David Allsop
19 22 Jun 91
20 6/7 Jul 91, Terry Hands
21 13 Jun 91, Alan Lee
22 24 Aug 91, Carey Fletcher
23 Jan 92
24 Aug 91, Maggie Alderson
25 Mar 92, John Yardley
26 Mar 92, Carah Samuel
27 20 Dec 91, Richard Cork
28 Aug/Sep 91, Reg Vallintine
29 Feb 92, Tom Robb
30 Aug 91, advert
31 13 Jul 91, Alan Henry
32 17 Jul 91, Michael Evans
33 Mar 92, Keith Merse
34 21 Aug 91, letter

4 THE GERUND

1 Jul 91, Sharon Maxwell Magnus
2 Mar 92, Jay Aspen
3 nd.
4 Mar 92, Janet Boulton
5 17 Aug 91, Antony Dore
6 Jan 92, Steve Mills
7 Mar 92, Sheila Sang
8 Jan 92
9 13 Nov 91, letter
10 24 Aug 91, Terry Tavner
11 Aug 91, letter
12 22 Nov 91
13 18 Jul 91, Victoria Glendinning
14 Issue 7, Summer 91, Jon Futrell
15 13 Jul 91, Robert Maycock
16 Mar 92, Spring Books
17 Feb 92, Jeremy Laurance
18 Feb 92
19 Aug 91, Tom Harvey
20 14 May 93, Harry Thompson
21 Jun 91, Eve Cameron
22 Aug 91
23 Feb 92, Andy Barnet

5 THE 'GERCIPLE' ATTACHED TO A NOUN

1 22 Jul 91, Neil Mackinnon
2 Sep 91
3 24–30 Jan 92, Caroline Sefton

4 14 Feb 92, Michele Martin
5 Aug 91, Suzanne Wilkinson
6 21–7 Aug 91, Derek Hand
7 7 Feb 92, Rachel Kelly
8 6 Feb 92, Colin Vogel
9 2 Jul 91, Peter Jenkins
10 24 Jun 91
11 Feb 92
12 14 Feb 92, Michele Martin
13 12 Aug 91, John Andrew
14 12 Jul 91, Nicholas Timmins
15 17 Sep 93, Jonathan Brynn
16 12 Sep 91, Hugh Barnes
17 Mar 92
18 19 Aug 91, Lynn Faulds Wood
19 24 Jul 91
20 Mar 92, Dipesh Chakrabarty
21 2 Sep 91, Roger Nightingale
22 4–17 Mar 92
23 17 Apr 92, letter
24 8–16 Jun 91
25 19 Aug 91, Chris Arnot
26 9 Sep 91, Jane Bartlett
27 Sep 91, Patrick Kingston
28 11 Apr 92, Peter Barnard
29 Mar 92, Jay Aspen
30 18 Jul 91, Colin Narbrough
31 24 Jul 91
32 24 Jul 91
33 27 Jul 91, Tom Walker
34 18 Jul 91

6 THE 'GERCIPLE' ATTACHED TO A PRONOUN

1 Aug 91, quoted
2 27 Mar 92
3 4–17 Mar 92, letter
4 Mar 92, letter
5 Aug/Sep 91, Tony Warburton
6 Feb 92, Marina Cantacuzino
7 Sep 91
8 Sep 91
9 9 Sep 91, quoted
10 Issue 7, Summer 91
11 26 Feb 92, quoted
12 Sep 91, quoted
13 4 Sep 91, Bernard Levin
14 23 Jan 92, Bernard Levin
15 10 Sep 91, Janet Daley
16 Sep 91, quoted
17 Sep 91
18 24 Aug 91, story dialogue

35 14 Feb 92, Sue Elms
36 14 Feb 92, Michele Martin
37 Feb 92, Wyn Francis
38 Dec/Jan 92, Karl Stedman
39 25 Oct 91, Diary

4 MISUSE OF 'WITH'

1   18 Jun 91, Anthony Bevins
2   Sep 91, advert
3   Feb 92, Peter Gotzl
4   12 Jun 91, Sean French
5   Feb 92
6   Feb 92, Liz Hoggard
7   Feb 92, Caroline Collins
8   Feb 92, Chris Baines
9   Jan 92, John Darling
10 Sep 91, Jessie Anderson
11 Feb 92, Richard Mabey
12 Feb 92, Karen Suzuki
13 Feb 92, Richard Fawkes
14 24–30 Jan 92
15 Feb 92, Nicholas Campion
16 Aug 91, Alex Dingwall Main
17 12 Feb 92
18 Feb 92
19 8 Jun 91, Books & Arts
20 Mar 92
21 31 Jan 92, 2nd leader
22 24–30 Jan 92
23 Mar 92, Nicole Swengley
24 13 Jun 91, Michael Harrison
25 Mar 92, Andrew Ayton
26 Aug 91, Andy Harris
27 10 Jun 91, Graham Searjeant &
    Philip Bassett
28 10 Jun 91, Nicholas Timmins
29 2 Sep 91, Carol Leonard
30 13 Jul 91, Teresa Hunter & Nick
    Pandya
31 Mar 92
32 6 Feb 92, advert
33 12 Jun 91, 2nd leader
34 24–30 Jan 92
35 24 Jul 91, Matthew Bond
36 Mar 92, Andrew Barrow
37 Feb 92, Karen Suzuki
38 29 Jun 91, obit
39 Feb 92
40 6 Feb 92, advert
41 Mar 92, Mary Lambert
42 20 Aug 91, Geoff Brown

43 Dec 91/Jan 92, Richard Evans
44 4–17 Mar 92
45 6 Feb 92, advert
46 Feb 92
47 Mar 92, Judi Goodwin
48 Feb 92, advert
49 Jan 92, Michael Wigan
50 29 Feb 92, Michael Watkins

5 PREPOSITIONS

1   Sep 91, David Wilcock
2   16 Aug 91, Martin Whitfield
3   Feb 92, John Hatt
4   21–27 Aug 91
5   19 Aug 91, 2nd leader
6   2 Oct 91, Jamie Dettmer
7   Dec 91, Cathy Farmer
8   Mar 92, Paul Morrison
9   Dec 91, Christopher Springate
10 24 Feb 92, Charles Bremner
11 Sep 91, quoted
12 Jan 92
13 Issue 7, Summer 91
14 7 Sep 91
15 6 Feb 92, letter
16 Feb 92, Edward Cooper
17 15 Jun 91, Sarah Lambert
18 22 Jul 91, Neil Mackinnon
19 9 May 93, leader
20 Dec 91, Lisa Sykes
21 Dec 91/Jan 92, Bill Trigg
22 30 Jan 92, Peter Davenport
23 Sep 91, Dr Dennis C. Turner
24 18 Jun 91
25 Feb 92
26 Apr 87, Jackie Burgoyne
27 6 Feb 92, advert
28 Jan 92, Steve Mills
29 7 Mar 92, 2nd leader
30 Feb 92, Gus van Hensbergen
31 Mar 92
32 1 Jul 91, letter
33 24 Aug 91, Roger Black
34 18 Sep 91, advert
35 4 Jul 91, leader
36 12 Jul 91, obit
37 Aug 91, Hazel Martin & Donna Hay
38 Dec 91, Rufus Bellamy
39 13 Jul 91, obit
40 20 Nov 91, Peter Davenport
41 14 May 93, Patricia Morison

42 Jul/Aug 91, William Hardy
43 Feb 92
44 Sep 91
45 Sep 91
46 Feb 92, advert
47 Feb 92
48 4–17 Mar 92
49 24–30 Jan 92
50 Aug 91, Gill Page
51 9 Jan 92, Fiona Beckett
52 24–30 Jan 92
53 Dec 91
54 Sep 91, Adrian Bloom
55 31 Aug 91, Andrew Longmore
56 Mar 93, University College, Oxford
57 Feb 92, Liz Shaw
58 Feb 92, letter
59 Spring 92, Bryan Sage
60 30 Dec 92, Lord Ridley
61 Mar 92, editorial
62 3 May 93, Peter Riddell
63 11 Jan 92
64 2 Jul 91, Annika Savill
65 Aug/Sep 91, David Trew

VI PRESERVING DUE SEQUENCE

1 GRAMMATICAL CONTINUITY

1 Aug 91
2 Mar 92, Judi Goodwin
3 6 Feb 92, obit
4 Aug/Sep 91
5 19 Jul 91, obit
6 19 Jul 91, Tim Jones
7 Dec/Jan 92
8 nd., Melvyn Bragg
9 Jun 91, Ros Miles
10 14 Jun 91, John Kay
11 19 Aug 91, quoted
12 Xmas Gift Catalogue 91
13 12 Jun 91, John Pienaar
14 Sep 91, advert
15 Feb 92
16 Feb 92, advert
17 23 Aug 91, Neil Bennett
18 21–27 Aug, Meg Bond
19 2 Jul 91, obit
20 13 Jun 91, Peter Jenkins
21 6 Feb 92, Colin Vogel
22 16 Jul 92, obit
23 Aug 91

24 Aug 91
25 12 Jun 91, 2nd leader
26 Nick Breckenfield
27 Feb 92
28 Spring 92, June Chatfield
29 13 Jul 91, Jan Smaczny
30 19 Aug 91, Chris Arnot
31 8 Aug 91, Comment
32 Aug 91, Fenton Bresler
33 10 Aug 91, Roy Hattersley
34 28 Jun 91, Neil Bennett

2 COHERENCE AND INCOHERENCE

1 27 Jun 91, Colin Brown
2 17 Jul 91, Liz Smith
3 27 Aug 91, The World at One
4 18 Feb 92, John Russell Taylor
5 21–27 Aug 91, Ann Bowling
6 Feb 92
7 Jul 91, Louise Pearce & Sarah King
8 25 Sep 91, Charles Bremner
9 9 Mar 92, Peter Riddell
10 24 Aug 91, quoted
11 10 Aug 91
12 3 Sep 91, advert
13 11 Mar 92, leader
14 17 Sep 91, John Kendall
15 5 Jul 91, Brian Unwin
16 19 Aug 91, 2nd leader
17 13 Jul 91
18 Sep 91, Geraldine Ranson
19 17 Jul 91, obit
20 Aug 91, Alison Wick
21 Mar 92, letter
22 17 Feb 92, 2nd leader
23 19 May 93, leader
24 Dec/Jan 92, advert
25 Sep 91
26 11 Jul 91, Gordon Creig
27 27 Feb 92
28 Mar 92
29 1993, circular
30 Jan 92, advert
31 21–27 Aug 91, Margaret Smith
32 9 Sep 91
33 Summer 91, Matthew Fort
34 nd.
35 Jan 92, Jason Smalley
36 Feb 92, Dan Cruickshank
37 Jan 92, Tony Skinner
38 Jan 92, David Steel

5 Mar 92
6 13 Aug 91, letter
7 Aug 91
8 Mar 92
9 Jan 92, Michael Wigan
10 Jan 92, Mel Russ
11 Aug/Sep 91, Richard Platt
12 Sep 91
13 Feb 92
14 Feb 92
15 Feb 92, Dr Debbi Hastings
16 Dec 91
17 28 Apr 92, Richard Morrison
18 Feb 92, Caroline Clifton-Mogg
19 Feb 92, letter
20 Feb 92
21 8 Apr 92, leader
22 Sep 91
23 9 Sep 91, Kerry Gill
24 Feb 92, advert
25 Feb 92, Chris Baines
26 Aug/Sep 91, Reg Vallintine
27 No 2, nd., Liz Gilbey
28 13 Jun 91, Charles Bremner
29 9 Sep 91
30 19 Jun 91, obit
31 nd.
32 8 Nov 91
33 10 Sep 91, Jon Ashworth
34 Summer 91, Gordon Burn
35 14 Jun 91, 2nd leader
36 5 Aug 91, letter
37 Mar 92, Alan Thomas
38 Jul 91, advert
39 Jul/Aug 91, Kate Constable
40 Feb 92, advert
41 14 Mar 92, leader
42 Jun 91, Hilary Burden
43 27 Jun 91, quoted
44 Feb 92, Tamsin Walker
45 Annual Review 91
46 Feb 92, Peter Gotzl
47 Feb 92, Chris Baines
48 6 Feb 92, Carol Allen
49 14 Feb 92, Sarah Macdonald
50 Mar 92, quoted
51 Dec 91, Paul Gosling
52 21–27 Aug 91, Colin Beacock
53 Mar 92, Alan Thomas
54 13 Jun 91, Hamish McRae
55 Feb 92, Chris Baines
56 Feb 92, Jennifer Mourin

VIII Vocabulary

1 Some over-used and ill-used words

1 Jan 92
2 Sep 91
3 Feb 92, Tom Robb
4 Jan 92, Guy Wallace
5 Feb 92, Jim Budd
6 Feb 92
7 16 Aug 91
8 8 Jan 92, quoted
9 Feb 92
10 14 Feb 92, Michele Martin
11 29 Jun 91, Keith Botsford
12 Jun 91, Esme Newton-Dunn
13 9 Sep 91
14 Feb 92
15 Dec 91/Jan 92, John Hooper
16 7 Feb 92, Sean French
17 Aug 91
18 Aug 91
19 1 Feb 92, Robin Young
20 Mar 92, John Teague
21 2 Sep 91, Roger Nightingale
22 2 Sep 91, Colin Narbrough
23 Mar 92, Eric Sawford
24 Jan 92, Alan Yates
25 4 Sep 91, leader
26 Dec 91
27 Aug 91, Kathy Robinson
28 Mar 92, Ros Chissick
29 Mar 92, advert
30 21 Aug 91, letter
31 Sep 91, Keir Laurence
32 14 Feb 92
33 14 Jan 92, Nick Nuttall
34 Mar 92
35 April 92, Sharon Kingman
36 Mar 92, Maureen Connett
37 Aug 91
38 24 Aug 91, advert
39 Jan 92, Ron Hodges
40 Aug 91, Peter Randall
41 14 Feb 92
42 24–30 Jan 92, Craig Breheny
43 Jul/Aug 91, William Hardy
44 Mar 92
45 Aug 91, Lesley Abdela
46 14 Jun 91, letter
47 Aug 91
48 6 Feb 92

18 13 Jul 91, advert
19 28 Aug 91, advert
20 26 Aug 91, letter
21 nd.
22 Jan 92, Sir Derek Barber
23 27 Feb 92, Vic Chapple
24 Jun 93
25 Feb 92, Geraldine Trembath
26 Sep 91
27 10 Aug 91, obit
28 Sep 91, Editor's Notebook
29 Mar 92, Mark Bennett
30 6 Sep 91, Janet Daley
31 24 Aug 91, Gillian Thornton
32 Feb/Mar 92, Robin Page
33 13 Jun 91, quoted
34 Aug 91, quoted
35 27 Jul 91, obit
36 29 Jun 91, quoted
37 Feb 92
38 Jan 92, quoted
39 29 Aug 91, Mary Dejevsky
40 3 Jan 92, Kate Muir
41 Feb 92
42 Aug 91, Alan Castle

43 21 Feb 92, quoted
44 27 Feb 92, advert
45 Sep 91, Nick Pigotí
46 3 Sep 91, David Watts & Catherine
    Sampson
47 Mar 92, Bernard Denvir
48 Aug/Sep 91
49 Jan 92, Robert Brooke
50 Feb 92, Gilly Smith
51 Feb 92
52 Jun 92, Robert Brooke
53 Sep 91
54 Sep 91, Sara Jane Evans
55 Sep 91, Veronica Robinson
56 Aug 91, Vivien Goldsmith
57 28 Dec 91, obit
58 Mar 92, Mary Lambert
59 Dec 91, quoted
60 Feb 92, Jonathan Plant
61 Feb 92, Noël Goodwin
62 Jan 92, advert
63 Jun 91
64 No 2, nd.
65 Sep 91

SYNOPSIS

INDEX